MODERN TEACHING OF EXCEPTIONAL CHILDREN

Modern Teaching of
Exceptional Children

[Teaching Methods for Physically Challenged, Handicapped and Abnormal Children]

Bharat Singh

ANMOL PUBLICATIONS PVT. LTD.

NEW DELHI - 110 002 (INDIA)

ANMOL PUBLICATIONS PVT. LTD.
H.O.: 4374/4B, Ansari Road, Darya Ganj,
New Delhi-110 002 (India)
Ph.: 23261597, 23278000
B.O.: No. 1015, Ist Main Road, BSK IIIrd Stage
IIIrd Phase, IIIrd Block,
Bangalore - 560 085 (India)
Visit us at: www.anmolpublications.com

Modern Teaching of Exceptional Children

First Published, **2006**
Reprint, 2008

PRINTED IN INDIA

Printed at Mehra Offset Press, Delhi.

Contents

Preface vii

1. **Introduction** 1
2. **Basic Concepts** 9
3. **Various Issues** 28
4. **Special Education** 45
5. **The Innovations** 56
6. **Special Education Services** 75
7. **Integrated Education** 89
8. **Teacher Training** 96
9. **The Physically Challenged-1** 117
10. **The Physically Challenged-2** 134
11. **Learning at Slow Pace** 146
12. **The Mentally Retarded** 159
13. **Juvenile Delinquency** 179
14. **The Socially Disadvantaged** 207
15. **The Gifted Ones** 225
16. **The Researches** 241
17. **Programmes and Policies** 259

Preface

Education is a vast discipline and Teachers' Training is a vital part of it. The responsibilities of the educationists and educators are focused on the task of providing better training to the future teachers for their better learning and proper development. Needless to say that this responsibility can only be exercised, if the trainers are equipped with the required knowledge of the subject concerned. That's why it becomes essential for making adequate provisions for each course to the student-teachers or teacher trainees. The present series is designed for providing a solid workable base for all course-papers. It has been prepared strictly according to the syllabus of the B.Ed class, prescribed by the UGC for different universities.

No doubt, there are so many other books on the subject, available in the market, written by worthy authors. However, every writer has his or her own style and way of presentation. The present work also has its own features and characteristics.

In preparation of this series of texts, the editor had to refer to the works of other authors and information sources. The editor feels a deep sense of gratitude for incorporating their ideas in the text. Hopefully, this series would serve as a 'ready to refer' tool for all teachers, teacher-students and others.

—**Editor**

1

Introduction

Education of exceptional children is a challenging field. The term "Exceptional Children" refers to children whose needs are very different from those of the majority of children in society. These children deviate from average children to the extent they cannot receive classroom instruction in regular schools. This was the belief prevalent for several years.

Many children are hard of hearing but every such child is not exceptional unless the loss is such as to impair communication skills. Within a particular group of exceptional children, there are also variations. There are different degrees of hearing loss. Hence, it is appropriate to define exceptional children as those who differ from the average to such a degree in physical and psychological characteristics that the traditional school programme does not allow all round development and progress for them. They need special education or special ancillary services to grow according to their ability.

Special education refers to instruction that is specifically designed to meet the needs of exceptional children. It involves designing the physical environment in the classroom (e.g., use of ramps) teaching procedures, teaching content and equipment (hearing aids for the deaf) for a particular type of disability.

Several terms have been used to describe exceptionality: subnormal, handicapped, disabled, exceptional, special, impaired etc. These have added confusion to understanding and placing the children who are different from the average. As a result of widespread debate, discussions and research, the World Health Organisation has clearly distinguished the use of three terms: impairment, disability and handicap.

Impairment means, abnormalities of body structure and appearance and organ or system function resulting from any cause in principle. Impairment represents disturbances at the organ level (WHO, 1976).

Disability reflects the consequences of impairment in terms of functional performance and activity by the individual (WHO, 1976).

Handicap on the other hand, refers to disadvantages experienced by the individual as a result of impairments and disabilities; handicaps thus reflect interaction with an adaptation to the individual's surroundings (WHO, 1976).

These terms are based on an organic model having functional interrelationship.

Impairment → Disability → Handicap

The inter-relationship between the three can be explained by means of examples:

- A child born with a finger-nail missing has a malformation—a structural impairment but this does not in any way interfere with the function of the hand and so there is no disability; the impairment is not particularly evident, and so disadvantage or handicap would be unlikely.
- A myope or a diabetic individual suffers a functional impairment but, because this can be corrected or abolished by aids, appliances, or drugs, he would not necessarily be disabled; however, the disadvantage is considerable, e.g., he may not be allowed to take part in group activities or may have to give himself regular injections.
- An individual with colour blindness has an impairment but it would be unlikely to lead to activity restriction; whether the impairment constitutes a handicap would depend on circumstances-if his occupations were agricultural he might well be unaware of his impairment, but he would be at a disadvantage if he aspired to drive a railway engine, because he would be prevented from following this occupation.

"Subnormality of intelligence is an impairment, but it may not lead to appreciable activity restriction; factors other than the impairment may determine the handicap because the disadvantage may be minimal if the individual lives in a remote rural community, whereas it could be severe if he lives in the midst of university graduates living in a large city, of whom more might be expected."

Hence, children are considered exceptional when they have some characteristics that deviate from the normal or average child. It is for this reason the term "Exceptional Children" is used more often. It is more inclusive in the sense that it consists of the handicapped in one extreme and of the gifted at the other. These children are classified into certain categories for the purpose of placement and educational care.

The following categories of children represent the various types of exceptional children:

- The Educable Mentally Retarded
- The Trainable Mentally Retarded
- The Profound or Severely Mentally Retarded
- The Visually Handicapped
- The Hearing Handicapped
- The Emotionally Handicapped
- The Disabled Learner
- The Physically or Neurologically Handicapped
- The Speech and Language Handicapped
- The Slow Learner
- The Gifted
- The Multiple Handicapped
- The Socially Handicapped

The operational definitions of all these categories and a brief overview of their characteristics are given below in order to help the reader understand the text easily.

The Educable Mentally Retarded (EMR) children have IQs between 60 to 85 (earlier 50-75) accompanied by impaired behaviour. These children can learn minimal academic skills by their late teens with special educational support. They are capable of social and vocational independence with proper education and training. Some of them need supervision and guidance. On an average 2.5 per cent children are within educable range. They come from low socio-economic backgrounds and are classified as non-pathological or cultural-familial. They are slightly below normal children in physical development. Their greatest difficulty is with learning of abstract concepts. They have a higher expectancy of failure than the intellectually normal. They need to make more effort, immediate and tangible reward and language training. Special teachers work hard to teach the EMR social-emotional adjustment, academic knowledge, physical and motor activities. These children are deficient in information processing habits and have low aspirations. Their rate of forgetting is rapid. But they do profit from training.

Trainable Mentally Retarded children have IQs between 40-60 approximately. By adulthood they have the intelligence of 4 to 8 year old. They can only learn selfcare socialisation and oral communication skills. They need personal attention and care throughout their lives. They can be partially self-supporting after training in sheltered workshops. They contribute 0.5 per cent of the retarded children population. They usually live with parents, relatives or are cared for by some social agencies. They display behaviour problems withdrawal, distractibility, and unusual emotional states. Special school setting sometimes is the answer to their training and care.

Visual handicap is defined in terms of visual acuity, field of vision, and visual efficiency. Visual ability is the ability of the eye to see distant objects clearly using Snellen chart. Individuals who see the letter capital 'E' from a 20 feet distance instead of 200 feet are legally blind. There are children who have low vision or residual vision. These children are sighted and their visual acuity does not exceed 20/70. These children have orientation and mobility problems. Low vision is defined in terms of clarity whereas partial sightedness is defined in terms of distance from the Snellen Chart. Education of these children is based on multi sensory approach, use of plus curriculum, use of Braille, etc.

An emotionally disturbed child is one whose reactions to life situations are unrewarding to himself and unacceptable to his peers and other members of society. They vary in degree. They show over a long period of time and to a marked degree certain characteristics which affect their academic performances. These are:

a. Inability to learn, that cannot be explained by intellectual, sensory or health factors.

b. Inability to build and maintain satisfactory interpersonal relationship with peers and teachers.
c. Inappropriate behaviour or feelings under normal circumstances.
d. General and pervasive mood of unhappiness or depression.
e. Tendency to develop fear associated with personal and school problems.

Educational programmes are planned quite cautiously to handle these children.

Hearing handicap is defined in terms of degree of hearing loss. These are classified as mild (20-30 dB), marginal (30-40 dB), the moderate (40-50 dB), severe (60-75 dB), and profound 75 + dB. The deaf hardly profit from auditory training but the hard of hearings do. They have poor self concept, inferiority feeling, temper tantrums, submissiveness, lack of cognitive functioning and language reading difficulties. Interventions and psycho-educational programmes have proved helpful for them including speech therapy.

Learning disabled children exhibit disorder in one or more of the basic psychological processes involved in understanding and using the spoken or written languages. These disorders are manifested in listening, thinking, talking, reading, writing, spelling, arithmetic. They include conditions which are referred to as perceptual problems, brain injury, minimal brain dysfunction, dyslexia, developmental aphasia. They do not include learning problems which are primarily due to visual, hearing or motor handicaps, to mental retardation, emotional disturbance or to environmental disadvantage. These children are near or above average in intelligence, impulsive, distractible, poor in language organisation, and abstract ideas, hyperactive as well as hypo-active in different situations. They have severe reading problems. Emotionally unstable, these children are over dependent. They display deficiency in memory processes and thinking.

A variety of interchangeable terms have been used to describe persons with physical handicaps e.g., physically handicapped, crippled, orthopaedically handicapped, multiple handicapped. But the legal definition for orthopaedically impaired is a severe orthopaedic impairment that adversely affects child's educational performance. The term includes clubfoot, poliomyelitis, bone tuberculosis, cerebral palsy, amputations, fractures or burns that cause contractions.

Health handicap is manifested by severe communication and other developmental and educational problems, or having limited strength, vitality or alertness because of heart condition, tuberculosis, rheumatic fever, asthma, epilepsy, lemophillia, lead poisoning, leukemia or diabetes.

From an educational point of view, crippling and neurological handicaps would include all children with non-sensory physical handicaps whether or not they are accompanied by a neurological damage whether they result in chronic health condition or crippling. Muscle weakness, paralysis, non-coordination are grouped under neuro-muscular impairment. The difficulty usually occurs in nerves which innervate the muscles. This may result from infection or injury at any time during the individual's life. Poliomyelitis otherwise known as infantile paralysis comes under neurological impairment. Spina Bifida, Cerebral Palsy and Epilepsy are known neurological handicaps. They require special educational-services and treatment. These children show perceptual problems, inability for spatial orientation and judgement.

Speech impairment is the most common disorder among exceptional children. Speech is defective when it deviates so far from the speech of other people that it calls attention to itself, interferes with communication, or causes the child to be maladjusted. Much can be done for these children by the regular classroom teacher and speech therapist. These children have articulation problems, stuttering, voice disorders, delayed speech and language problems. Language disorders are characterised by abnormal comprehension and/or production of symbols, grammatical structure and words. These are corrected by appropriate language training and intervention from early stages. Speech defects are corrected by speech therapy. .

Slow learners are seen in the classroom. They are regarded in numerous ways. Slow learner refers to children and adolescents who learn or underachieve in one or more academic areas. Intellectually they are within 80 and 95 IQ points range i.e., on the borderline between average low average classification of intelligence. Slow learners are not special education students. They receive remedial education and for them the regular classroom curriculum and learning are applicable. There is no diagnostic or descriptive profile that characterises the slow learner. They are under achievers and they come from low socio-economic backgrounds. They have low self-concepts. They need educational attention but not special educational services.

Gifted are those children whose cognitive abilities place them in the upper three to five per cent of the population. The gifted children have an IQ of 130 and above. They have superior cognitive ability, creativity in thinking and production. They display superior ability in problem solving and possess high aspiration, high motivation, goal oriented behaviour, analytical ability, perseverance, action oriented, linguistic competence and physical abilities. They learn faster and remember for longer time than average or normal children. But for rare exceptions they are well adjusted in home and school. They can be future problem solvers, innovators, and evaluators of culture if adequate educational experiences are provided.

The presence of more than one type of disability in an individual is referred to as multiple handicap. Most multiple handicapped children are characterised by mental retardation along with another physical disability. Emotional disturbance is also often associated with other disabilities i.e., cerebral palsy, epilepsy and mental retardation. Much thought is currently being given to the education of multiple handicapped children. The term does not include deaf-blind children.

Social Disadvantaged Children refer to children who come from socio-economically backward sections of the community who cannot profit from school because of deprivation of one sort or another. They live in interior tribal and rural areas of the country where educational facilities are minimal. These children have been identified by various types of tests which are either in conflict with one another or are not comprehensive enough, (Panda, 1995). The disadvantaged children show progressive decline in intellectual functioning, cumulative academic deficits, and premature school termination and, high dropout rates. Besides these, the behavioural characteristics include: distractibility, poor self-concept, low motivation, and impulsive behaviour.

Can these children be called as "Children with Special Needs?" It is true that these children have special educational needs and the term special needs children is also used simultaneously for exceptional children. A brief discussion on this point is imperative.

The concept "children with special educational needs" is of British origin. Prior to 1944, provision of education was made on the basis of a specific handicap i.e., visual and hearing impairment, essentially through charitable initiatives. The emphasis was more on training than on education. Originally, provision for children with sensory and physical disabilities and mental handicaps were made, and subsequently extended to those with emotional and behavioural problems.

In the period following World War-II an increasing amount of research was directed at children with special education needs, particularly in the USA. It was recognised that this could not be achieved through the classification of children into handicap categories which had no direct educational implications. Parents became conscious and concerned that their children's educational needs should be met and in the period following the War many parents' organisations were started which then exerted pressure to improve educational provisions. This was the second cycle of development in special education.

Research on social deprivation indicated that children's educational progress did not reflect factors within the child but within the child's environment. This led to the Head Start programme in USA and "the educational priority area" programme in Britain. The third development was growing concern for the rights of the minorities. Equal educational opportunities were seen as essential to realising the rights through participation in the general system of education.

Integrated education was regarded as necessary to enable an individual to become an accepted member of society. These views led to a strong demand that those with special educational needs should be educated in ordinary schools. Integrated education in different forms was introduced, but in Britain it waited to be implemented till the 1988 Education Act was formulated about special education needs.

2

Basic Concepts

The term "Exceptional Children" refers to those children who deviate from normal children in any way. The Committee for the National Society for the Study of Education has described exceptional children as "those who deviate from what is supposed to be average in physical, mental, emotional or social characteristics to such an extent that they require educational services in order to develop their maximum capacity. H.J. Baker has emphasised that these children do not form a separate class. Even they are not also distinct from normal children (Baker, HA; 1953). These children are far enough below or far enough above the average range. They need specialised attention which is not provided in regular classrooms. The basic educational aim is similar to that of all other children. But only the means of education differ. Here, the basic guiding principle is equality, not identity.

In the classroom, children are so distributed that a majority of them may be classified as average or normal. Some children are there who deviate mentally socially, educationally or physically from normal children. Such children require special educational care and their adjustment problems have to be tackled in an exceptional manner. These deviated children come under the designation of "Exceptional Children".

According to Barbe, "exceptional" refers to those children who differ from the average to an extent that their differences warrant some type of special school adjustment, either within the regular classroom or in special classes. According to psychologists, all children are "exceptional" because they are unique in themselves and are different from one another. In other words, children differ from each other in a variety of ways. Anyhow children are not alike in any way. Every child is unique. The difference in the case of exceptional children is only one of degree. The word "exceptional" according to Barbe, is only used to obtain a better understanding of the child. The difference lies in learning or behaviour of the child. For example, many students have impaired vision, but most of the cases can be corrected by glasses. Only a few require special helps like large print, magnifiers or braille materials. These students can be categorised under "exceptional children".

Crow and Crow say: "the term typical or exceptional is applied to a trait or to a person possessing the trait if the extent of deviation from normal possession of that trait is so great that because of it, the individual warrants and receives special attention from his behaviour responses and activities are thereby affected." The following classification may be made taking the above definition of "exceptional children" into consideration.

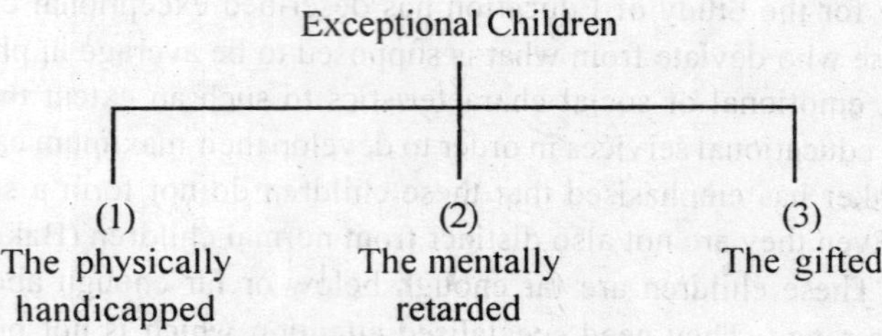

The physically handicapped, can be sub-grouped under the category of the crippled, the blind, the near blind, the deaf, and those having defective speech and delicate health.

Presently, only a small number of exceptional children are receiving the special services they need. In some affluent societies, special instructional techniques, equipment and school schedules are being organised to meet their needs. Teachers, with professional qualifications, are also being employed to educate them. Special training programmes are also being undertaken by governments to help the teachers.

Teachers who work with exceptional children need to have abundant confidence, self-control and self-direction. Sometimes, patience and perseverance bring success. The education of the exceptional child should be taken as a problem to be solved. The teachers must develop a scientific attitude in dealing with it. If some methods do not work, they should try out other methods. If certain materials are not productive, they should be done away with. The teachers should keep themselves physically and mentally fit, otherwise they are likely to develop a habit of fault finding or become over-critical towards the children.

In a developing country like India, the facilities available to educate exceptional children are not as sophisticated as in developed countries. Although Article 45 of the Indian Constitution says that free and compulsory education should be provided for all children, including those who are physically, mentally and socially handicapped, no steps have been taken to extend this benefit to the handicapped children. Recently, some guidance centres were opened in metropolitan cities to enable parents and teachers to deal with such students. Of course, in the last few decades, interest in behavioural therapy has greatly increased. In the 1950s behaviour modification was not even considered a major technique for application to children; but in the 1970s, there were several treatises devoted exclusively to behaviour modification.

In India, the guidance movement started in Calcutta in 1938. Later guidance centres were opened in Patna (1945), Bombay (1947) and Allahabad (1948). In 1954, a Central Bureau of Educational and Vocational Guidance was established at Delhi by the Ministry of Education. It offered financial help to the state governments to start their own bureaus.

In the developed countries, child guidance has become an integral part of their health and educational services. They have child guidance centres just as they have schools and hospitals. At these centres, parents, teachers, doctors, nurses and juvenile court magistrates are given advice on the management and upbringing of problem children.

Generally, a child guidance centre has a psychiatrist or psychotherapist, a social worker and a psychologist. At some centres, there are also paediatricians, play therapists and speech therapists. Unless remedial measures are adopted during childhood, the life of the child becomes miserable. As an Indian proverb puts it, what cannot be bent as a plant, cannot be bent as a tree. If proper attention is paid, a number of maladjustments can be easily rectified.

Specific Needs

Exceptional children need special education services. Emphasis is placed upon three factors. These are:

(i) In institutions where special educational programmes are to be taken up, trained professional personnel should be appointed by the authorities. They should include teachers, teacher educators, administrators, consultants, psychiatrists, psychotherapists, psychoanalysts, speech therapists and physiotherapists.

(ii) Special courses of study suiting different areas of exceptionality should be prepared by experts. Depending on the severity of the problem, specialised courses should be undertaken for mental retardation, giftedness, deafness, blindness, orthopaedic handicaps, cerebral palsy, etc.

(iii) Exceptional children should be provided greater facilities than normal children. These should include special building features, equipment, materials and crafts.

In special classrooms, study courses should be taught by experts. Recently, stress has been laid on special education programmes development for exceptional children as a part of the general education. Earlier, special education was confined to those exceptional children who were assigned to special classes. Now special programmes laying emphasis on separate special classes is discharged as much as possible.

Need for Special Education

The following objectives of special education should be borne in mind:

(i) The most important goal of special education is to reach the maximum level of effectiveness in tool subjects.

(ii) Both physical and mental hygiene of the handicapped school children are to be considered.

(iii) Preparation of curricular matters that strategically determine effective living for a particular type of handicapped children.

(iv) Development of motivational patterns in the exceptional children which produce achievement in the school.

(v) Interest in the handicapped for participation in the activities of the non-handicapped is to be created.

(vi) Priority to be given to the development of a realistic self-concept in handicapped children.

Educational psychologists have formulated a set of axioms on which the total edifice of special education stands. These can be enumerated as follows:

(i) Every child in this world is unique. First, each exceptional child is a child. He has the same right to acceptance and understanding as other children. So he should get the same educational privileges.

(ii) Studies reveal that there are wide individual differences among children in each domain of exceptionality.

(iii) Early screening, identification and placement in special educational programmes are essential because exceptional children make optimal progress in educational institutions.

(iv) In order to have proper placement, a team approach is essential. The team should consist of psychologists, educational specialists, psychiatrists and medical personnel.

(v) Since the team requires well-trained and competent persons, programmes should not be augmented till these personnel are available.

(vi) A special curriculum should be prepared to match the needs of the exceptional children.

(vii) The domains of exceptionality will determine the quantity and nature of materials required.

(viii) Emphasis must be placed on the fact that education for exceptional children should form an integral part of a total educational programme.

(ix) To ensure progress, there should be continuous reassessment of exceptional children. Sometimes, revaluation of institutional programmers is also necessary.

(x) The school must take the responsibility of placement assistance for each student.

(xi) When clarification is sought by the public and parents, special educational programmes should be interpreted lucidly.

(xii) For promotion of research activities, selection of teachers and training programmers, the central, state, and local agencies should have joint responsibility.

Various Types

Psychologists have classified exceptional children into many broad categories each of them having one or more types. Some of the major divisions are discussed below:

Physically Challenged Kids

This category is generally known as physically handicapped children. "An individual who is afflicted with a physical impairment that, in any way, limits or inhibits his participation in normal activities may be referred to as physically handicapped." In other words, we can say that any person having a disability is called handicapped. A disability consists of the objectively defined impairment of structure or function. For example, the loss of vision in one eye or the hearing in one ear is a disability.

The extent to which any disability handicaps its possessor always depends upon circumstances. There are some disabilities which do not operate really as a handicap. For example, colour blindness is a handicap for a navigation officer at sea, a car or train driver on the road or rail. But it is not a handicap in securing a job not requiring colour vision. A stammerer cannot be a good orator. It is a handicap for him. He may not be a good lawyer. But he may be a good scientist. Of course, some of the disabilities can be mitigated with the aid of sophisticated instruments like hearing aids for hard-of-hearing and self-propelled chairs for parapalgies.

As a rule, a handicap is a partial disability. In handicapped children, the disability usually affects one organ, sense or system, the rest remaining unimpaired, or being even better than average. The handicap does not necessarily reduce all the power and abilities, though it does restrict their range. For example, a blind child may have strong legs, but he will find it difficult to walk in unfamiliar places. It is important to note that some disabilities can produce secondary handicaps. For example, a child with normal speech organs but with other severe defects is likely to have speech defects.

Now we will discuss some more physical handicaps found in children.

Visually Handicapped Children : Blindness is regarded as the most severe and traumatic of the physical handicaps. The visually handicapped have always been the favoured group compared to those with other types of disabilities. Social and educational provisions have been made considering them as the most important group. Special rights and privileges are given to them. This group has attracted more public concern than any other category of the handicapped.

Blindness is caused by certain environmental and genetic agents. These etiological agents include infections, diseases, accidents, poisoning, tumours and cancer. However, much of the incidence of blindness is attributed to pre-natal factors. The blind are easily identified, but the partially sighted require a detailed examination. Total blindness is an obvious condition, easy to recognise and define, but partial blindness is rather difficult to recognise and define. Blindness is viewed from different angles. There is "educational blindness", "legal blindness", "medical blindness", "occupational blindness", etc.

The professionals and the authorities have two important objectives: (i) to prevent blindness and other types of visual impairment by finding the causes: diseases, malformations, accidents, etc., and (ii) to make adequate provisions for those already affected.

Children, with a defective vision, may be classified into two categories educationally. These are (i) The blind, whose vision is so defective that they cannot be educated through visual methods; they have to be educated through channels other than vision; (ii) The partially sighted are able to utilise vision in acquiring educational skills. Partially sighted children are those who have defective vision even after correction. Adaptation of the visual materials and special methods of instruction are required for them. While a partially sighted child can utilise vision as an important channel of learning, a totally blind child must rely on other approaches, primarily auditory and tactual. For this reason, a distinction between normal vision, partial sight and blindness is made on the basis of visual equity.

When the child is one year old or even earlier, total blindness can be detected. But the detection of a partially sighted child is a much more difficult job. The reason is that such a child has little concept of vision and hence it is difficult for him to report about his visual problems. Sometimes visual impairment is detected even after the child reaches school age. Very often, such a child may appear to be clumsy, careless or mentally backward. Anyhow, the degree of blindness and the age of its onset must be given priority in planning for the education of the blind child. A child who is born blind depends upon hearing and touch for acquiring knowledge. But a child who becomes blind after birth may retain his visual imagery and correlate what he hears or touches with it. Research works on blind children have revealed that the deviations in vision have not caused significant discrepancies in growth patterns. So such children may be educated along with visually normal children if adaptations are made in equipment and instructional methods.

When both vision and audition are seriously impaired, the problems of education and social adjustment become cumulative. Education of these children becomes demanding, tedious and a one-to-one teaching-learning process. Here the role of a teacher becomes very complex. He often becomes a friend to the handicapped child and provides him constant social contact. In the first stage, education is directed at establishing contacts with the external world and arousing interest in learning. For this purpose, special educational programmes for the blind have been devised. Here the emphasis is placed on the individualisation of instruction and formation of small groups. That means the class must consist of four children only. Here the special educational needs of the blind are learning of braille, extensive use of auditory, tactual and kinesthetic experiences and special mobility training. With the help of large prints and magnification, the partially educated children are educated. Nowadays, sheltered workshops are playing a vital role in vocational training and employment of the blind. Previously, the vocational emphasis at these workshops was almost exclusively on things like brooms, rugs and brushes. But now, the workshops often subcontract for various industrial concerns. In Mumbai, one such workshop has been set up at Worli. It imparts good vocational training and employment to visually handicapped individuals.

Aurally Handicapped Children : Verbal communication and speech development through hearing are major sensory pathways for a human being. If a child hears imperfectly, there is every possibility that he will speak incorrectly. Hearing also influences learning and other aspects of maturation. If a hearing impairment is detected in early childhood, there is every chance of its being corrected. If detected late, there is every chance of the child developing a functional disability.

Auditory defects can be found in either one or both ears. Sometimes children have no power of hearing at all. Some terms are used to denote auditory impairments. These are: "deaf', "hard of hearing", "partially deaf" and "deaf mute". However, no classification has been found totally correct. Some of the major variables are the degree and type of hearing loss and age of its onset.

The term :'deaf' is applied only to a person who has never had hearing or who lost his hearing before he learnt to speak. A person who loses his hearing after he has acquired speech is known as "hard of hearing". Deaf children have a profound hearing loss. They have to be educated through a sense modality other than the ear. These children can be placed under separate categories according to the onset of the hearing loss. Children born deaf are known as "congenitally deaf" and children who are born with normal hearing but later lose it are called "adventitiously deaf". "Hard of hearing" children have slight, marginal and moderate losses. They are educated through the auditory channel.

Hearing Defects

The aurally handicapped children are subdivided according to the organic hearing loss. These are as follows:

Conductive Hearing Loss: This is the most common hearing impairment among children. In this case there is reduction in the loudness of sound so that its clarity is distorted. This often results from pathological changes in the middle ear due to congenital or acquired defects of the ear. If it is mild, then a surgical or medical therapy is sufficient to cure it. Proper and timely treatment of acute infections in the middle ear and the prevention of chronic infections of the ear will often greatly reduce the incidence of hearing defects. Hearing aids and sound amplification systems are also conducive to mitigate conductive defects.

Sensori-neural Hearing Loss: This abnormality is generally caused by defects in the inner ear or in the auditory nerve. Medical or surgical therapy is of no use in curing it. Hearing aids employed for the amplification of sound are also of no help. Here, the sound is conducted without any difficulty, but the problem lies in analysing or perceiving it properly.

The most important therapy for children suffering from sensori-neural defects is educational. Hearing aids, auditory training, lip-reading and language training can help children having moderate defects. However, special schooling is needed for children with profound hearing impairments.

Psychogenic Hearing Loss: Here, the cause of the difficulty is purely psychological. Exaggerated symptoms of hearing impairment are often shown by the child. Very often, there is a history of ear infection which appears to act as a shock organ for localisation of the psychic symptom. Sometimes, under a stressful situation, the child may unconsciously develop hearing loss as an escape from what according to him is an intolerable situation. It is a very difficult job to distinguish between organic defects and psycliogenic losses. Appropriate audiological techniques and meticulous observation can often help to bring out a correct diagnosis.

Central Auditory Defects: These defects are extremely complex. Their causes and pathogenesis are not known. Children having them seem to be aware of sound but are unable to get its meaning. So they cause severe communication problems. During early infancy, use of certain life-saving drugs can also affect the auditory system. Such children require an extensive and prolonged therapy because they are difficult to manage.

Coming to the etiology of hearing defects, we can say that some hearing defects are predetermined by the genetic structure of the individual. Such anomalies may also be present at birth or may develop later in life. Sometimes these defects are caused by disease, trauma or accidents. The causes of profound deafness are not yet known. Physiologists have often found a hereditary type of degenerative disability in children having hearing defects. Post-natal causes include measles, mumps and scarlet fever etc. Defects in the auditory mechanism are also found to have been caused by typhoid fever and pneumonia. In early childhood, deafness is caused by encephalitis or meningitis. Chronic middle ear infection (otitis media) is another etiological factor contributing to deafness. Certain traumatic experiences, lack of oxygen at the time of birth and accidents are known to cause deafness. Studies reveal that psychological and emotional factors are also responsible for deafness. Very often psychogenic deafness is confused with malingering. But it can be detected by audiological tests.

Special schooling is needed for deaf children. The curriculum is somewhat similar to that for normal children. By adequate education and training, persons with hearing defects can be helped and later employed in all types of jobs not requiring much hearing capacity. At present, they hold semi-skilled and unskilled jobs. They often work as tailors, clerks, painters, typists and carpenters.

Sometimes, we show a lack of interest in and sympathy for aurally handicapped children. We become impatient towards them. Children having mild hearing defects often give the impression that they are inattentive, mentally retarded, clumsy and unmotivated.

Speech Handicapped Children : As we know, communication is an essential feature of interaction. Human interaction involves language. Most people confuse 'speech' with 'language'. As we see, quite a wide range of speech patterns is considered normal. When the speech of an individual differs significantly from that of others and it affects communication, it is diagnosed as a speech defect. The number of children suffering from speech defects is much more than the number of those having any other handicap.

Development of speech and language depends upon the speech mechanism and the psychological environment in which the child lives in. There are physical, social and psychological conditions which greatly affect the normal development of a child. These conditions can disrupt the development of the speech and language skills of the child ultimately.

The classification of speech defects depends mainly on the purpose of classification. A speech defect may be categorised according to such major symptoms as articulation disorders, voice disorders, delayed speech, stammering and disturbances of rhythm. Another typology is based on the cause according to which it may be organic or functional.

Organic causes include speech handicaps due to palatal defects, dental irregularities, paralysis, tumours in the larynx and brain damage, etc. Functional group comprises speech handicaps caused by general personality and emotional disturbances. But this dichotomy does not hold good for various reasons. Now we shall consider some of the major speech defects in detail.

Disorders of Articulation: The symptoms of this type of disorder include distortion, omission, addition or substitution of speech sounds. Very often it includes the mispronunciation of an entire word or words. This is a defect which is most commonly found among children. Statistics reveal that 70 to 80 per cent of speech defects are of this kind. In young children, this defect appears as immature speech. However, a good number of children soon outgrow it.

Disorders of Voice (Phonation): This type of disorder is found more often in adults than in children. It includes marked deviations in terms of loudness, quality, pitch or intensity of sounds. In addition, some other anomalies like breathiness, huskiness, nasality and hoarseness are also found. The causes may be emotional, vocal abuse, overuse or infections. Tension and shocks in life are also contributory factors.

Delayed Speech: Among children, the frequency of delayed speech is much higher than any other defects in communication. The chief causes of delayed speech are hearing loss, mental retardation, cerebral dysfunction, emotional disturbances and environmental deprivation. Very often, children are not able to speak at the usual age due to lack of motivation. Professional help should be sought for the treatment and diagnosis of delayed speech.

Stuttering and Stammering: Stuttering is a type of repetitive speech. Very often stuttering is confused with stammering. These are most serious forms of speech disorders. They are chiefly caused by emotional difficulties, fear of failure, fear of authority, anxiety, frustration, insecurity, hostility, over prodding by adults, etc. Ridiculing the children will aggravate the situation.

Stuttering is often considered a disorder of rhythm. In stammering, there appears to be a difficulty in producing any speech sound. A stutterer can articulate, but he is unable to enunciate the first consonant letter of a word. He, therefore, says: “g-g-garden”. The situation becomes embarrassing for both the sufferer and others with whom he desires to communicate and this tends to intensify the difficulty.

In both the cases, the affected children need to be treated by a specialist. Studies reveal that stammering does not cause any handicap in intellectual capacities. Many persons reach high positions in spite of the fact that they are stammerers. It has been found that between the ages of 2½, and 3½, stuttering is often due to a lack of correlation between thought, and language. In grown-up children it appears as a result of poor vocabulary, over-protective, dominant and overanxious parents.

Therapeutic procedures reveal that there are two approaches for the treatment of stammering: (i) Symptomatic treatment and (ii) Psychotherapy. Through symptomatic treatment, the patient seeks help for removal of the symptoms. He wants to stop stammering and speak fluently without hesitation, repetition or blocks. But in the later kind of treatment, stuttering is considered as a neurotic disorder. Here the professionals try to remove the symptoms, deal with the basic problems and conflicts based on the belief that speech will improve personality orientation and lead to better adjustment.

Disorders Associated with Cerebral Palsy: Children who suffer from cerebral palsy, i.e., spastics, as well as athetoid and ataxic children develop speech defects. In spastic children, articulatory deviations are found. The athetoid child shows slurring in thythm. The cerebral palsy children often lack the motivation to speak.

Research experiences indicate that more male children than female children develop speech defects. The etiological factors accounting for this speech disorder include anatomical defects, disturbed feelings, attitudes and emotions. Faulty language habits due to social pressures and unsatisfactory speech models are other contributory factors.

Mentally Retarded Children

Generally, we consider mental retardation as a disease. Earlier some people described it as a 'condition'. At one time mentally retarded children were rejected by society as they were thought to be possessed by demons. Nowadays, there is greater acceptance of and awareness about them among the general public. Certainly, mental retardation is a very complex medical, social and educational problem. It presents a strong challenge to our sophisticated society. It is a condition of arrest or incomplete development of mind existing before the age of 18 years.

Hebber (1962) was the first to attempt a standard definition of "mental retardation" taking intelligence, adaptive behaviour and developmental level into consideration. A more adequate definition was developed by the American Association of Mental Deficiency (AAMD) in 1973. It states: "Mental retardation refers to significantly sub-average general intellectual functioning existing concurrently with deficits in adaptive behaviour and manifested during developmental period". This developmental period includes the life span from birth to 18 years of age.

The study of mental retardation began with the work of Itard, a French physician. He tried to develop his ideas while studying the case of "The Wild Boy of Aveyron". Later, Seguin focussed on the appropriate educational placement of and provision for the low intelligent group of children.

Mental retardation implies impairment in intelligence from early life and inadequate mental development throughout the growing period. Studies have shown that 75 per cent of the retarded have no physical disability. They have sensori-defects, language disorders and neuro-muscular impairment.

Who is "Mentally Retarded?"

How can we know that a child is mentally retarded? I.Q. is taken as the criterion for identification of retardation and its classification. Of course, there is a controversy over the term I. Q.

If 100 is taken as the mean I.Q. and 15 as the standard deviation (S.D.), then all those who are two standard deviations above or below the mean (i.e., 70 I.Q. to 130 I.Q.) will be considered to have average intelligence. Those above 130 I.Q. (i.e., more than two standard deviations above the mean) are persons with "superior" intelligence and those with I.Q. below 70 are individuals who are mentally retarded.

There are many tests to measure I.Q. Two well-known tests are: (i) Standford-Binet and (11) Wechsler Scales. These tests offer deviation I.Qs. Besides these criteria, the concept of adaptive behaviour is also used in the classification and identification. Adaptive behaviour refers to the effectiveness with which an individual copes with the natural and social demands of his environment.

Clinical Classification of Mental Retardation

Taking I.Qs. into consideration, the following classification has been made by psychologists.

Level of Mental Retardation	*Wechsler I. Q.*	*Standford-Binet I.Q.*
(i) Mild	(55-69)	(52-67)
(ii) Moderate	(40-54)	(36-51)
(iii) Severe	(25-39)	(20-35)
(iv) Profound	Under 25	Under 20

The educational classification of retardation taking I.Qs into account is as follows:

	Level of Retardation	*I.Qs*
(i)	Educable	(60-85)
(ii)	Trainable	(30-60)
(iii)	Custodial	Below 30

Clinical evidences indicate that on an average 2.5 per cent of children in India are mild to moderately mentally retarded and 0.5 per cent severely retarded.

Since most parents of such children in India are not educated and affluent, they do not believe that their offspring are mentally retarded. They have a strong notion that if the child is not doing well in his studies, it is because he does not work hard. They strongly resent being told that their child is mentally retarded and needs special attention. So the first thing to do is to educate the parents to accept the situation. Tests of mental ability should be applied to the children and the parents made conversant with them. For the mentally retarded, adjustment problems are different from those faced by normal or gifted children. They should be treated with sympathy and patience.

If a mentally retarded child is admitted into school, his performance is very poor. There is every chance that he will discontinue his studies or he will remain in the lower grades for a long span of time. He is unable to compete with his classmates. Others expect him to show a performance equally that of a normal child. This attitude will make him frustrated.

In the table below, UNESCO has given the estimated proportion of mentally subnormal children in a school.

Degree of Mental Subnormality	*Terms in Current Use*	*Approximate I.Q. Level*	*Approximate percentage in Population of School Age*
(i) Severe Subnormality	Idiot	(0-19)	0.06
(ii) Moderate Subnormality	Imbecile	(20-49)	2.56 0.24
(iii) Mild Subnormality	Feeble-minded	(50-69)	2.26
(iv) Dull-Normal	Dull and Backward	(70-85 & 90)	10.00

(Estimated Proportion of Various Grades of Mentally Subnormal Children in the School Population)

From the above table it will be seen that in a school nearly 2.56 per cent of children have an estimated I.Q. lower than 70. So it is essential that mentally retarded children should be given special attention. They should be taught a simple vocabulary. The reading materials for them must be written around their life interests. Also they should be provided with vocational training.

Causes of Mental Retardation : There are many etiological factors related to mental retardation. These have seen classified in several ways by the psychologists. Broadly they may be classified into three groups: (i) Genetic, (ii) Organic, and (iii) Social. However, it is very often impossible to differentiate genetic or hereditary factors from the organic factors or from the environment or cultural factors.

For a long time, it was believed that mental retardation was the result of inherited defects. The famous Goddard story placed emphasis on inherited defects. During the American Revolutionary War, Martin married a barmaid who was considered to be mentally retarded. After the war he married again, this time an intelligent girl from his own class. Goddard (1912) traced both the lines of descendants for a number of generations. Astonishingly, he found many more feebleminded persons among the descendants of the feeble-minded barmaid than among those of the intelligent wives. Lastly, Goddard concluded that mental retardation is hereditary. Some recent research findings reveal that 20 to 25 per cent of the cases of mental retardation are due to genetic defects.

Coming to the organic causes of mental retardation, it can be said that this is characterised by a definite pathology in the central nervous system which is not hereditary. Such anomalies in the brain or nervous system may arise before birth, during birth or after birth. Organic causes also include birth injury, disease or toxic conditions. Mal-development of the embryo or foetus due to infection, such as 'German Measles', is another potent factor of mental retardation.

Social factors also play a major role in mental retardation such as adverse socio-economic conditions in which children are brought up. Children coming from the lowest social classes obviously have poor educational facilities.

Educating the Mentally Retarded : The educational goals for the mentally retarded are social competence, emotional security, occupational competence, academic achievement and adjustments in the home and family. Another important area is vocational adjustment. Retarded children who are eligible for vocational rehabilitation are often associated with vocational guidance. Retarded children who are unable to enter competitive employment may be eligible to work in workshops. These employed have often contributed a lot to society. They develop a feeling for work and accomplishment. No longer are they a liability to society. It is a matter of regret that many people do not think that mental retardation is a universal problem. It is true that the majority of mentally retarded children come from the disadvantaged strata of society. These children are generally poorly nourished and subjected to acute and chronic illnesses. They also receive less medical care than others.

Gifted Children

During the later part of the 19th century, the study of gifted children took a different turn. In the Greek and Roman periods of history, education of the gifted children was emphasised. After the publication of Galton's Hereditary Genius (1869) and Lombroso's The Man of Genius (1891), genius and insanity, were thought to be intimately related. However, the emphasis on the gifted children became more prominent after 1905, i.e., after the development of Binet's I.Q. tests and Terman's famous longitudinal study. During the later half of the 20th century, we find a renewal of interest in the gifted and talented.

Who is a Gifted Child? Gifted children are those whose cognitive abilities place them in the upper 3 to 5 per cent of the population. A gifted child has an I.Q. of 130 or above. These children have superior cognitive ability, creativeness in thinking and superior talent in specific domains. Not more than 2 per cent of the school population all expected to have this degree of intelligence. There is every possibility that gifted children present problems for the school management and organisation.

According to Guilford (1950), "The gifted are those students whose potential intellectual powers are at such a high ideational level in both productive and evaluative thinking that it can be reasonably assumed that they could be the future problem solvers, innovators and evaluators of the culture if adequate educational experiences are provided."

Different studies reveal that a large number of gifted children come from families of unusual ability and attainment. Development of this potentiality is dependent upon the combined efforts of the family, school and community. The incidence of giftedness is equally present in both boys and girls.

Research works in this field indicate that the gifted children are free from maladjustment problems. Some extremely gifted children have adjustment difficulties, but they are readily accepted by other people in their social behaviour.

The gifted children always prefer companions of their own level to those of average children. Also they want to develop friendship with those children who are slightly older than them. They are not at all introverted and disinterested in their communities. Their memory is very sharp and long-lasting. The rate of learning is also fast. Their language development is refined and elaborate. They have a high problem solving capacity. They exhibit novelty in expression. Always they want immediate rewards.

Early identification of the gifted is very essential to make adequate educational provision. The teacher of gifted children must be very flexible, who should allow them time to make new discoveries. The teacher must provide inspiration, encouragement and opportunities for them. Of course, guiding the gifted children towards effective living and productive learning is very difficult.

QUESTIONS

1. What do you understand by the term "exceptional children"? How will you arrange for their education?
2. Define "exceptional children". How many types of exceptional children are there?
3. Define "mental retardation". Discuss its different types.
4. "The gifted children" always create problems in school. What steps can a psychologist take to solve them?
5. Discuss the steps that should be taken to educate the physically handicapped children.
6. How do exceptional children differ from normal children?
7. What do you mean by "special education"? Why is it essential for exceptional children?
8. Prepare a plan for the education of exceptional children.
9. Distinguish between a "mentally retarded child" and a "gifted child". Give some characteristics of gifted children.
10. What are the special needs of gifted children that the school should cater to?
11. Write short notes on the following:
    a. Handicapped Children
    b. Gifted Children
    c. Exceptional Children
    d. Mental Retardation
    e. Special Education
    f. Stammering
    g. Stuttering
    h. Aurally Handicapped Children

3

Various Issues

Here, we deal with various issues and measures relating to the education of exceptional children. The focus is on issues such as:

- The concept of labelling a child and referring him/her for placement.
- Assessment in Special Education.
- The effects of special class placement of exceptional children.
- Deinstitutionalisation.
- Mainstreaming and/or Integration of exceptional children in regular schools.

Issues relating to integration and innovation are also covered such as:

- Small group instruction.
- Mastery learning strategy.
- Resource room instruction.
- The role of the resource teacher.
- The role of the regular teacher.
- Peer tutoring.
- Programmed Instruction.

Micro Computer in Education.
Ecology and Special Education.
Physical Education in Special Education.

Labelling

"Labelling refers to the act of assigning a child or a condition to a general category or to a particular position in the classification system" — (Hobbs, 1975). By implication it is generally negative. A label indicates that a stigma is present, particularly with mild handicapping classifications e.g., mental retardation, specific learning disabilities, emotional disturbance. In day to day life we often use labels for various purposes. Labels exert direct influence on our behaviour towards persons, objects, situations and issues. In the case of the handicapped the theory of deviance explains the attributions we make.

Referrals precede a child being labelled as disabled in one way or the other. It is initiated when significant learning or behavioural problems in the classroom are noticed. Although anyone can refer a child for special education, it is usually the regular teacher or parent who exercises this responsibility. A regular classroom teacher can use observation, criterion-referenced assessment, curriculum-based assessment for referral purposes. A teacher can observe systematically and collect baseline data, and develop the Criterion Referenced Test (CRT) to know how well or poorly a child is being compared to others. Recently, the Concept Based Assessment (CBA) has received considerable attention. This is an assessment procedure in terms of the expected curricular outcome of the school. The teacher simply monitors the progress with respect to school's curriculum.

After referral, the children are labelled on the basis of their eligibility and educational needs. Labels are used to provide some degree of communication among professionals. There are both positive and negative sides to labelling. Hobbs (1975) stated that labels led to improved legislation, improved communication, and the development of advocacy agencies. On the negative side, there are possibilities of stigmatisation, peer rejection, and wrong labelling of minority group children on the basis of inappropriate tests. The labelling process is not the easy as there are overlapping characteristics i.e., Mild mental retardation and learning disabilities. Hence, to provide a specific educational programme based on a label alone is obviously and inappropriate step.

Most severely handicapped students are identified prior to school age by parents and physicians. The majority of mildly handicapped students are usually identified by administration of educational and psychological tests. The physical or sensory disabilities are identified by non-educational procedures. Psychological and educational tests are non-referenced tests. These are relevant to most exceptional students. Labels are given according to test scores obtained by the child.

Some of the commonly used tests of intelligence and achievement used in assessing children for labelling purposes are:

1. Wechsler Intelligence Scale for Children-Revised.
2. Kaufman Assessment Battery for Children (sequential and simultaneous processing).
3. Wide Range Achievement Test-(Revised).
4. Peabody Individual Achievement Test-Revised.
5. AAMD Adaptive Behaviour Scale.

Following placement, the education of exceptional students is largely placed in the hands of the special education teacher. Of course, the regular teacher too takes responsibility, as well as the school counsellor, specialists and therapists wherever available. However, once a student has been deemed eligible to receive special education it is essential to develop an Individual Education Program (IEP). After the labelling and placement in a special setting, the question is asked how much of its is justifiable? Are there efficacy studies to substantiate this? Is the assessment correct?

The Assessment

Assessing children for identifying handicaps is a necessary step for placement. These are done in various ways. As a matter of fact, assessment in the field of special education has been more controversial than any other area of special education. For effective placement of a child in special education institution and for mainstreaming, two issues are of special concern: (i) assessment principles, and (ii) assessment procedures. Test measures or scores are not the *sine qua non of* assessment as assessment here means much more than simply a calculated figure. It requires proper screening for identification of all possible plus and minus points to prescribe guidelines for immediate and intermediate interventions and for the child's future placement in continuum of special education delivery processes.

An attempt has been made in this chapter to present an analysis of the salient features of psycho-educational assessment used for various categories of the handicapped and make the readers, practitioners and professionals aware of the shortcomings.

Traditionally assessment and intervention were regarded as independent processes but in Special Education both are integrated and dynamic. Assessment forms an integral part of the process of intervention. Assessment data should dictate intervention and the nature of pupil on the other hand would specify the assessment procedures. The form of psychological assessment now most prevalent in education fails utterly to do this.

The Deviations are:

1. Use of the test for purposes other than those for which they were designed e.g., use of intelligence tests for remedial and compensatory intervention whereas its function is for classification and placement. Intelligence score does not tell the teacher how best to teach. It simply shows the extent to which an individual child differs from others who took the test.
2. Use of technically inadequate tests in decision making and lack of concern for the type of culture to which the child is exposed as well as using inadequately constructed norms as reference pointy. Diagnostic Personnel should not routinely administer in such tests to children, nor use normative scores, and interpret and make important decisions. Careful consideration of the target group is necessary with reference to its cultural background. Measurement instruments must have empirical evidence, for their validity and reliability for use in such groups.
3. Use of Deficit Score to identify handicapped children is very much in vogue in case of learning disabled children. Discrepancy between capabilities (IQ test) and achievement levels are often used to identify the disabled learners. In fact, measurement errors accumulate when difference scores are used to identify children. One needs to carefully use the different scores.

4. Bias in assessment has been a subject of regular debate. Tests used should not only be non-discriminatory but decision makers should not be biased while making decisions basing their judgement on race, sex, SES, physical characteristics, parental power etc. Labelling has a tremendous effect on teacher's expectation and assessment of cognitive competence and achievement.
5. Assessment of abilities versus skills is another issue. It is better to use skill development models than the ability training model for design of instruction of the disabled. These are related to:
   a. To what extent does ability deficit account for achievement of academic skills?
   b. Does change in ability scores improve achievement skills?
   c. Should we design intervention on the basis of norm reference tests?
   d. Is intervention necessary when efficacy of intervention is marginal?
6. Competence of persons who assess the child varies very widely in our country. There is virtually no certification for test users in India.
7. Should we avoid assessment of disabled children? Certainly such a step is not desirable but a test administrator should know the kind of data to be collected; the kind of behaviour to be sampled; adequacy of tests to measure such traits; relevance of tests; and test administration and scoring procedures.
8. Certain ethical issues also deserve attention. These include:
   — No placement or denial of placement should occur without a full and individual evaluation of each child's special educational needs.
   — Evaluation must be in the primary language of the child.
   — All evaluation devices must be professionally and properly validated for the specific purpose for which the school proposes to use them.
   — Tests should be administered by trained personnel.

— Assessment should contain more than an IQ test.
— No one test can be used for placement.
— Adaptive behaviour, physical condition, and cultural background are to be ascertained.
— Re-evaluation should be a necessary condition of psycho-educational assessment and diagnosis because "when a programme talks about labelling someone as a particular type and such label could remain with him for the remainder of his life, the margin of error must be almost nil".

9. Cost effectiveness and feasibility in terms of time and objective of assessment need attention. For screening purposes one can use the Group Administered Norm Referenced Test; or the Multiple Skill Test (Iowa Test of Basic Skills); Cognitive Abilities Test; California Achievement Test; Stanford Achievement Test; Peabody Picture Vocabulary Test.
10. For placement purposes, for example, use of the Norm referenced criteria is appropriate enough using the Wepman Auditory Discrimination Test; Illinois Test of Psycholinguistic Abilities; Development Test of Visual Motor Integration; Development Test of Visual Perception; Bender Gestalt Test; American Association of Mental Deficiency; Adaptive Behaviour Scale; Edward's Personal Preference Schedule, California Personality Inventory, Thematic Appreception Test, or the Rorschack Ink Blot Test.

Special Class Placement

Special education services were designed to help handicapped children. But much can be said about the effectiveness of special education. It is effective, and it is not effective. There are several reasons for the equivocal nature of this generalisation. One important reason is the vaguely defined parameter of the group "the mildly handicapped", mildly retarded, learning disabled, emotionally disturbed etc. These mask treatment effectiveness, and do not provide an accurate picture of intervention efficacy in general.

Secondly, the Illinois Test of Psycholinguistic Abilities (ITPA) has served as the clinical test in various intervention programmes. The belief is that language training provides better scope for helping special children. This is not so. Efficacy studies on the basis of language intervention are divided. Meta analysis of the findings revealed that ITPA total score and subtest scores based on psycholinguistic training are quite effective and encouraging. For a basic area like language, the average elementary pupils gains about one standard deviation over the school year and exceeds about 84 per cent of the pupil's score made on the language achievement measure at the beginning of school year (Hamill and Larsen, 1978). Perceptual motor training has essentially no effect on achievement and cognitive outcomes and only a modest effect on the areas of which training is directed i.e., perceptual motor ability.

Visual or auditory training failed to produce any significant difference, in achievement on reading skill. But when a child's preferred mode of learning matched with the teaching method, modest improvement for auditory mode, visual mode or kinaesthetic mode of teaching were observed. But special class placement was most disadvantageous for handicapped children whose primary problem was lowered IQ levels. (EMR-.14, slow learner (76-90 IQ)-.34). The emotional and behaviour disordered pupils in a special class were better off than those in a regular class.

One significant factor which appears to lower the efficacy of special class placement is the lowered expectancy. It diverts instructional efforts away from academic pursuits towards a maintenance function. On the other hand, teacher's expectations are not dampened for learning disabled, behaviour and emotionally disturbed children of normal intelligence. This gives a direct focus to a system focusing on individual learning needs and abilities, in order to design the most effective programme of academic improvement necessary to overcome academic deficits. Hence, special education must seek out not new technology, but a frame of reference emphasising the potential for growth in all its clientele. Such a position must be "special" in special education to operate more effectively. It must come out of labelling effects.

It has been observed that a special education intervention that works in, one place may or may not work in another. The variability inherent in special education practices is compounded by the fact that it is essentially indeterminate. Special education interventions may or may not produce benefits but the final outcome is largely unpredictable.

Hence, special education does not require prescriptive pronouncement (Dunn, 1968).

Therefore, during the present decade great stress has been given to mainstreaming, normalisation, and integration of special needs children under the rubric of least restrictive environment. This trend is in sharp contrast to that of the past years prior to 1980. Concern is being expressed in implementing programmes that truly enhance the academic and social skills. The concept of handicap has undergone a change, the responsibilities of the special educator and regular education have also received recognition. Special education services in the form of integrated education are a response to this need.

Research attempting to observe developmental changes in self-concept and peer acceptance before and after labelling has resulted in mixed results. Labelling either improves or has no significant effect on self-concept and other acceptance. It is true that there is a strong case against use of labels, but some kind of generic classification and categorisation system is necessary for placement and for organising programmes for the handicapped. Negative connotations cannot be totally avoided but they can be reduced to a minimum if they are directly related to the special educational programme.

Deinstitutionalisation

Several concepts are used in this field to connote mainstreaming or integration such as deinstitutionalisation, normalisation, least restrictive environment (LRE). They are interrelated to the extent that a discussion of one is difficult without reference to the others. "Deinstitutionalisation" means that removing retarded persons from institutions and placing them in other environments. "Mainstreaming" means educating retarded persons as much as possible in classes with non-retarded persons. "Integration" basically means mainstreaming. "Normalisation" means that the individual's total environment should be as close as possible to that of non-handicapped person's environment. Segregation is only desirable when the nature of the handicap is such that education in regular classes with the use of supplementary aids and services cannot be achieved satisfactorily.

Deinstitutionalisation is a trend which grew in reaction to institutionalisation. In institutions, disabled children were considered physically or mentally ill and received treatment but no care and education. Around 1800 such institutions sprouted and as they grew in size they became less cost effective and housed people without much of treatment either. The trend continued. In the 1950s and 1960s a number of social movements took place to help the retarded e.g. President Kennedy's approach to mental illness which led to the establishment of community centres which provided impatient and outpatient care, treatment, consultation and education.

Deinstitutionalisation includes three processes (1) reversing institutionalisation by finding alternative placement, (2) returning to the community all residents who have developed the skills necessary for successful transition, (3) establishing residential environments that protect rights and lead to a rapid transition to the community. At the initial phase there also negative reports on deinstitutionalisation; (a) placement in nursing homes where the quality of care is less than at institutions, (b) primarily medication was the treatment, (c) readmissions to institutions since community facilities are not available, (d) poor medical diagnosis, (e) regression in adaptive behaviour, and (f) incompetent staff to look after the inmates.

Mainstreaming

Over the years, things have improved, diagnosis has become multidisciplinary, education has become the emphasis, trained professionals are available. Hence, the need for integration and mainstreaming is more felt. Mainstreaming is an approach that emphasizes integration and as such it is the antithesis of the earlier institutionalisation movement which emphasized segregation. But not until the 1970s was it thought fit to integrate retarded children, even though it was known earlier that special classes were not superior to regular classes, and that placement in special classes stigmatised those children. Hence, efforts are directed toward a less restricted educational environment.

The Council for Exceptional Children (CEC) has specified the essentials of mainstreaming the mildly disabled.

1. Providing the most appropriate education for each child in the least restrictive environment (LRE).
2. Concentrating on specific educational needs than on labelling.

3. Developing means by which regular classroom personnel can serve students with adjustment problems.
4. Writing the skills of regular and special educators to best serve the students.

Has mainstreaming a sound footing in research in special education? As early as 1968, Lloyd Dunn, the doyen of the special education movement, wrote a paper based on a decade of research called 'Special Education for the Mildly Retarded, Is much of it justifiable?' His arguments were quite understandable that in terms of cost, energy training of specialists and resource allocation, special schools and special classes for the mildly retarded did not yield substantial results in the area of academic achievement although improvements did occur in the areas of personal-social adjustment. Attempts were made to make the efficacy studies more objective but the findings virtually remained the same. Rather, placement of a mildly disabled child in a regular class contributed to a slightly better educational performance with the assistance of resource teachers, aids, and care. The differences appeared to be bridged due to pre-school intervention, built-in programmes of language, physical-motor coordination exercises, and manipulating personal social interaction among the peers in the classroom. Hence, in the late 1970's the cry was not for special education of the mildly disabled but integration and mainstreaming.

Mainstreaming is a relatively recent development in special education. In fact, the origin of the term 'mainstreaming' is not known. During the mid-twentieth century, several factors came together to precipitate change in the direction of mainstreaming. The research literature that relates most specifically to the mainstreaming movement deals with the mentally retarded.

"Mainstreaming is the education of mildly handicapped children in the regular classroom. It is a concept that is compatible with the least restrictive environment .... All the handicapped can be educated with their normal peers whenever possible. It is based on the philosophy of equal educational opportunity that is implemented through individual planning to promote appropriate learning, achievement and social normalisation." (Stephens, Blackhurt, and Magliocia, 1983, p. 3).

Mainstreaming does not mean placement of all exceptional students in regular classes. The key to mainstreaming is the placement of the mildly retarded in the regular classroom environment that best fits their needs. It can even be a regular classroom for the part of the day. Sometimes, it may not include a regular classroom but a special class in the regular setting, and extra-curricular activities determined by consideration of how best we may promote learning, achievement, and social normalisation.

Mainstreaming is a particular orientation towards supplying special education to the majority of the mildly retarded in particular and the handicapped in general. Environmental stimulation has significant positive effects on the development of retarded children. This was observed in the 1940s and gave a hard blow to the concepts of institutionalisation and segregation prevalent then. It opposed the idea that retardation was permanent and irreversible. Although the Skeels and Dye (1939) study was a landmark, the subsequent studies furthered the research into environmental factors which serve to diminish retardation. Multisensory approaches reduced learning disability. VAKT Multisensory approach (Visual-Auditory-Kinaesthetic-Tactual) approach became widespread.

While sociometirc studies admittedly showed low acceptance, by non-handicapped peers of handicapped children in mainstream classes they also showed that in special classes there is lower academic achievement and few social models from whom the handicapped could learn interpersonal skills. Efficacy studies have shown better academic achievement of regular class special children than those in special classes as highlighted by Dunn, 1968. Dunn's article was frequently cited as the consciousness-raising article that began the mainstreaming movement in earnest. It virtually led to an unwarranted assumption that all mildly handicapped children should be placed in the mainstream.

Mainstreaming, is no longer a fad or slogan. It has outgrown that stage. Mainstreaming is a workable process. It needs a comprehensive support system for its success in the school. Are the schools ready for it? What is meant by readiness? It means an individualised education programme, the least restricted environment and parental effort, particularly in the context of a developing country. Further the concept of integration and mainstreaming aim at bridging the differences between milder conditions of disability and the normal peers by providing access to equal educational opportunity under the least restrictive environment. The delivery models of such integration include placement of a mildly disabled child in a regular class with resource teachers for all purposes of acquisition of academic and social skills, an itinerant special teacher plan for a cluster of schools; partial integration where the disabled child lives in a residential setting but attends most of his classes in the regular class of a day school; on special classes with the children however, taking part in co-curricular and other activities of the school.

The objectives bridge up the initial entry differences in-

a. academic achievement,
b. social skills, and
c. economic sufficiency through development of vocational skills within the limits of the special children's educability.

The aim is never to replace special education classes or schools which could meet the demands of the severely disabled/ retarded. In a word, the objective of integration and mainstreaming is normalisation under the least restrictive environment (LRE).

Mainstreaming had its roots in the civil rights movements of the 1950s and 1960s which recognised segregation as illegal. Although the terms mainstreaming and LRE share historical antecedents they are not equivalent. LRE mandates that, to the maximum extent appropriate, handicapped children should be educated with non-handicapped children. In cases of severe handicap, the educational agency may remove a student to a special institution. Resource room or itinerant instruction, in which a visiting teacher takes special classes, is to be provided as a supplementary service to instruction in the regular classroom. Thus, if school personnel or others involved in evaluating and developing individualised educational programmes (IEPs) for students can justify a more restrictive placement than a regular classroom, that placement is acceptable with parental consent.

Mainstreaming has often been interpreted to mean that handicapped students must be instructed is regular classroom settings. According to the US Department of Education (1984) 68% of handicapped students receive most of their education in regular classes in the US, while an additional 25% are enrolled in special classes located in the same buildings as regular education classrooms. Placement in regular classrooms or in school buildings within these classrooms is presumed to give handicapped students more opportunities to be in contact with non-handicapped peers. Such exposure is thought to present behaviour patterns for handicapped students to emulate.

Placing handicapped students in the same classroom as non-handicapped students seems to result in desegregation. These students may occupy the same space but they may not be engaged in activities with one another. However, placement in regular classroom per se does not result in improved achievement or social status.

Handicapped students' social status has been improved when programmes were planned to help integrate them into the regular class setting. Kaufman, Gottlieb, Agard, and Kukic (1975) and Wang (1981) emphasized this as follows:

1. "Mainstreaming refers to the temporal, instructional and social integration of eligible exceptional children with normal peers. It is based on an ongoing individually determined educational needs assessment, requiring classification of responsibility for coordinated planning and programming by regular and special education administrative, instructional, and support personnel (Kauffman et. al., 1975; pp. 40-41)."
2. "The term mainstreaming is used to mean an integration of regular and exceptional children in a school setting where all children share the same resources and opportunities for learning on a full-time basis", (Wang, 1981, p. 196).

Several excellent works have discussed the historical and philosophical underpinnings of mainstreaming and LRE, and have analysed research studies conducted on the mainstreaming of handicapped students in regular classroom settings.

Integration

Integration is another expression used to mean mainstreaming. Integration cannot be reduced simply to an educational issue, or an employment issue. Its achievement will require the successful coordination of a whole series of transitions for the handicapped, ranging from early identification, to early intervention, to school programmes, to community, jobs and finally to community living.

An approach to integration that takes the individual needs of the special child into full consideration may result in one or more of following:

Physical integration - Planning for the location of special programmes in school buildings with regular education programmes.

Social integration - Planning for regular personal interactions between students who have handicaps and those who do not.

Academic integration - Planning to ensure students with and without handicaps simultaneously use school resources.

Societal integration - Planning designed to enable students with moderate and severe handicaps to work, live, and spend leisure time with their fellow non-handicapped citizens.

Integration means:

- Providing special services within the regular schools.
- Supporting regular teachers and administrators.
- Having students with disabilities follow the same schedule as non-disabled students.
- Involving disabled students in as many academic classes and extra-curricular activities as possible including music, art, field trips, assemblies and exercises.
- Arranging for disabled students to use library, playground, and other facilities at the same time as non-disabled students.
- Encouraging helper and buddy relationships between disabled and non-disabled students.
- Arranging for disabled students to receive their education in regular community environments when appropriate.
- Teaching all children to understand and accept human differences.
- Enrolling disabled children in the same schools they would attend if they did not have disabilities.
- Taking parents' concerns seriously.
- Providing an appropriate individualised programme.

Integration does not Mean:

- Dumping students with disabilities into regular programmes without preparation or support.

- Locating special education classes in a separate wing at a regular school.
- Grouping children with a wide range of disabilities and needs in the same programme.
- Exposing children to unnecessary hazards and risks.
- Ignoring children's individual needs.
- Placing too much demands on teachers and administrators.
- Ignoring parent's concerns.
- Isolating children with disabilities in regular schools.
- Putting older students with disabilities in classes for younger children i.e., age appropriate placement.
- Maintaining separate schedules for students in special education and regular education.

How to achieve mainstreaming and/or integration ?

Reynolds (1980) has suggested a set of specific targets in 10 different areas for effective mainstreaming and/or integration.

1. *Curriculum* - The preparation of all teachers should include the study of, and first hand experience with curricular principles, guides, and structures from pre-school through secondary school levels. The means and procedures by which curriculum is developed, adopted, and changed should be understood and there should be practice in designing and modifying curriculum and materials, especially to suit the individual needs of students.
2. *Teaching Basic Skills* - The preparation of all teachers should include necessary elements to assure competency in teaching the basic skills (defined to include literacy, life-maintenance, and personal-development skills).
3. *Class Management* - All teachers should be proficient in class management procedures, including a variety of ecological interventions, group techniques, crisis interventions, etc.
4. *Professional Consultation and Communication* - It is essential now that all teachers have opportunities to master the knowledge and practices involved in effective consultation and other forms of professional communication. All teachers should be skilled at group problem-solving.

5. *Teacher-Parent-Student Relationship* - All teachers should have skills and sensitivity for dealing with parents and siblings of handicapped students.
6. *Student-Student Relationships* - All teachers should be able to convey to students the positive attitudes necessary for productive interactions with normal peers.
7. *Exceptional Conditions* - All prospective teachers should have full knowledge about exceptional children, about school procedures for accommodating children's special needs, and in the functions of specialists who serve exceptional children. Moreover, opportunities for direct experience with the children and with specialists should be provided.
8. *Referral* - Teachers need to learn the procedures for referrals, the responsibilities involved, and the ways to capitalize on referral resources to obtain better education for individual pupils.
9. *Individualised Teaching* - All teachers should be competent in the assessment of the individual student's educational needs and in adapting instruction to the individual. Teachers should, have working knowledge of the IEP development process.
10. *Professional Values* - Professional educators' values ought to reflect a primary emphasis on the needs and rights of individual students.

The following issues emerge from the above for the purpose of implementing the integrated /mainstreamed education scheme.

1. Degree of segregation in the educational setting has to be spelled out for the mildly disabled. What type of integration would best fulfil the objectives needs to be decided.
2. Supportive systems and services for psychological, recreational, and vocational skill development have to be visualised and introduced.
3. Instructional procedures have been stereotyped due to the lack of exposure of existing teachers to special teaching techniques. There is need for in-service as well as pre-service teacher training.
4. Existing negative attitudes of teachers and normal peers towards mildly disabled children's capacities need to be changed.

5. Parental involvement and community participation in the total scheme of integrated education is important. The parents constitute a vital factor in the child's care and acceptance at home.
6. Integrated schools should use sensory stimulation and life skill training.
7. Routine placement of a mildly disabled child in regular school without due process of identification and diagnosis, and prescriptive teaching, is meaningless.
8. Normal and mildly disabled teacher-pupil ratio, in classes needs major attention.
9. Preparation for early intervention programmes, quality of intervention, and management must be made.
10. Behaviour management resource specialists should be used and resource rooms installed.
11. Professional intolerance and alienation among specialists of different disciplines should be minimised.
12. Delineation of activities by different service delivery systems in the total scheme of integrated education is required.
13. Development of infrastructure and instructional materials in regional and state languages for the resource room is needed.

QUESTIONS

1. Explain the concept of labelling. What is the effect of labelling?
2. Is the special education system justified for handicapped children?
3. What is mainstreaming or integrated education? How can it be effective?
4. How can a resource room plan contribute to effective mainstreaming?

4

Special Education

The very term "Special Education" includes all aspects of education which are applied to exceptional children-Physical, Mental, Disadvantaged and Gifted children. But these methods are not usually adopted for average children. Special education has a long history. The basis of caste system is connected with the concept of Special Education. In the primitive era, the Brahmins were supposed to be academically talented, the Kshatriyas talented in warfare. Similarly, the trainings of Vaisyas and Sudras were also different. This was done primarily to bring out the different categories of people with various talents.

Students have been individually tutored by their parents or teachers who recognised their talents. Modern educational techniques also follow the same procedures for educating gifted children. Our educationists pay little attention to gifted children due to preoccupation with the normal and backward children. The different views taken on Special Education have sparked off controversies of segregating- some children from the mainstream and providing them with extra opportunities.

As generally considered, special education is not a total programme which is entirely different from the education of ordinary children. Rather it includes those aspects of education which are specific in addition to the regular programme for all children. In some developed countries like USA and UK, these types of schools are mostly residential. But in a developing country like India, residential schools are very rare and now care is being taken to provide certain facilities to these types of children in some metropolitan cities.

The Importance

It is true that the backward children and the talented children need specific facilities for their development. So educationists feel the importance of special education for them.

(i) Special classes are necessary for backward children because they require specific teaching methods.

(ii) Talented children face difficulties in adjusting themselves with average children because they belong to a higher I.Q. group. In general, it is found that the teaching expert moves at his speed which suits average children. But a child with superior intelligence finishes the task much earlier. Here the problem is how a talented child will spend the rest of his time while the teacher continues the same task for the average children. Very often, the talented child is up to mischievous pranks. Also the curriculum meant for the average child is too simple and gets monotonous for the gifted one. Here the talented children do not get any kind of stimulation and lose interest in their studies.

Anyhow, in due course, the gifted children become aware of their superiority. The possibility of such awareness is more when they are kept with the children of average ability than when they are grouped with other talented children in a special class. So in regular classes, there is every possibility that the talented children run the risk of developing conceit in their attitude. They become self-conscious about their own ability. There is a strict boundary line between their ability and the ability of the average students. The separating line is pertinent and sharp.

Very often the class teachers ask questions to the talented students in the class and they also anticipate correct answers from them. By doing that, they boost the ego of the talented students. Sometimes the teachers also ask the bright children in the class to help the average students in solving some problems. So it provides the opportunity for gifted children to realise their superiority. On the other hand, the presence of bright children in regular classes invites certain problems for average children. The average children develop a feeling of inferiority which may lead to further psychological problems.

Considering the above two points, it can be suggested that the backward children as well as the gifted children should be separated from normal children for their upliftment. But arguments were advanced in favour as well as against the segregation. The supporters of segregation reveal that the backward children feel more secure when they are forced to work with children of their own type and ability. They feel inferior when they are forced to work with better achievers. On the contrary, the educationists who nullified the idea argue that these children have to live with normal children in the long run, and should not be denied the experiences of learning with them.

The best compromise, some psychologists feel, is that a special class is necessary for exceptional children in the average school where they may spend a part of their school time span with children of specific backwardness.

(iii) Special teaching facilities are required to meet the personal and social needs of exceptional children. So additional facilities enable the children to realise their potentialities and to minimise the handicaps arising from their anomalies. Here superior children are provided with the opportunity to work according to their talent. In an average class, a bright child feels the handicap. With little endeavour he comes out exceptional. He can stand and keep a position in the class with minimum effort. Of course, accelerated promotions call for many drawbacks.

(iv) Experimental data reveal that social maladjustment is found to be rampant with bright children in regular schools. The talented children stay idle in the class due to the light load of work. So they engage themselves in mischievous pranks and unapproved behaviour.

(v) In the special classes, the bright children get a chance for proper stimulation; but it becomes a problem for teaching experts to provide proper stimulation to both the talented and average students in an average class. Generally gifted children are more sensitive in comparison with the average children. They are quick and alert in thinking. So they require special techniques for being handled.

(vi) In a special class of gifted children, every student feels that he is not superior alone, but there are some other brighter ones. This thought helps a great deal in developing confidence. Again, special classes also provide opportunities for developing leadership in special branches. Among the group, there may be some children with special interest in poetry, drama, games and in other branches of knowledge. Proper encouragement and training under special programmes of education may help them in the long run.

(vii) Selective placement is entailed through special education. It involves the complete assessment of children as well as their social environment by professionally qualified experts from different fields. Physical examinations and evaluations by specialists and experts like ophthalmologists, audiologists, pathologists, psychiatrists, paediatricians, neurologists, psychologists and educational personnel are necessary for proper selective placement of many types of exceptional children.

(viii) Special education requires many auxiliary services. For example, the orthopaedically handicapped require physical therapy, occupational therapy and periodic physical examination. Some exceptional children need to be kept under constant medical supervision. Periodic examination may be necessary for blind children and the children who are partially blind and hard-of-hearing. Occupational and physical therapy with psychiatric and psychological services are also necessary for some exceptional children.

Of course, some special equipments and additional training are necessary for teaching experts and sometimes these are very expensive. As a matter of fact, neglect of exceptional children as well as the handicapped is more expensive than adequate training.

(ix) The importance of special education can be associated with the problem faced by a teacher in the average class. An average class, generally, consists of children of many categories such as handicapped (both physically and mentally), gifted (bright and superior) and some average or normal. The teacher has to devise a method of instruction which is suitable for all. But in putting this into practice, it is difficult for the teacher, for the students also face problems to understand the instructions. Some students also underestimate the instructions. Here the need for a special class is seriously felt. In a way, special education is not only meant to help the exceptional children but is also conducive for the regular class teachers.

(x) Very often, it is said that education begins where medicine ends. Providing a hearing aid to a hard-of-hearing child is, of course, of medical concern. But teaching the child to use his vision or hearing capacities effectively is certainly an educational function. If the hearing anomaly is corrected, then it is also a medical concern. But if it is not corrected, then it becomes an educational concern. For totally blind children, instruction in Braille, provision of special Braille materials, travel training and counselling are advised by educationists through special education.

Unfortunately only 5 per cent of the physically handicapped children (i.e., blind and deaf) are estimated to be in special schools and special care is being taken to educate them by experts in different disciplines. But most of these special schools are located in the metropolitan cities or in urban areas. But children by having rural background remain practically unserved by these educational schools. This accentuates the fact that a large number of special schools are needed to accommodate these children.

The Need

First, special education needs the identification of exceptional children and some provision made for experts to take them into account. This special education may be imparted in the regular classroom, special classroom or in a combination of both. Previously it was primarily confined to special classes. But now, a special education programme development for exceptional children is a part of total general education.

However, exceptional children require special education which include three elements, and these are:

(i) Trained professionals including teachers, educationists, physiotherapists and others are required.

(ii) Special curriculum is made for the children which suit different areas of exceptionality such as mental retardation, giftedness, deafness, blindness, orthopaedic handicap, cerebral palsy and social and emotional problems.

(iii) Some facilities including special building features, study materials and equipments are also collected for this purpose.

The Objectives

Considering the goals and objectives of special education, we come to the following points:

(a) By means of this, the realistic self-concept of that strategically determine effective living.

The NPE (1986) and the Programme of Action Relating to Special Schools

In the year 1986, the National Policy of Education (NPE) has suggested the following measures for the education of handicapped children.

- ***Development of Vocational Training Centres:*** The National Policy of Education suggested the establishment of special schools at the district and sub-district levels.

In addition to this, in every district where a special school is set up, a vocational training centre would also be developed. The establishment of special schools is based on the decision of sending the disabled children to the educational institution and to provide them the opportunity of post-education rehabilitation courses. Some parents are reluctant to send their children to the schools located at distant places. So the establishment of special schools as well as vocational centres solve their problem because residential classes would be possible through this policy. Again these children will get the opportunity to share with the specialists, therapists and psychologists under the same roof. These experts would support the educational efforts. The NPE has also felt that in a particular district, if the number of children afflicted by a particular disability becomes large enough (i.e., 60-70), separate special schools for that area of handicap can be established at a later stage. In the composite special schools, the children with different handicaps will be educated in different departments/groups/classrooms.

Vocational training centres provide opportunity to the students to choose the vocations of their interests. Special care is taken for training the craftsmen for locally available jobs. Separate hostel facilities are also provided for both boys and girls. The capacity for boys hostel should be around forty and that of girls around twenty.

Training of Teachers: NPE assumes that each special school will require 8 to 10 special teachers; so about 3,500 to 4,000 teachers will be required during the current plan. Training of special teachers (disability-wise) has to be taken up immediately if the proposed special schools at district headquarters have to function at the suggested speed. NPE also suggests that this task may be undertaken by the Ministry of Human Resource Development and Ministry of Welfare through UGC, NCERT, Regional College of Education, National Institutes of the Handicapped and selected university departments of special education. The in-service training programmes should be reinforced by the authorities and organisers of these programmes which should be carried out by the National institutes through its regional centres and the regional college of education in collaboration with SCERTs.

It has been mentioned in NPE that sometimes the voluntary agencies do not depute untrained teachers for training. Here, the grant may be made contingent on appointing trained ones or getting them trained within three years of their appointment. Any delay in this regard may be accomplished by proportionate reduction in the grant. Again, the grant-in-aid may be associated with the quality of the service provided by the institutions. Besides that NPE has felt that the special and vocational teachers for the handicapped children may be given additional special 20 per cent of the basic pay.

Special Schools in Plan Period: The NPE has also suggested to open another 5,000 special schools at sub-district level during the Eighth Five Year Plan, raising the total number of schools to about 7,500. There is also another proposal to increase the number of schools to 10,000 during the Ninth Five Year Plan. Again, establishment of special schools should come under the central scheme implemented through the state, or through the state machinery or through the voluntary sector. At least 400 special schools should have been established during the Seventh Five Year Plan itself. Priority should be given to establish the schools in the districts which have no such schools at all. Each of these schools must have at least 60 different types of handicapped children.

Orientation Programme for Personnel: At least 400 psychologists and 2 doctors in each district need to be specially trained for the task of assessment and rehabilitation of the handicapped children besides teachers. Service training for counsellors is also suggested for 4 to 6 weeks to assess the handicapped children meticulously. Orientation programmes for medical staff, physiotherapists, occupational therapists and speed therapists may also be arranged. Coordination and development of these programmes of training may be done with the help of Health and Welfare Ministry.

Modification of Curriculum: Modification of curriculum of these schools is a must keeping the specific learning problems in the forefront arising out of a particular handicap. For example, limitation of the blind child for science practicals and limitation of the deaf child to study more than one language need to be adjusted in the courses of study. Experts should note that these children should not miss the curriculum component that they can do. The NCERT should take the responsibility of preparing the curriculum and supply the curriculum guides and teacher's handbooks to special schools.

Special Examination: Flexibility in the examination system is a vital characteristic included in the schedule and it is a must for severely disabled children. Evaluation guides and tools for educational assessment should be made available to these schools. NCERT and the National Institutes may collaborate for the production of such materials.

Use of Technology in Special Education: Attention must be drawn to the use of technology in special education. This involves modification, adjustment and adaptation of the equipment and material in the learning resource centre. The Ministry of Welfare and electronic media may collaborate to produce such materials for improving learning opportunities for the handicapped. Television, computers, and video may come to the help of deaf children.

Strengthening of the Existing Special Schools: The NPE has suggested that the existing strength of the special schools should be increased wherever possible. The group also agreed to the recommendation made by the National Commission on teachers that "grants to special schools should be given on the same basis as the regular schools with adequate provision to meet the special needs of the disabled children."

Effective Supervision for Schools: Récently lack of supervision due to absence of infrastructure for maintenance of standards of special education in the institutions is very pronounced. NPE suggests that the Ministry of Welfare and Ministry of Human Resources Development may cooperatively develop an infrastructure for developing supervisory services to the special schools. A panel of supervisors may be introduced. The members of the staff at the district level may be provided with the knowledge and competence for carrying out such supervision. The staff members of District Rehabilitation Centres may also be associated with this supervision.

Promotion of Research Activities: Research works on education of the handicapped in Indian socio-cultural context is to be taken with immediate effect. The institutions like NCERT, ICSSR, UGC and the National Institute for the Handicapped should help in promoting research. The universities, research personnels and teaching experts show very little interest to work in this area. That is the reason why promotion of research activities comes to a standstill these days. The National Institute should take an active part in promoting the training of research workers, developing the designs for research and providing incentives to research workers.

Strengthening the Information System: The information system regarding the education of the handicapped is now very weak. Steps must be taken for strengthening the information system in every respect. The Ministry of Human Resource Development and the Ministry of Welfare should take an active part in it. The NPE also suggested to locate an Integrated Information System in the Ministry of Human Resource Development. The statistical report of the Ministry of HRD must include the data regarding the institutions made for handicapped children. Periodical surveys conducted by NCERT should also be included. Evaluative studies should be conducted by the Ministry of HRD and the Ministry of Welfare to assess the situation. Designs of evaluation should be developed by NCERT and the National Institute of the Handicapped to incorporate qualitative and quantitative aspects of special education.

Critical Assessment

A severe criticism of the special education for exceptional children is that the very idea is not democratic. A big question mark in the minds of the parents reveals that when all parents pay the same education fee why should the exceptional children be shown special preference towards these programmes?

So the critics say that "equal opportunity of education" should be provided for one and all. But arguments against this fact spell out that equal opportunity should be defined with reference to the needs of the individuals. According to some experts, who argue in favour of special education, if the programmes meant for the average do not meet the requirements of the gifted, that means no provision is made for the education of this particular group.

Taking a different stance, the educationists say that if the superior group is separated from the average group, then the gifted children tend to develop conceit. It has already been discussed that there is every probability of such conceit when they are left with the average children than when they are put with children of their own calibre. Some people consider that such programmes give rise to a kind of intellectual aristocracy and that there is a possibility of average children developing jealousy towards the talented ones.

Another criticism of special classes reveals that average children tend to lose when the talented ones are separated. They are deprived of learning many new and sophisticated things. Another counter-argument brings into focus that average children are deprived of leadership and become jealous when they are put together. Again, when the superior children are not separated, the competition becomes stiff. Consequently, the average chaps have to work hard to meet the goals. This may have a setback on their physical health.

Besides the above facts, selection and screening procedures are very important for exceptional children. Screening depends primarily on mental testing and achievement tests. Very often, psychological tests have been criticised as imperfect tools of assessment. Priority was given to teachers'reports, cumulative records of the pupils and other supplementary techniques. Meticulous examination is needed for selecting curriculum, methods, equipment and institution for gifted as well as average children. Enriched curriculum for gifted children and well planned curriculum for dull and average ones will be a boon to register significant progress.

QUESTIONS

1. Discuss the recommendations of the NPE for the education of physically handicapped children.
2. What is "Integrated Education?" Discuss its importance in educating the disabled children.
3. Discuss how physically handicapped children can be integrated into common schools.
4. What is "Special Education?" State the recommendations of the NPE for education in special schools.
5. State the role of "Special Education" in educating physically disabled children.

5

The Innovations

Innovative steps have been visualised and are in operation in recent years to make mainstreaming and/or integration effective. Teachers who know how to individualise instruction will have little difficulty integrating disabled pupils in the classroom. Individualised instruction in a classroom does not mean 30 students doing 30 different things at the same time. It means that after a general discussion, the class can be divided into three to five small groups for part of their instruction. It is in the small groups that the most pressing needs of the children can be met.

Teachers should be managers of learning, facilitaters of the learning experience rather than disbursers of information. All teachers need time to work with individual pupils or groups of pupils. Experienced teachers keep catch up time in the few minutes before recess, during lunch, or after school to help those pupils who need extra instruction. During this time they also help children to begin homework.

Small Group Instruction

Using small group instruction is another way to make mainstreaming more effective. Before using this technique the teachers should have sufficiently developed their classroom grouping skills to enable small pupil groups to function smoothly. They should be taught how to work in groups. The following instructions could be a starting point:

- Choose your two most trustworthy pupils.
- Assign them each a specific task to be completed outside class, such as preparing for a science demonstration.
- Excuse the pupils from regular class work. Make the assignment a choice one.
- Have the pupils put on their demonstration.
- Compliment pupils for a job well done.
- Get ready for complaints from others for such choice assignments. Now the stage is set.
- Select a reliable pupil and one of the less reliable ones.
- Gradually extend this procedure over five or six weeks to more and more small groups.
- Make sure that having a group assignment remain a privilege; this will encourage good behaviour.

Learning Strategy

Mastery learning techniques offer a systematic way to give pupils longer periods of time to master skills and concepts without penalty. In the long run mastery learning can save time by reducing the time for revision. Bloom (1964) has found that mastery learning hinges on pupil perseverance and aptitude, and on the clarity of the teacher's instructions. Pupil's perseverance tends to increase as pupils realise that they are learning.

In order to use mastery learning the following steps may be used. Use Mastery Learning by-

- Restricting mastery learning to the basic curriculum.
- Beginning with the most essential basic skills.
- Providing pupils with a short list of skills to learn.
- Having each pupil study, practice, self-test, recycle, and retest, with final checking (testing) by the teacher until mastery is achieved.
- Initially, allowing about 10 to 15 per cent more time for handicapped children.
- Drawing on assistance of tutors from other grades or the same grade, teacher aides, parent volunteers, programmed instructional units, microcomputer drills.

Mastery learning is an optimistic theory about teaching and learning that any teacher can virtually get all students to learn excellently, swiftly and self-confidently. Both exceptional and non-exceptional children can benefit from the system of instruction if it is systematic, if the tasks are broken into small steps, if goals are clearly stated, if sufficient time is given to the learners and there is some criteria of what constitutes mastery.

Bloom asserts that native intelligence matters in learning. But when instruction is matched to learner's present level of functioning, all students can learn fast. Mastery learning programmes are used successfully in special education programmes under IEP. Some of the materials used in special education classes are based on mastery learning principles. In order to make it more effective a resource room with a resource teacher are required.

Resource Room

The concept of resource room gained popularity following the declaration that the tracking system was illegal. ("Tracking" system is one by which children, based on IQ test achievements are placed in different classes, according to their ability. This was judged to violate the law on education of the disabled). This was the forerunner to mainstreaming and LRE. The resource room concept is a promising alternative to placement in self-contained classes or regular classes without support services. Usually students attending resource rooms are mildly handicapped and gifted exceptional children.

A resource room is a class which special needs students attend for less than 50% of their school hours. The resource room is staffed by a resource room teacher. Attendance in the resource room is determined by a multi-disciplinary staff according to the student's individual needs. Students attend in specific time slots when they receive remedial instruction from a trained specialist in their deficit areas. A resource room should be well equipped with a wide variety of instructional material. Individualised instruction may include perceptual training, language development, motor training, social and emotional development, and academic skills development. Resource room class size should be small. A recommended size per teacher would be no more than 20 students at any one time. Class sessions are either individual or in small groups of up to five students per session. The sessions continue for a minimum of 20 minutes and a maximum of 45 minutes in length. The resource room should have the same comfortable characteristics of a regular classroom, should be at least 150 square feet size with adequate lighting, and ventilation. The resource room should be easily accessible to teachers and students and possess adequate storage space for folders and materials. In general, the resource room should provide a positive learning environment.

Placement in the resource room is intended to be of short duration. As students progress toward specified goals they are returned to full-time placement in the regular classroom. Return to the regular classroom should progress through a gradual phasing out of support services. The resource room is to be considered as one type of service delivery within the continuum of services available.

Resource Teacher

'A resource teacher's role is open ended and limited only by time, talent and acceptance of the teacher by the school administration and staff. The resource teacher is a trained specialist who works with, and acts as a consultant to other teachers, providing materials and methods to those who are having difficulties within the regular classroom. Usually the resource teacher works with the mildly handicapped population in a centralised resource room.

The role of Resource Teacher has been identified as follows:

a. He should conduct and participate in the screening of children with learning disabilities, determine their learning abilities and prepare final report for referral.
b. He should provide instruction in small groups and individually.
c. He should prepare lessons for a child who cannot function in a regular classroom.
d. He should provide resource room help till the child is fully integrated in the regular class.
e. He should provide consultation to the regular classroom teacher and parents.

Requirements of Equipment for Resource Room Disability-Wise Inventory of Equipment and Material

Disability	*Aids and Equipments Individuals*	*Materials Shared within a School*	*Materials Shared amongst Schools*	*Instructional Material*
Orthopaedic	Adjustable furniture, special writing material, thick pen.	Adjustable furniture provision for development of improvised prosthetics.		
Visual Impaired Blind.	Braille slate and stylus Abacus, Taylor frame, Mobility canes.	Brailler, Abacus, Taylor frame, Cassettee and Talking books, Maps, Recreational material, Embossed recreational materials.	Braille sheets, Thermoform machine, Indu Brailon Maintenance services for Brailler, Embossed recreational materials.	Braille Material on cassette and talking books.

Contd.

Partially sighted and low vision children.	Special adaptive equipment like hand magnifiers to be used with spectacles, reading lamps.	Specially designed desks with adjustable magnifiers and white boards	Special arrangements for producing large print	Large print materials. materials,
Hearing Impaired.	Individual hearing aids.	voice trainer, Mirror 3' x 6' size for speech therapy, big mirrors 10' x 6' in each classroom, Group hearing aids, cell hearing aids.	Audiometer Voice trainer Maintenance facilities for hearing aids.	Special learning materials like flash charts, educational games, handouts of classroom activities.
Mentally Retarded		Sensory apparatus and kits prepared on the lines of Maria Montessori Kits or produced by NCERT for early Childhood Education Programmc.	level than	Material written on a lower reading average.

The resource teacher may be categorical, non-categorical, itinerant, teacher consultant to regular class teachers, parents and other personnel connected with the education of the child.

A resource teacher is a highly trained professional who is capable of diagnosing the child, planning and implementing the teaching programme, assisting the classroom teachers, providing continuous evaluation of the child and conducting in service sessions with other educators, and the community. The role of the resource teacher includes direct service to individuals and small groups of children, consultant services to classroom teachers, and assessment and delivery of individualised programmes.

The Special Education/Resource-room Teacher should

- find out ıf the student has the skills to function in the classroom,
- identify the physical or academic adaptations needed for the student to function in the regular class,
- identify the student's strengths and weaknesses,
- provide the handicapped student an opportunity to visit the regular education class and meet the teacher before he is enrolled there,
- determine the adapted equipment or the special services needed by students to function in the regular class,
- participate in planning for mainstreaming activities,
- participate in parent and community orientation programmes on mainstreaming,
- seek out consultative relationships with specialists on the school staff,
- develop programmes to prepare special students for entry into regular classes,
- prepare members of regular classes for the entry of special students into the class,
- gather information to determine the educational needs of each students,
- evaluate each student's present level of functioning,
- determine goals for each student that are appropriate, realistic and measurable,

- determine group goals for the class as a whole and for subsets within the class,
- involve parents in setting goals for their children,
- design teaching procedures that provide for individual differences among students,
- prepare a variety of activities that will involve the entire class in grouping patterns that are varied and flexible,
- design a variety of alternative teaching strategies,
- develop plans for using human and material resources,
- develop a flexible time schedule that provides for learning, as well as the physical and social needs of each student.

Regular Class Teacher

The regular class teacher where a child with special needs has been admitted should:

- learn about the student's handicapping condition,
- its common characteristics,
- the child's expected performance,
- common difficulties the disabled child will experience,
- learn about the appliances and special materials the child uses, e.g., pushing a wheel chair up or down stairs, storing wheel chairs, etc.,
- determine if any special methods, techniques, or adaptations are needed for the disabled child to function more independently and successfully,
- meet the special education teacher to determine specific strengths, weakness and needs of the handicapped student,
- prepare the classroom, remove obstacles, make necessary adaptations to furniture, rearrange furniture to help the special needs student, and so on,
- use various techniques to manage individual and group behaviour:
  - (i) Reward self-directed behaviour;
  - (ii) Teach how to respond to disruptive behaviour;
  - (iii) Use peer role models to advance goals;
  - (iv) Teach students to relieve aggression in acceptable ways.

- acknowledge appropriate behaviour in order to stimulate continuous effort;
- conduct class activities in ways to encourage student interaction;
- provide instruction in the development of coping strategies;
- plan with the students for systematic appraisal and improvement of the psychological climate of the class;
- collect and record data to evaluate student progress;
- develop a feedback system that will furnish continuous data to students, teachers, and parents;
- use evaluation data to assess the attainment of goals and to set new goals.

Stating it more realistically the regular as well as the special and resource room teachers for teaching exceptional children must be cognizant of their Rights, Roles, and Responsibilities. Mainstreaming therefore is the "End of the Quiet Revolution." The Rights of the exceptional learners are to be safeguarded while mainstreaming them in terms of their right to

— Public education,
— Individual education programme (IEP),
— Non-discriminatory evaluation,
— Due process of law,
— Least restrictive environment.

The IEP is the management tool that specifies the child's educational needs, annual goals for the child, the service provided and effectiveness of the programme. The IEP holds that individual educational needs of the child should be determined rather than the needs of categories of children.

Teaching exceptional children in the regular classroom does not mean watering down or slowing down the rate of curricula presented to the student. The disabled learner has problems with language facility, learning styles, motivation, consistent work and therefore the teacher has new roles to play. He does not simply slow down the speed.

The teacher must be careful and give specific directions to the student, many times if necessary. These should be presented both visually and verbally. The task must be presented at the students response level. The need of frequent praising and reserving criticism is important in motivating students who keep failing in school related tasks.

New learning tasks must be analysed by the teacher and broken into small sequential steps. Different sensory modalities may be used in combination. Repetition of difficult materials, review of earlier materials, use of several response modes e.g., tape recorded response, models, and drawing, for knowing comprehension may be used.

The teacher must evaluate the student's performance fairly. The teacher has to create a climate of acceptance for the learning disabled students without which they will feel rejected and isolated in the regular classroom.

Teamwork with other professionals gets importance in mainstreaming, particularly the principal, special-education teacher and school psychologists. Teachers dealing with exceptional pupils must be adequately trained through in service programmes. They should be acquainted with referral processes.

In a regular school the critical person is the special teacher or resource room teacher. A resource room setting involves movement of students through the resource room from the regular class on regular basis. Constant liason between the regular and resource teacher is required to help the exceptional child. There are other specialists who can assist the regular teacher i.e., speech therapists, language teachers, parents etc.

But the greatest obstacle to mainstreaming should be first removed i.e., negative attitudes towards the handicapped. Many students who are mainstreamed are identified prior to the time that they enter school, although the majority of them are identified by classroom teachers and are referred thereafter for assessment and placement.

Just as the resource room/special teacher, the regular teacher and other staff members have specific roles to play for successful mainstreaming, the special and regular students are no less important.

Regular Education Students should :

- listen to a special education teacher when he speaks to the class about the physically handicapped program;
- use a set of crutches or a wheel chair, to have experience of how it feels to be in a wheel chair or on crutches;

- spend a day in the special education class, simulating the handicap for the entire day, and then report the experience to the regular education class;
- read materials about handicaps.

Special Education Student should :

- engage in normal activities in the regular classroom, such as copying from the board, completing assignments with little assistance;
- invite one or more pupils from the regular class to become acquainted with students before mainstreaming. This is best accomplished through cooperative involvement in a task. The students will have buddies in the regular classroom; and
- get an opportunity to meet the regular classroom teacher before placement.

The Tutoring

Training pupils to teach one another, one to one or in small groups provides an extensive opportunity for individualised instruction. Peer tutoring is defined here as two, three, and sometimes four, or five pupils working together on the same task. Typically one pupil is being taught by another. Peer tutoring is mutual and interactive. In order to ensure it, the classroom teacher has to work out how to start, monitor, evaluate and terminate. Peer tutoring has salutory effects.

Resource Unit

A resource unit for various subject areas from which a teacher can make a selection for a target group of impaired children in mainstreamed classroom can be developed by following certain guidelines and activities.

These are:

- Decide the subject area for the resource unit.
- Prepare the curriculum by writing behavioural objectives for possible knowledge, skills, and concepts, for each unit.
- List related study skills that might be developed while completing the unit e.g., letter writing, public speaking, library use.

- Describe ways to initiate the unity to create pupil interest e.g., Bulletin boards, dramatizations, reading a poem or story etc.
- Prepare an extensive list of activities for the unit.
- Prepare list of available publications for pupils.
- Prepare a list of resources to include sites for a study trips, records, filmstrips, tapes, songs and dances, charts, maps, and so on.
- Describe a variety of ways to evaluate the unit.

Programmed Instructions

Programmed instruction is well suited for individualised instruction and for mastery learning. Programmed instruction can be effective in meeting the needs of several types of exceptional pupils:

- Because the material content has been thoroughly task-analyzed, slow learning pupils experience success.
- Visually impaired pupils can benefit from those programmed materials that have verbal responses using auditory presentation.
- Hearing impaired pupils can benefit from visual responses formats.
- Pupils with superior abilities can often experience an enriched curriculum by using programmed material.
- Programmed materials also help pupils who have health problems to catch up on content when they have been absent for a period of time.
- Physically handicapped pupils whose upper extremities are affected can benefit from programmed materials that do not require written responses, especially if the machine is easily advanced to the next frame.

Programmed materials can provide regular classroom teachers with another method of meeting the individual needs of a variety of pupils. The up-to-date mode for presenting programmed instruction is the microcomputer.

Use of Microcomputer

Microcomputers in the classroom are another very powerful tool for the mainstreaming teacher. The computer is probably the most powerful tool ever developed for helping pupils of widely varying needs, achievement levels, learning problems, or interests. The computer promises to bring teachers extra pairs of quality hands. It is highly motivating to most pupils.

For Pupils the Computer :

- Writes extremely large words on a screen particularly for the partially visually impaired pupil.
- Provides auditory accompaniment to visual symbols on the screen. What is typed on the computer is read back immediately by the microcomputer.
- Allows 30 pupils to work at 30 different skill levels in spelling, arithmetic, or other subject areas.
- Provides practice in typing.
- Provides eye-motor coordination skill drills.
- Increases reading speed and comprehension.
- Provides opportunities for creative thinking.
- Presents visual simulations of difficult concepts in animated form, slow or fast, repeatedly.
- Furnishes endless drill and practice on virtually any skill or concept to be mastered.
- Provides practice in problem solving.

For Teachers, the Computer :

- Facilitates data-based management such as storage and, retrieval of individual and class pupil records with the data analysed, summarized, and in consumable form for easy interpretation.
- Provides information retrieval such as finding specific references to go with special pupil needs.
- Develops daily pupil schedules.
- Observes demonstration teaching. There is a large screen which magnities everything on the microcomputer so the entire class can see what is happening. Using this, teachers can show and explain very abstract ideas, repeating them as often as necessary.

Why does the Microcomputer Work ?

The major reason why microcomputers really work as educational tools are stated below:

1. The machine is interactive; it is not passive like television.
2. The machine can be infinitely patient, unlike a human being
3. The pupil tends to become more relaxed, less tense and uptight than the presence of a human being.
4. The drill and practice programmes are similar to programmed instructional materials and work for the same reasons of immediate feedback, reinforcement, and pacing.
5. Many of the learning activities resemble actual games; there is a fascination about these games which we have yet to define precisely.
6. Micros are different in kind, not just in degree, from any learning system.
7. Sound programmes have been field-tested, revised and revised until they do work, until pupils do learn.
8. Microcomputers are incredibly fast and accurate.
9. Microcomputers enable both competency-based mastery learning of skills and open-ended, divergent-type thinking.

Technology for the Disabled

During the last 15 years things have changed greatly. Silicon chips and micro processors have changed society. Technology is gradually changing the life of disabled. The Computer has two characteristics that have significance and meaning for the disabled (a) decrease in size of hardware (b) increasing sophistication, while makes it easier to use. Micro computers can be attached to wheel chairs to improve mobility. They are more accessible for use by handicaps because mere key strokes are needed to perform computer functions.

The micro processor facilitates communication (a) as a compensatory device for sensory disabilities (b) as an assistive device for individuals whose physical impairments make communication difficult. Talking computer terminals can translate text into speech, special adaptive devices for micro computers that can provide visual displays of auditory information by translating sound into text. For motoric disabilities communication aids have developed that allow them to operate computers with single switch input devices. Key board enhancers and emulators help individuals with restricted movement by reducing the number of actuations necessary for communication, e.g., minispeak system adaptive communication devices can be linked to micro computers that can help the disabled to control his living environment in some ways: answering telephone calls, etc.

Telecommunication system helps the disabled to gather information and disseminate information. These should not be confined to schools alone. Computer networking also enables people to use information from far off remote places. Electronic Bulleting Boards and electronic mails, use of word processors and telecommunication software are beneficial to the disabled in sending and receiving information from large information libraries using telecommunication hook ups.

Often telecommunication is tele text, a one way transmission to television viewers. Current tele text applications include: news headlines, weather forecasts, school holidays. Closed captioning in a tele text is useful to hearing impaired individuals.

A video disk is a table top device that is interfaced with a monitor to play video programmes stored on 12 inch disks. When interfaced with a micro computer it becomes a powerful tool for instructional use. It can allow students to move ahead or go back according to learner's needs. Information can also be shown in slow motion. California school for the deaf has developed a system to use the video disk to teach language development and reading. With this system, students use light pens to write their responses on the screen. It is available on low cost at present.

Artificial intelligence refers to the use of computer to solve the same types of problems and to make the same kinds of decisions faced by humans. This has potential benefits to disabled individuals. Robots is a device that can be programmed to move in specified direction and to manipulate objects. To some extent, robots are being used in classrooms to teach computer logic. Robots are able to acquire information, understand it, and plan and implement appropriate actions.

Role of Ecology

Ecology means study of relationship between an organism and the environment. Its applications to special education is relatively new although it originated from Strauss, Lehtinen, and Cruickshank with brain injured children in 1940s.

Hobbs (1966) started the first Re-Ed project with emotionally disturbed children and recognised socialisation problems did not occur within child; it existed rather in the environment and its interactions with the labelled child. It is an environmental misfit. Therefore, the child has to be removed from the environment for helping him to be temporarily away from it, and then change the environment to suit him. Segregation was to be as brief as possible; normalisation was always the goal. Normalisation was possible for ED children through ecological intervention.

Broadly, the approach emphasized that disturbance or defect is not intrinsic perse, but the description of the interaction of a particular child with a particular environment. The search is for the mismatch in the eco-system. The study of the child occurs not in the sterility of the psychological laboratory, but in the naturalistic real world, holistic settings in which the problems occur. This is not to deny that emotional disturbance, mental retardation, learning disability are not real. The ecological focus in special education tries to show that looking only at internal factors cannot give the whole picture and that treatment approaches based on simplified, historical, etiological views can limit the success that parents and professional might face with disabled children.

Special education ecologist looks at both how child acts on the environment and how the environment acts on the child. They look for establishing an equilibrium by using appropriate coping skills, which may be taught to the child and engineered in the environment.

The ecological special educator studies the cultural relativity of the child's behaviour and tries to promote cultural conformity and adaptation between the child and the environment. It is not limited to emotionally, disturbed only but to all areas of disability. School related factors produced disability, learning and behaviour. Infact, we place regular and special education students for about 1100 hours per year in school without changing the school environment or designing the school environment. Partial attempts have been made for the physically handicapped children. Special educators must move away from the child focus approach to more of a pedagogy in which they test, observe and teach in the real world settings where skills must ultimately be generalised and demonstrated successfully.

Physical Education

The aim of physical education for the handicapped is to aid in achieving physical, social, and emotional growth commensurate with their potential. Accordingly handicapped students are required to take a battery of motor, physical fitness, and perceptual motor tests for the making of the yearly IEP.

Physical education programme has 3 basic functions: (i) input functions (ii) abilities (iii) motor skill. Basic input functions include equilibrium reflexes, vestibular system, vision, audition, tactile and kinaesthetic success. Perceptual motor abilities include: balance, laterality, directionality, body image, spatial awareness, cross-lateral integration. Physical fitness parameters consist of strength, muscle and cardiovascular endurance, and flexibility. Motor abilities include: speed, power, agility and motor coordination. If both there are intact, then skill acquisition occurs through movement and sports exercises. Hence, physical education instruction is a must for the disabled. The regular sports activities should be suitably modified to suit to the capabilities of the disabled. Play and sports for the disabled should be more organised and structured than those of the normal child.

Understanding special education processes are significant in planning the programmes for the handicapped. Infact, identification, referrals, placement, management in a particular service system is of crucial importance. More important at the moment is application of technology, computer, mastery learning techniques, programmed texts and several other innovations to the advantage of special needs children and their education. It is necessary, that practioners, teachers resource team should have a thorough understanding of the various aspects of disability and processes. The chapter highlights the need for mainstreaming the mildly handicapped.

Highlights

Several issues are at the crossroads in the development of education of exceptional children. Use of labels such as Mentally

Retarded, Physically Handicapped etc. put children at a disadvantage for no fault of theirs. Labelling has a negative/ stigmatising effect which further accentuates the shortcoming of the handicapped children.

Labels are used sometimes by way of discrimination, and have racial, ethnic, social class or personal basis and are the result of inadequate assessment procedures. The prevailing referral system based on use of psychometric assessment suffers from poor use and selection of tests, improper test, administrative bias in testing, etc., leading to wrongful placement of the handicapped child in a special school or special class. Assessment should be culture representative and comprehensive.

Studies on the efficacy of the special class have often led to improvement in socio-metirc relationships whereas arguments favouring better achievement of the handicapped in the regular setting are becoming common and sensible for the mildly handicapped children.

Advocacy programmes for mainstreaming the handicapped have gained momentum in theory and practice, although in most cases, integration has remained by and large at the physical level. This is but a transitional phenomenon. Mainstreaming provides most appropriate education for each under LRE; fulfils specific educational needs; helps in adjustment problems; develops skills in the handicapped. Effective mainstreaming and/or integration would further involve: curricular changes, class management, teaching of basic skills, teacher-parent-student relationships, appropriate referral services, individualised teaching and assistance in resource rooms.

In order to further speed up the process of normalisation, various innovative procedures are under way in the field which include: teaching handicapped children in small groups, using peers as tutors, adapting mastery learning and task analysis techniques, utilising resource rooms, resource teacher competencies, programmed materials, micro computers, and revitalising the regular classroom teacher in terms of new experimental inputs for handling the handicapped children in the regular classroom. Ecological understanding with a view to providing wholesome conducive educational environment and design of suitable physical activities for the handicapped have been a few major breakthroughs in special education.

QUESTIONS

1. What are the uses of micro-computers in special education?
2. What kind of technology can be used for the education of the disabled?
3. Explain ecology and special education from the point of view of integrating the disabled into the community.
4. What is the role of physical education for the disabled?
5. What is the role of a regular teacher in a mainstreamed class for the disabled?
6. What is the role of a resource teacher in a mainstreamed class for the disabled?
7. What is the role of the peer group on disabled peers in a mainstreamed classroom? What is the role of normal peers in this setting?

6

Special Education Services

An examination of special education in the school system reveals an incremental continuum or ordered array of special education classes designed to serve the individual needs of children. Special educators agree that a range or continuum of placement alternatives must exist for exceptional children (Deno, 1973).

Four aspects are unique about special education: specialized educators, special curricular content, special instructional methods, and special instructional materials. Prior to the mainstreaming trend these four services were almost always provided to children within the context of special classes or schools. These classes and schools were categorized along a continuum reflecting their degree of separation from the mainstream. Resource rooms, self-contained classes, special day schools, and residential treatment centres reflect this continuum, with resource rooms being a relatively less restrictive environment than residential centres. The goal is to place a child in the least restrictive environment relative to the severity of his or her handicapped condition. Therefore, even with the current trend toward mainstream programmes, many exceptional children will receive some of their education in one or more of the special environments outside regular classes.

Residential Schools

The residential school has two purposes:

a. The residential schools are primarily meant to provide 24 hour comprehensive education and care.

b. In certain cases where the care and management of the severely disabled child poses problems, it is necessary to send disabled children to residential institutions. In this case, the aim is not education. It is just a residential facility for care. Education is an adjunct to the total programme.

The children of either category are permitted to have as much contact with parents as possible, either by home visits, parental visits or both. But the greatest disadvantage of residential institutions is that they deprive children to mingle with normal children.

Home Bound or Hospitalised Instructions

The instruction is provided to children in Home/Hospitals in case they are under prolonged treatment for emotional problems, heart ailments, poliomyletes, chronic health problems. The special teacher goes to Home/Hospital to teach these children for a short period. It is psychologically and educationally useful.

High ↔ Cost for Service ↔ Low

Severe ↔ Severity of Handicap ↔ Mild

Most ↔ Environmental Restrictiveness ↔ Least

- Regular Classroom With Minor In-Class Support
- Regular Classroom With Weekly Itinerant Services
- Regular Classroom With Daily Resource Room Supplemental Programming
- Resource Room With Several Hours Of Daily Regular Classroom Instruction And Non- Instructional Activities
- Resource Room With Limited Hours Of Weekly Now Instructional Activities With Regular Classmates
- Self Contained Special Classroom
- Special Day School
- Homebound Or Hospitalization
- Residential

Figure : Continuum of Special Education Services

Special Day Schools

In many countries special day schools for various categories of handicapped children have been set up. These tend to be cheaper than special residential schools. In large cities, special day schools cater to the needs of one type of disability but in small cities they are meant for two disabilities. The defect in this system is that children are isolated from normal children.

Special Classes

Special class is a self-contained classroom in a regular school where a category of disabled children are admitted. There may be more than one special class depending on the number of children and the type of disability. This is specially meant for mentally retarded children. The children receive instruction in the special class and are separated from normal peers.

Resource Room

In this programme exceptional children, or children with special needs usually belonging to a single category, may be placed in a school for normal children. They participate in the regular classroom programme to the extent possible. For some time they go to a resource room where a specially qualified teacher instructs them in the use of special equipments and in overcoming special problems they may encounter in keeping up with academic or extra-curricular activities.

The resource room activities can be of three levels:

a. Resource room with limited hours of weekly non-instructional activities with regular classmates.
b. Resource room with several hours of daily regular classroom instruction and non-instructional activities.
c. Regular classroom with daily resource room supplementary programmes.

In this system which varies in degree of integration and use of resource room, the exceptional child is enrolled in the regular classroom. He receives much of his instruction there but he goes to the resource room to receive specialised instruction and use specialised equipments.

This plan is suitable for any type of child who can succeed in regular classes when provided with extra assistance. The resource room is well equipped with staff and equipment. The child becomes integrated with normal children academically and socially, in addition to his physical integration.

Regular Classroom

Under this system an exceptional child receives assistance from an itinerant teacher but is enrolled for all his classes under a regular teacher in the neighbourhood public school. In view of the fact that disabled children are often widely scattered it is not feasible to organise a resource teacher programme in every school. In such a situation it is advisable to have a travelling teacher assisting handicapped children in resource rooms in different schools. These schools should not be located at great distances from one another. It is quite similar to the resource room programme. Regular classroom teachers may also be trained to handle exceptional children in the regular class itself with more support from the special teachers.

The various types of special education services mentioned are representative ones. Three critical dimensions that define this continuum of special education services are: Environmental Restrictiveness, Severity of Handicap, and Cost of Service. Each dimension has been qualitatively anchored with reference to regular education classes. Thus, as placements get further away from the mainstream, they become increasingly more restrictive and costly, and are generally designed to handle more severe types of handicap. Ideally, placement decisions should be based on an analysis of an individual's needs and a system of methods for treating such needs.

Individualized educational programming calls for flexible use of settings and supporting staff. It seems logical that when support staff is skilful and motivated, the possibility of successfully educating a child in the mainstream is high. In a typical resource room arrangement, the exceptional child is enrolled in a regular program but is provided with additional educational and emotional support in one or may be two areas of weakness. The resource class would most likely be organized in a small group. In the self-contained special class arrangement, exceptional children are usually physically segregated from other groups of children and receive all academic instruction from special educators. But on a limited basis throughout the day they share in other activities such as sports and assemblies with non-handicapped peers.

Special day schools have been organised for different groups of exceptional children, especially the emotionally disturbed, physically handicapped, trainable mentally retarded, and multiple handicapped. Special schools are located some distance from the regular schools; this segregates children and staff, and limited interaction with non-handicapped peers takes place. Homebound or hospital services are provided primarily for children with serious health complications and/ or multi-handicapped preschoolers. Finally, there are residential schools or institutions for children with various severe handicapping conditions. Children live at the school and thus are able to receive intensive, daily educational, psychological, and medical services. Researchers have begun to investigate the effectiveness of services for exceptional children in the mainstream, and its variants.

The Variants

Portage: Portage training is used for children at risk, or for those having learning difficulties, developmental delays or mental retardation. It is a need based participatory family training in child care and development. It is home based. Yet it can be institution or centre based non-formal a cost effective pre-school early intervention programme for removing obvious learning difficulties or reducing delays in various areas of development such as cognition, motor, social, language etc. It involves parents, grandparents, siblings who act as the child's primary therapeutic teachers. The model is community based and it involves the utilisation of existing community resources.

Besides this, para professionals, professionals, non-professionals all cooperate and act as a team in this programme. It aims at motivating awakening and mobilising the community, parents, for changing the development of their children through service delivery. In the field of special needs children the programme has tremendous utility.

The Portage Model assumes that competencies are simply transmitted from professionals to parents, easily measurable and retained once learned. Children's development does not occur in a linear manner, but results from mutual transactions between children and their social and care giving environments.

Pre-school Intervention: Besides the educational services provided to the disabled children, attempts have been made to minimise disability by way of pre-school intervention. The portage project is one much innovation.

A comprehensive peripatetic teaching service has been conceived which would cater wherever possible, exclusively for children below school age with disabilities or significant difficulties.

These peripatetic teachers should

(i) assess children's educational needs on the basis of trained observation,

(ii) work with parents towards an educational programme for the child in the light of his assessed needs,

(iii) work directly with and teach children on a regular basis,

(iv) maintain contact with other professionals in the various services concerned with meeting the needs of young children with disabilities and their parents,

(v) encourage and participate in meetings of groups of parents of young children with special needs,

(vi) put parents in touch with toy libraries, iocal forms of pre-school provision-play groups, opportunity groups, day nurseries nursery schools, classes in ordinary or special schools and voluntary organisations.

The Development

The West: Education, Care, Training and Rehabilitation of exceptional children has a long past, but a short scientific history. An understanding of the origin and development of the special education movement would help to understand where we stand now in the field, particularly in India. Children with defects were not cared for in prehistoric societies. Defects like mental illness in the good old days were considered the result of some kind of sin. Children suffering from them were either killed or punished. The physicians and scholars in ancient Greek and Roman societies made some efforts to treat and preserve the lives of the handicapped and provided asylums for them. The Renaissance brought a small change in the earlier attitudes. This was the state of affairs until the late 18th and early 19th centuries.

The early history of special education started with the hearing handicapped as early as 1555 when the Spanish monk Pedro Ponce de Leon (1520-1584) taught a small number of deaf children to read, write and speak and learn academic subjects. Jnan Pablo Bonet in 1620 wrote the first book on the education of the deaf and developed a one handed manual alphabet that is being used even today. In England John Bulwer published another book on the education of the deaf in 1644, followed by the Deaf and Dumb Man's Tutor by George Dalgamo in 1680 which set out instructional methods.

The first school for the deaf in Great Britain was established in 1767 in Edinburgh by Thomas Braidwood. Braidwood's method combined oral and manual method teaching alphabets and signs.

At about same time Samuel Heinicke (1729-1784) developed the oral method emphasizing lip reading and speaking skills in Germany at Leipzig in 1778 which was further developed by F.M. Hill (1805-1874).

In France, Michel del' Epee (1712-1789) who established the first school in Paris in 1755, and Ambroise Sicard (1742-1822) were developing sign language. The French system also emphasised training of the senses of sight and touch which became the forerunner to Montessorie's sensory training approach.

Education of deaf children in USA started with Gallandet (1787-1851) using the French method. Gallandet established the first school of the deaf in 1847 (which is today known as the American School for the deaf). The New York School for the deaf opened the next year. By 1863 there were 22 schools for the deaf in USA. The first oral school of the deaf in Massachussets was established in 1867. Day school classes for the deaf were started in 1869 at Berton. Adult education for the deaf began in New York City in 1874.

Subsequently Grahma Bell (1847-1922) worked tirelessly for the deaf. Helen Keller (1880-1957) who was deaf and blind herself from early childhood, was a living example of the effectiveness of special education in overcoming the disability. The development of services for the deaf were hindered because the conflict over oral and manual method of instruction, but these have been reconciled over the years. In 1880, an international congress of education of the deaf was held in Milan, Italy. It made two recommendations:

a. Oral method must be preferred to the manual method.
b. Oral method must be preferred to lip reading/ sign language.

In Europe, oral method continued to prevail unchallenged during more than half the 20th century. After World War II the progress in electoacoustic technology gave new impetus to oralism. The increased belief that early education and intervention would allow most deaf children to attend ordinary schools for normal hearing or special units to these schools. The mainstreaming movement progressively gathered more and more strength in great Britain, then in the United States. and continental Europe.

Education of the blind began in France with Valentin Hany (1745-1822) a French philanthrophist who in 1784 founded the National Institution for the Blind in Paris. It is an integrated school and its success led to the establishment of seven schools in Europe during the next 15 years. The first school for the blind in Watertown, Massachussets was instituted in 1829 by Samuel Grindley Howe (1801-1876). This gave rise to residential schools for the partially sighted until the development of special classes in public schools in 1900 at Chicago. Special classes for the partially sighted was begun 13 years later in Boston. Hany developed embossed letters to be read with fingers and using this he printed the first book for the blind. Louise Braille (1809-1852) blind from childhood himself developed the system of Braille using raised dots to represent letters or alphabets, manually prepared for many years. The Braille typewriter was developed by Frank Hall (1843-1911), and a Braille printing system was standardised internationally in 1932.

Education of children with mental retardation began with the attempt by a French physician Dr. Itard (1775-1835) to educate an 11 year old boy who had been found living as a savage in the woods. This was documented in the book "*The Wild Boy of Aveyron*". Edward Seguin (1812-1880) followed the technique in France and United States and Maria Montessorie (1870-1952) in Italy. Seguin published his book "Idiocy and its treatment by the Physiological method" in 1866. It contained ideas which are relevant even now—total education of the child, individualisation of instruction, beginning instruction at the child's current level of functioning, and rapport between teacher and pupil. These were included in the famous method of Montessories for the education of the handicapped and non-handicapped.

Decroly (1871-1932) in Belgium developed a curriculum for mentally retarded children early in the 20th century and established schools throughout Europe. Binet (1857-1911) made an immense contribution with the invention of intelligence testing.

In 1839 the first blind and mentally retarded (MR) child was enrolled in the Perkins Institute for the Blind in the USA. In 1848 the first residential school for the MR was opened in Massachusetts. By 1917 all states except four provided instructional care for the mentally retarded in the USA.

The first public school with special classes for children with mental retardation was formed in Germany in 1859 and thereafter in other European nations in the next decades. In the USA the first public school with special classes for the MR was opened in 1896 at Providence, Rhodes Island.

There were very few special treatments and provisions for the orthopaedically handicapped and the health impaired prior to the 20th century. In the USA the first special class was established in Chicago in 1899, for children with low vitality in 1908 at Providence, Rhodes Island, and a class for children with epilepsy in Baltimore, Maryland in 1909.

Esquirol (1772-1840) published the first description of childhood psychosis in 1838 in a volume on scientific treatment of mental illness. For the first time in 1871 the New Haven Connecticut Public Schools provided a class for emotionally disturbed (ED) boys in New York City in 1874. These were first attempts made in USA. It was not until the 1930s that ED children were studied in a systematic way. The years since World War II have been characterised by the rapid development of services for handicapped children.

Special education services expanded rapidly after World War II both in numbers and types of children served. Legislative measures, parental involvement, early education or pre-school education for handicapped children all took off, including the education of those suffering from cerebral palsy, the learning disabled and the physically handicapped. By the 1970s facilities were available for all categories of the handicapped in the advanced countries of the world, and after 1981 in the developing nations.

Vocational Rehabilitation, occupational therapy, physical therapy were brought into the services for the handicapped. Expanded technology, use of computers, transportation devices, learning and visual aid technology, telecommunication systems, tele typewriters for the Deaf all came into use. Talking boons for the blind, which convert print into vibrating images that can be read with fingers were invented. The Kurzwell Reading Machine which converts print into spoken English, mobility aids etc. have further revolutionised the education of the disabled.

Besides, the 1970s have seen the emergence of mainstreaming and least restrictive environment as dominant concepts in special education. The special class has doubtful efficacy and that is why there is a shift from placement in residential schools and special day schools and increased enrolment in regular classes. Segregation is now discouraged unless the handicap is very very severe.

India: The first attempts at educating handicapped, children were made in the last two decades of the nineteenth century with the establishment of the first school for the hearing impaired in Bombay in 1885, followed by the first school for the visually impaired in Amritsar in 1887. Growth of schools for the handicapped in the sixty years until the advent of independence was extremely slow and sporadic. By 1947 India had just 32 schools for the blind. The number rose to 170 in 1980. Now there are 243 schools for the visually impaired in the country. Prior to independence there were only eight codes available in the country but Bharati Braille has replaced all other codes now. Thirteen Braille presses are available in the country.

The number of schools for the hearing impaired was only 35 in 1947 but had risen to 180 by 1980. The present figure of schools for the hearing impaired is about 478 as per the Rehabilitation Council of India (RCI) directory of which 97 are secondary schools. The largest number are in the state of Maharashtra (139 schools).

Schools for the mentally retarded were just three in 1947, but rose to 200 by 1980 and at present there are 600 schools for mentally retarded children. The first school for the cerebral palsied was started in 1973. There are 12 schools run for the cerebral palsied at present, but no facility is yet available for autistic children. As regards the orthopaedically handicapped most of them go to ordinary schools.

Teacher Training

Since 1981, systematic attempts have been made in the field of teacher training for handling special needs children. The leadership in this direction has been taken up by NCERT in designing courses of short term duration, mainly to implement the Integrated Education (IED) Scheme floated by the Govt. of India under centrally sponsored schemes which has been now named as Project Integrated Education of the Disabled (PIED). NCERT has designed three level courses which are:

Level I. One week training of all primary teachers in the project area,

Level II. In-service training for six weeks for selected teachers,

Level III. One year multi-category training of teachers since 1987 in its Regional Colleges of Education.

Besides, a six months training course has been given to key persons at the NCERT headquarters. Several courses have been designed by the Rehabilitation Council of India. Degree courses have been started in some universities leading to B.Ed. and M.Ed. in special education.

Rehabilitation

Vocational Rehabilitation Centres (VRC) have been established. National Institutes have started functioning. A three per cent job reservations for the handicapped has been brought in and special employment exchanges set up. National Awards, Tax concessions, self-employment schemes, sheltered workshops are also available for the handicapped. District Rehabilitation Centres (DRC) have been setup.

Community Based Rehabilitations (CBR) are in operation, where it is the responsibility of the community to rehabilitate the disabled of all categories. Each level is equipped with trained personnel. Regional Research Training Centres (RRTC) have been set up in the four regions of the country. A rehabilitation technology centre and the National Information Centre on Disabled and Rehabilitation (NICDR) have been set up at Delhi. The NGOs have done commendable work in the area of disability over the years.

Documentation

The National Information Centre on Disability and Rehabilitation (NICDR) undertakes collection, classification and storage of data on 12 different aspects of disability.

1. Concessions and facilities provided to the disabled by the central and state govt.
2. Organisations and institutions working for the disabled.
3. Professionals working for the disabled.
4. Statistics about beneficiaries of various rehabilitation schemes and programmes.
5. Demographic statistics about the disabled.
6. Aids and appliances available for the disabled.
7. Statistics about national awards and awardees.
8. Schemes of scholarships-beneficiaries.
9. Scheme of assistance for purchase /fitting of aids/ appliances.

10. Scheme of organisations working for the disabled.
11. Employment statistics.
12. Research and Development Projects.

It is proposed to have Regional Centres of NICDR too.

Non-government Organisations (NGOs) have contributed substantially to the care, training and rehabilitation of the disabled in India. There are 315 voluntary organisations working for the disabled in the country at present. Among them, prominent are the Mahavir Viklang Kendra, Jaipur, Nevedic Prosthetic Centre, Chandigarh, Thakur Hariprasad Institute of Mental Retardation, Hyderabad, Amar Jyoti School, New Delhi. Pandey and Advani (1995) have given an exhaustive list of the voluntary organisations in this sector.

An All India Federation of the Deaf has also come up.

The Rehabilitation Council of India is now regulating the training, recognition and de-recognition of the special education centres, institutes.

Training programmes for physiotherapists, occupational therapists, prosthetic and orthotic professionals, speech therapists, audiologists, mobility instructors of the blind, vocational instructioners and counsellors, placement officers, clinical psychologists, rehabilitation workers and others are being held in various national institutes and universities as per the norms of the Rehabilitation Council of India.

The major changes as regards exceptional children have been change from medical diagnosis to multi-professional assessment and treatment, treatment to education, meeting categorical needs to individual needs and change from category specific curricula and methods to appropriate variations in curriculum for all. There is a growing recognition of special education needs, training of special needs teachers, reorganisation of remedial teaching services, development of much closer relationships between the staff and pupils with special needs.

Highlights

Children who differ from the average or normal in their physical sensory motor and psychological characteristics (intelligence memory, learning, thinking, personality etc.) are designated as exceptional children such as: mentally retarded, visually handicapped, hearing handicapped, physically handicapped, learning disabled, gifted etc. Some of them are called handicapped when they fall below the average in terms of competencies and a few other are called gifted when they deviate in higher direction particularly on intellectual competence.

Not all children are disabled or handicapped to the same degree. It depends upon the degree of impairments. Not all impairments lead to be disabled and/or handicapped. These exceptional children are at times grouped as children with special needs, but the term exceptional children is more comprehensive.

There are different categories of special educational services for education training and care of exceptional children: Residential School, Special Day School, Special Class, Itinerant Teacher, Resource Room Teaching, commonly known as Cascade System based on degree of their separation from the mainstream.

The recent trend however is deinstitutionalisation, mainstreaming and integration is of the exceptional children in the regular school system where least restrictive environment are provided for their growth and development.

Comprehensive care and educational readiness is planned involving community and parents under the portage system and pre-school intervention programmes. These attempts to educate, take care and rehabilitation of the handicapped have started since the early sixteenth and seventeenth centuries in the West and India towards the closure of the 19th century.

Rapid strides and challenging development in education of exceptional children particularly have taken place only after the mid twentieth century in the West and after and IYDP-1981 in India, both by the Governmental sector and voluntary organisations. NICDR established in Delhi augmented the expansion of the programme with full information support and the establishment of National Institutes in major areas of handicap: hearing, visual, mental, orthopaedic, and the Rehabilitation Council of India, under the Ministry of Welfare have brought man power development programmes into the wheel.

QUESTIONS

1. Explain the concept of exceptional children. Mention the types of children who come under this category.

2. Differentiate between Impairment, Disability and Handicap. Are these terms inter-related?
3. Explain the conceptual and practical issues in the use of terminology "children with special needs."
4. What kind of special educational services can be provided to the exceptional children?
5. Outline the origin and development of special education in the west.
6. Briefly outline development of special education in India.
7. State and explain some variants of special education services.
8. Write short notes on:

Educable Mentally Retarded	Trainable Mentally Retarded
Emotionally Disturbed	Slow Learning Children
Disadvantaged Children	Gifted
Hearing Handicapped	Visually Handicapped
Orthopaedically Handicapped	Learning Disabled
Speech and Language Handicapped	Special School
Portage System	Resource Room
Special Class	Itinerant Teacher

7

Integrated Education

The National Policy on Education, 1986, has given priority on an equity basis in the field of education and recommends to provide equal opportunity to all not only for access but also for success. "Equalisation of educational opportunity" includes the opening of schools within walking distance, providing residential facilities to children, admission of children of all communities to schools, reducing the dropout rate and increasing the retention rate of children through various measures. Besides all the above facts, provisions should be made for non-formal education centres for non-attending children and various ancillary services to facilitate schooling of children.

The very term "integration" signifies the process of interaction of disabled children and normal children in the same educational setting. Of course, there are two separate terms which are very often synonymously used with "integration". These terms are – (i) Mainstreaming and (ii) Normalisation.

Basically "Integrated education" is the result of "Mainstreaming movement" in America. This movement makes provision for mainstreaming the disabled children. In other words, mainstreaming refers to integrating handicapped or disabled children into regular classes and helping them through specialised techniques.

Again, sometimes integration is interchangeably used with normalisation. The reason is that in integrated education, the disabled children are treated with normal children. There is every limitation to think that these two groups are different from any aspect.

Moreover, integrated education is an educational programme in which exceptional children attend classes with normal children on either a part or full-time basis. Such a combination may be taken as social integration or academic integration or both. Some educationists think that integrated education is the placement of the disabled children in ordinary schools with some specialised educational help and services.

The definition given by Stephens and Blackhurt reveals that "Mean-streaming is the education of mildly handicapped children in the regular classroom. It is based on the philosophy of equal opportunity that is implemented through individual planning to promote appropriate learning, achievement and social normalisation."

Various Types

Various types of integrated education for disabled are found. Among them seven important types of models are worth noting here.

(a) The first type of integration is the full time integration in normal schools. In regular classes, the teachers teach the disabled children throughout the day. Students also get support from teaching experts only when they are in need.

(b) Another category of such children attend regular classes. But some classes are suspended due to the arrangement of special classes.

(c) The third category includes the education of the disabled in a special class. But the students are required to maintain their attendance at normal classes. Again, they have to engage themselves in co-curricular activities of the normal school.

(d) The fourth type of integration includes the education in residential schools with some lessons in neighbouring normal schools.

(e) The fifth model includes reverse integration. Here a large number of normal children are placed with the disabled children to ensure academic and non-academic participation among themselves.

(f) Education in normal classes with home tution or homebound programme is included in the sixth category of integrated education.

(g) The seventh type of integration is the short term education in hospitals or in other establishments.

The Importance

As we have discussed earlier, many educationists nullify the idea of special education on the grounds that it never equalises educational opportunities, rather it creates a feeling of differentiation among children. Special classes create a feeling of inferiority complex among disabled children. Recently, psychologists think that integrated education should be introduced in our school system to provide equal opportunity for education of all children. Educationists justify this type of education under following points:

Normal Mental Growth is Possible: Psychological complexes are prominent under special educational settings. The disabled children think that they are inferior to others for which they are being treated separately. In integrated educational system, the disabled get the chance to enjoy along with normal children. In a way, the integrated education saves the disabled children from developing psychological complexes. Every child feels that he is, in no way, inferior to anyone. Thus, the integrated educational system leads to normal mental growth of children.

Social Integration is Ensured: Certain social qualities are very much pertinent with the disabled children when they tend to get education with normal ones. Children get wider community integrated set-up and this is conducive for the disabled ones to learn social virtues along with normal ones. These social virtues include love, affection, cooperation, sympathy and adjustments etc. The students in integrated settings not only get special attention but are also taught in a wider educational arena.

Integrated Education is Less Expensive: No doubt, special educational set-ups are very costly and expensive. Besides that, training programmes for special teachers and teaching experts are time-consuming. Considered from another angle, integrated education is less expensive and advantageous. To establish a special school, generally we seek the assistance from various corners, i.e., trained personnel, experts, physiotherapists, doctors etc. Again, keeping a disabled child in a normal class is less expensive than placing him in a special set-up.

Integration is Possible through Integrated Education: Social interaction is pronounced in integrated educational setups in comparison with special educational set-ups. A natural environment is created for interaction of the disabled with non-disabled peers. Learning to adjust in this environment, to accept and to be accepted by their friends are possible through integrated education. The students in nomal set-ups also acquire a sense of competency and emotional adjustment.

Academic Integration is Possible: Academic integration is possible through integrated set-ups. Educationists believe that once a child is placed in a special school, below par academic abilities of the disabled ones under the teacher are developed. The teaching experts always have the idea that the students in the special schools or the disabled children are under-achievers. Owing to the placement of children in special schools, they fail to score well in academic studies. In a way, we can say that, with a sophisticated environment and up-to-date curriculum, integrated education brings academic integration.

Principle of Equality is Maintained: Particularly in India, constitutional provisions were made to universalise the elementary education and to provide educational facilities to the disabled children. The very objective of equality should be maintained through integrated, set-ups, so that no student would think himself inferior to the other.

The Differences

The distinction between special education and integrated education can be described in the following manner:

Special Education	*Integrated Education*
(i) Special education for exceptional or disabled children is an old notion.	(i) Integrated education is relatively a recent development of special education.
(ii) This system isolates the disabled from the normal children.	(ii) The provisions of integrated educational system call for socialising the disabled participants with normal children in academic and non-academic area.
(iii) Special education is somehow clinical.	(iii) But integrated education is based on the principles of psychology.
(iv) Special education is based on the laws of discrimination.	(iv) Integrated education is based on the principles of equality.
(v) Special educational systems provide necessary arrangements for severely handicapped children. They are also benefited by special education.	(v) But mildly disabled children get benefit through integrated education. An all round development is possible through it.
(vi) Education for the disabled children is not considered as an integral part of the total education. Provisions for the establishment of special classes are rather encouraged by it.	(vi) Education for the disabled children is a part of total education.
(vii) Special education, provides vocational training and pre-vocational guidance etc.	(vii) Integrated education provides general education with some special provisions.
(viii) Special education is truly special in every aspect. It is established outside the ordinary school systems.	(viii) Integrated education is an educational programme in which disabled receive education along with the normal child.

Suggestions given by the NPE (1986)

Some suggestions were given by the NPE (1986) regarding the education of the disabled children. They are as follows:

(1) Children having severe disability should be admitted in special schools whereas children with locomotor handicaps and other mild handicaps should be placed in ordinary schools.

(2) Priority has been given by NPE to organise teacher training programmes in order to produce expert hands.

(3) Emphasis is placed on supplying additional materials and equipments to the schools.

(4) NPE suggests the supply of textbooks and uniforms free of cost to SCs and STs.

(5) Advice is given for mobilising support from the other establishments like health, sanitation, industry and public welfare departments etc.

(6) Steps should taken to remove architectural barriers in school buildings where at least 13 disabled children are enrolled.

Role of a Teacher

A teacher always tries to bring out the best in each child. When children stay away from their family, the teacher is the person who contributes a lot for them. Again teachers for deaf and disabled children have special roles in schools. Besides some additional qualities, they must have the primary aim of teaching and guidance. To make the children interested in the class is very important for a teacher. The teacher must try to satisfy the needs of the children as far as practicable, so that the relationship becomes strong. He should remain alert always in order to meet the needs of the students.

Again, the teachers should have pleasant personalities. They must try to develop a tendency to understand the child and the situation. Readiness to work hard is highly appreciated. Good teachers always have knowledge of up-to-date methods of teaching. Some teachers must develop skills in teaching and handling the problems of exceptional children.

No doubt, the education of exceptional children either in special school or in an integrated set-up depends on the efficiency of the teacher. The following steps are noteworthy for effective teaching:

(1) Problems of children should be intimated to the parents by the teacher within a minimum span of time.

(2) Records of every child should be maintained properly by the teacher, so that a programme of action can be executed immediately.

(3) A teacher must have a clear concept of special education and integrated education.

(4) Remedial teaching programmes should be worked out by the teachers which may be conducive for children with specific educational needs.

(5) A teacher should prepare instructional materials to teach in integrated set-ups.

(6) Cooperation of other faculty members must be sought by the teacher to provide best possible education for disabled children.

Emphatically speaking, education of exceptional children either in special schools or in common schools, is a tough task. Their early identification, assessment of disability, enrolment in school, specialised help and successful placement in a vocation and life is not limited to primary schools or secondary schools only. Through joint efforts and in collaboration with various departments, effective implementation of integrated education is possible.

QUESTIONS

1. Discuss the need, objectives and importance of special education.
2. Point out the differences between special education and integrated education.
3. Write short notes on the following:
   (a) Special Education
   (b) Integrated Education
   (c) Mainstreaming
   (d) Normalisation.

8

Teacher Training

Development of facilities for education of exceptional children are increasing day by day. Does manpower development, particularly that of teachers and rehabilitation personnel, go hand in hand? Are there such institutions and programmes in our country? This chapter describes the facilities with a historical perspective emphasizing the present state of affairs with respect to:

- Major handicaps: mentally retarded, visually handicapped, hearing handicapped, orthopaedically handicapped etc. in the country.
- Programmes of the National Institutes.
- Programmes of Rehabilitation Council of India.
- Programmes located in selected NGO level.

Special education movement in India is relatively of recent origin. However, the institutions have come up for education, care and rehabilitation during the last two decades in a significant number, if not proportion to the target clientele yet significant enough from near zero base. In the present chapter a review of teacher training programmes institutions in the context of manpower development will be described on the basis of available data, to give an insight into manpower planning and preparation in the field of education, training and rehabilitation.

- The nature and functioning of different national level organisations,

- The courses which are in operation in the field.
- The type of research undertaken.
- An overview of the teacher training programme is described in brief to create awareness among students and readers.

Mentally Retarded

Of all the areas of handicapped, the Mentally Retarded constitutes the largest segment but it is the most neglected field in India. There are a very few institutions of teacher training in India for training teachers of Mentally Retarded: Teacher Training in Special Education, Bombay; B.M. Institute of Mental Health, Ahmedabad; and All India Institute Speech and Hearing, Kamayani School of the Mentally Retarded, Poone; Bal Bihar Training School, Madras; Alakendu Bodh Niketana, Calcutta; Karnataka Parent Association for MR, Bangalore; Jai Vakeel School for Children in need of Special Care, Bombay; Thakur Hariprasad Institute of Mentally Handicapped, Hyderabad; YMCA; Nizamuddin East, Delhi: Central Institute of Mental Retardation, Trivandrum; North Calcutta Pratibandhu Seva Kendra, Calcutta; National Institute of Mentally Handicapped, Secunderabad and its regional centres. Banaras Hindu University, Jamia Millia Islamia, New Delhi, S.N.D.T. Women's University, Bombay; R.K. Mission Mahavidyalaya, Coimbatore who have undertaken the responsibilities of training teachers for MR in terms of certificate courses; Bachelor in Mental Retardation, Diploma in Special Education; B.Ed. and M.Ed. in Special Education, Post-graduate Diploma in Mental Retardation. The institutes addressed themselves to offer teacher training for the teachers of mentally retarded. These institutes also offer one/two year Diploma in teaching the mentally retarded. Number of students admitted in these institutions are quite limited i.e., about 400 in all in these institutions.

The curriculum includes: Education for handicapped children, psycho-educational assessment; - methods of teaching mentally retarded, behaviour therapy, psychology of the handicapped, medical care of handicapped, occupational therapy, auditory and speech therapy and project work. At present curriculum have been standardised by RCI.

Visually Impaired

Upto 1980, there were four centres for the training of teachers of the blind or visually impaired, one each in Madras, Calcutta, Delhi and Bombay. Each centre is providing specialised training for preparing teachers of blind and expenditure is met by the Central Government on 100 per cent basis. The annual intake of these centres is 50.

The Regional Training Centre for teachers of the blind, Poonamalle, Madras, Training Institutes for teachers of Blind, Bombay; National Institute for Visually Handicapped, Dehradun, Ramakrishna Mission Ashram Blind Boys' Academy, West Bengal; Regional Training Centre of the Blind, New Delhi; Alakenon Bodh Niketan, Calcutta are institutions in India which offer teacher training for the teachers of Blind. These courses vary from 60 days duration (inservice) to one academic year (preservice) and a diploma is given on successful completion of the course. At present there are about 15 such teacher training centres where B.Ed., M.Ed., Diploma and Certificates are given.

Recent centres include NIVH, regional centres and University Departments. Some of these are: Blind Relief Association, New Delhi; Divine Light Trust for the Blind, Bombay: Handicapped Welfare Department, Andhra Pradesh; R.K. Mission Training Centre, 24 Pragana, West Bengal; NAB, Karnataka; Poona School and Home for the Blind Trust, Pune; R.K. Mission Mahavidyalaya, Coimbatore; Jamia Millia Islamia, New Delhi; Kurukshetra University, Andhra University, Waltier Mahatma Gandhi Granyo Yog Yiswavidyalays, Chitrakoot.

The curriculum that is followed in these institutions include: Educational Psychology, Principles of Education, Education of Blind and Visually Impaired, Methods of Teaching, History of Education and Rehabilitation of the Blind, Anatomy and physiology of the Eye and Eye Diseases, Braille Technique.

These curriculum are almost identifical in all the training institutions and each institution offers practical training and practicals during the course.

Speech and Hearing Impaired

The teacher training curriculum for the teachers of the Deaf currently in vogue at various training institutes: Government Lady Noyce Secondary School, Ferozeshah; School for Deaf and Dumb, New

Delhi; Training Institute of Stephen's High School for the Deaf and Aphasics, Bombay; The Centres for the Teachers of the Deaf, Lucknow; Education and Audiology Institute for Teachers of the Deaf, Bombay; V.R. Raja Teachers Institute for the Teacher of Deaf, Pune; provide instructions for a period of one academic year and award a diploma or certificate which enables the graduates to enter into teaching profession. Clarks school for the deaf, Madras; Education Auditory and Research Society, Bombay; Holly Cross College, Tiruchirapally; Institute of Speech and Hearing, Mysore; K.L. Institute of the Deaf, Bhavnagar, Gujarat; Little Flower Convent Higher Secondary School for the Deaf, Madras; V.R. Rina Mook-Badhir Vidyalaya, Pune; Training College for the teachers of Deaf, Calcutta; Sheila Kothavala Institute for the Deaf, Bangalore; Central Institute of Teachers of Deaf, Bombay.

There are also graduate and post-graduate courses in about 15 centres in the country. The instructions include : Audiology and learning aids, Psychology, Principles of education and class management, Anatomy and physiology, History of education of the deaf, sound, curricular studies, Phonetics, Methods of teaching, Arts and Crafts, Problems of the deaf. This course provides practice teaching along with practical and theory classes. On the average 350 teachers are enrolled into the various courses every year.

Orthopaedically Handicapped

The Spastic Society of India, New Delhi; Spastic Society of West Bengal; the National Institute of Orthopaedically Handicapped, Calcutta; Spastic Society, Bombay; offer short term programmes of teacher training varying from 12 seeks to 60 days. Courses include: Medical and therapeutic aspects of the child development, normal psychology and the psychology of handicap, and educational aspects of normal and special children.

These short courses are inservice in nature since no special training for teaching is necessary for teaching the orthopaedically handicapped. These courses are very new and do not have a regular intake although each one is equipped with adequate trained personnel. The National Institute of the Regional Centres concentrate on short term teacher training as well as pre-service teacher training programmes.

With the assistance of UNICEF since 1979-80 courses were organised for teacher training-one by the spastic society of India and the other by the B.M. Institute for the teachers of Mentally Retarded children. Various courses on Orthotics, Prosthotics, OT, PT, Rehabilitation, Developmental Therapy etc. are conducted by several institutes such as: Christian Medical College, Vellore; Seth G.S. Medical College, Bombay; Institute of Social Sciences and Research, Vellore; Patna Medical College; Vikalanga Kendra, Allahabad; School of Prosthetics and Orthotics, Madras; Dept. of Rehabilitation, Safdarjang; All India Institute of Physical Medicine and Rehabilitation, Bombay.

All India Institute of Speech and Hearing

This Institute established in 1965 at Mysore is managed by Government of India. It has exceptionally well-qualified staff for imparting therapeutic services as well as teacher training the area of Mentally Retarded, Deaf, Orthopaedically handicapped. The graduate degree leading to Bachelor of Science is of 3 Years duration and the post-graduate degree leading to M.Sc. is of 2 years duration. There is also facilities for advanced research in all these areas of handicap including speech and hearing disorders leading to Ph. D. so far, 246 candidates have obtained the B.Sc. and 158 have obtained M.Sc. degree. The annual intake is 23 and 13 for graduate and post-graduate courses respectively. This institute is an ideal one for undertaking research and innovation in special education in the years to come. The institute brings out the journal on Speech and Hearing.

National Council of Educational Research and Training

The National Council of Educational Research and Training (NCERT) was established on 1st September, 1961 with its headquarters at New Delhi with a view to improving school education. It is an autonomous organisation registered under the Societies Registration Act, 1860 and functions as the academic adviser to the Ministry of Education and Social Welfare. In formulating and implementing its policies and programmes in the field of school education the Ministry of Education draws upon the expertise of the NCERT.

With reference to special education, NCERT has earlier a department of special education within teacher education and special education cells in all its four Regional Colleges of Education. It is pioneer in running six months key/ Resource Teacher Training at its headquarter and Multi-category Training of Teachers in the four Regional Institutes of Education. Besides, it has assisted in running one week course teachers training of primary teachers, six week's intensive course for selected teachers of PIED. The Regional Institutes of Education also run B.Ed, and M.Ed, courses with specialisations in one area of special education until recently. These courses are on the process of being phased out. The special education unit is now with the new department on disadvantaged groups.

At the centre, several inservice programmes also being run for Principals of DIET, special education faculty of SCERT/SIE, PIED Block supervisors at various times. The main contribution has been among others implementing of PIED project, development of instructional manuals, promotion of research and documentation, preparation of Handbooks: Hearing impairment, Visual impairment, PIED, etc. It has also been responsible for feeding information to data base for POA 1992 and Policy Guidelines NPE, 1986 and NCTE Committee on Special Education as well as to RCI.

NCERT has introduced MCT programme to prepare manpower for meeting the needs of integrated education in schools. The course is run in its four Regional Institutes of Education and in a few centres e.g., Amarjyoti Trust, New Delhi, and JSS Teacher Training Institute in Bangalore. The course is of one year duration and is not disability specific. About 100 teachers are trained every year. The course structure includes comprehensive coverage for enabling the teachers to develop competency to handle major disabilities.

Emerging Objectives

- To develop an awareness that all school teachers whatever the age group of their pupils or level of their work are likely to be concerned with helping some children who have special educational needs.
- To enable teachers to recognise early signs of variable special educational needs.
- To give the knowledge of the part which they can play in the amount of child's educational needs and in the execution of any special measures prescribed.

— To give teachers what special education is like together with the knowledge or range of various form of special educational provision and of specialist advisory services.
— To provide some acquaintance with the school classes and units.
— To give teachers understanding of how to communicate effectively with parent's anxieties and encouraging their continued involvement in their child's progress.
— To give teachers in-service training of when and where to refer for special help and knowledge in general terms of teaching to handicapped. The following skills are to be developed:
— Practical skills in observation of children both individually and in groups to help teachers sharpen their perception of variations in children's learning and behaviour and develop their awareness of variation in children's circumstances (home-school difficulties).
— Appreciation of the educational needs of children with developed difficulties -- physical, sensory, emotional behavioural or learning the needs of their parents, and the value of the contribution which parents can make to their children's development.
— Understanding of the practical steps necessary for meeting a child's special needs and an ability to adopt the attitude must suit to dealing with particular difficulties and to appreciate the need for modification of the school or classroom organisation the curriculum or teaching techniques.
— Appreciation of the special services available to children with special needs of their familiar and of the advisory services available to teachers. This might be developed by inviting professionals for the various services to visit the college so that through discussion, the students can learn about the work of teachers in relation to other professionals the contributions which different specialist can make the services to expect from them, and the kind of question to put to them
— Awareness of the range of career and professional opportunities in special education and the availability of further qualification in special education and the fact that special education offer the teachers engaged in it an intellectual challenge.

Rehabilitation Council of India

The Rehabilitation Council of India, New Delhi which was originally established in 1986 as a registered society has become a statutory body by promulgation of the Rehablitation Council of India Act, 1992, with effect from July 31, 1993. Its main function is to regulate training, its recognition and derecognition and quality improvement in special education.

Aims and Objectives: The aims and objectives of the Rehabilitation Council are as follows:

1. To regulate the training policies and programmes in the field of Rehabilitation of disabled people.
2. To bring about standardization of training courses for professionals dealing with disabled persons.
3. To prescribe minimum standards of education and training for various categories of professionals dealing with disabled persons.
4. To regular these standards in Government Institutions, Central as well as State, uniformally throughout the country.
5. To recognise institutions training professionals in the field and recognise the Degree/Diploma/Certificates awarded by these institutions and to withdraw recognition.
6. To recognise foreign Degree/Diploma/Certificates on reciprocal basis and to get Indian Degrees/Diploma/Certificates recognised abroad and to withdraw such recognition.
7. To maintain an Indian Rehabilitation Register.
8. To collect information on a regular basis, on education and training in the field of Rehabilitation of disabled persons from institution in India and abroad.

The Council has standardised several courses for different categories of manpower requirement in the field of special education.

Training Programmes

The Rehabilitation training programme mentioned below are being conducted by various institutes in the country have been standardized and approved by RCI. The Council keeps on updating and adding new training programmes as per requirement of the country.

Speech and Hearing

	Name of the Course	Duration	Qualification
(a)	M.Sc. Speech & Hearing	2 years	Degree
(b)	B.Sc. Speech & Hearing	3 years	Degree
(c)	Diploma Speech & Hearing	1 year	Diploma
(d)	B.Ed. (HI)	1 year	Degree
(e)	D. Ed. (HI)	1 year	Diploma
Mental Retardation			
(a)	Bachelor in Mental Retardation	3 years	Degree
(b)	Diploma in Mental Retradation	1 year	Diploma
Visually Handicapped			
(a)	B.Ed. Special Education	1 year	Degree
(b)	Course for Training Teachers of Visually Handicapped Children at Primary Level.	1 year	Diploma
(c)	Course for Training Teachers of Visually Handicapped Children at Secondary Level.	1 year	Diploma
(d)	Orientation and Mobility Training Course	6 months	Certificate
Locomotor Handicapped			
(a)	B.Sc. in Prosthetic & Orthotic	31 /2 years	Degree
(b)	Diploma in Prosthetic and Orthotic Engrs.	21/2 years	Diploma
(c)	Multi-rehabilitation Workers	1 1/2 years	Certificate
Multi-handicapped			
(a)	Post-graduate Course on the Education of Physically and Neurologically Handicapped Children.	1 year	Degree
(b)	Basic Development Therapy Course for Children with Cerebral Palsy.	1 year	Certificate

National Institute for the Mentally Handicapped

The National Institute for the Mentally Handicapped, Secunderabad was established in the year 1984 as an autonomous body under the Ministry of Welfare, Government of India. The Institute serves as an apex body with specific emphasis on training and research in the field of mental retardation. The NIMH offers specialised services keeping in view the various requirements of the mentally handicapped persons.

The aim and objectives are:

(a) To develop appropriate models of care and habilitation for the mentally retarded persons appropriate to Indian conditions.

(b) To develop manpower for delivery of services to the mentally handicapped.

(c) To identify, conduct and coordinate research in the area of mental retardation.

(d) To provide consultancy services to voluntary organisations in the area of mental handicap and to assist them wherever necessary.

(e) To serve as a documentation and information centre in the area of mental retardation.

(f) To acquire relevant data to assess the magnitude, causes, rural-urban composition, socio-economic factors etc. of mental retardation in the country.

(g) To promote and stimulate growth of various kind of quality services for persons with mental retardation throughout the country.

At the Institute's headquarter at Secunderabad, there are six departments namely as medical sciences, psychology, special education, speech pathology and audiology, information and documentation services and vocational training. The Institute has three regional training centres located at Bombay, Calcutta and New Delhi, while Model School for the Mentally Deficient Children at New Delhi was taken over by the Institute in the year 1986. Some of the Institute's training programmes are also carried by a network of supported and affiliated centres spread across the country. .

The National Institute runs the following preservice, inservice, seminar and other training programmes:

(a) Three years Bachelor's Degree Course in Mental Retardation (BMR) at Secunderabad.

(b) Diploma Course in Mental Retardation.

(c) Post-graduate Diploma in Mental Retardation.

The Institute organises 10 to 12 short term courses every year. The duration of such courses is 3 to 5 days and the courses cover (a) portage programme, (b) vocational training, (c) behaviour modification, (d) appreciation programme for AIR producers, (e) media workshop on disability.

Each year a national level seminar on mental retardation is organised by the Institute which serves as a platform to professionals working in the field of mental retardation to exchange information including parent training programmes.

The Institute provides multi-disciplinary team services for helping the mentally handicapped persons and their parents. Usually all the cases that come to NIMH are assessed by a general service team for psychological, clinical and educational assessments. After identifying the different requirements of the mentally handicapped individuals and their families, intervention programmes are decided which include appropriate referrals, further remediation in special services of the Institute and providing consultancy to organisations such as special schools. The services available include:

— Behaviour modification
— Early intervention for pre-school children
— Group activities
— Medical management
— Parent/family guidance and counselling
— Physiotherapy
— Special education intervention
— Vocational training and guidance
— Psycho social services.

Karavalamban Kendra

This special education centre located at NIMH headquarters at Secunderabad admits about 85 children with mental retardation in the age range of 3 to 16 years. Children are grouped into pre-primary, primary, secondary and pre-vocational levels. Admission is offered for a period of 2 years to children with mental retardation who have been regularly attending the group activity training programme of the Institute. This special education centre also runs group activities for children with mental retardation during the afternoon hours. About 250 children per week benefit from this programme. The children in the morning school programme as well as in the group activity programme are provided systematic training and in addition to participate in extra-curricular activities which include music, dance, drama, sports and other recreational activities. Special programmes such as special Olympics are also actively organised. Parents family interaction all programmes is encouraged.

The institute has 12 family cottage which offer stay and training facilities in its campus at Secunderabad. Parents who come from far to places and like to spend time with expert staff at NIMH find the facility of such a service extremely useful

The Model School which was established in Delhi in the year 1964 by Government of India and later in the year 1986 was transferred to NIMH. About 110 children both boys and girls in the age range from 5 to 18 years are currently on roll. Of them 40 stay in the residential hostel. There are 12 classes at various levels of pre-primary, primary, secondary, pre-vocational and vocational. Apart from regular school programme of training in skills, extra-curricular activities like sports, music, drama and recreational activities are encouraged.

Early intervention services are offered by the NIMH Regional Training Centre (North), Delhi for very young children with delayed development and mental retardation upto 5 years of age. Every month about 40 to 50 children benefit from this programme. The parents are given instructions for home management programme after demonstration of the skill training activities at the centre by the trained staff.

In 1992, the vocational training centre was established which offers services of vocational training to persons with mental retardation above the age of 16 years.

To reach people living in remote areas the Institute periodically conducts rural camps. The activities include (a) screening and case detection, (b) individual assessment and counselling, (c) training of parents, (d) creation of awareness, and (e) reference.

In collaboration with NCERT and Central Institute of Educational Technology, the Institute has produced programmes which are regularly telecast as a part of the school TV programmes on Doordarshan every alternate Saturday. This programme is directed towards parents having children with mental retardation and provides instructions for home management of children. This programme is telecast in different languages.

National Institute for the Visually Handicapped

The National Institute for the Visually Handicapped (NIVH) Dehradun, was established in July, 1979, amalgamation 9 the National Centre for the Blind. The latter was started in January 1950 with a training centre for the adult Blind, taken over from St. Dunstan's Hostel for the Indian War Blinded. Subsequently, other units such as a women's wing, a workshop for making braille appliances, a sheltered workshop, a central braille press, schools for blind and partially sighted children and a national library for the blind were added.

The basic objectives of the institute are:

- to promote research;
- to undertake the training of personnel; and
- to provide certain national level services.

The National Institute for Visually Handicapped is a registered society under the Ministry of Social and Women's Welfare. Its director is the executive head. The Institute has the following divisions: (i) School Division; (ii) Training Division, (iii) Aids and Appliances Division; (iv) Research Division; (v) Book Division and (vi) Industrial Psychology Division.

The activities of the institute include operating schools for the blind, imparting occupational training, running of a sheltered workshop, a braille press, a teacher's training centre, and conducting research on several aspects of blindness.

The institute operates two schools-one each for the blind and for the partially sighted children. These schools prepare the blind children for the secondary examination. It is the task of these two schools to try out new methods of teaching and equipment.

Adult blind persons are imparted occupational training in handicrafts, braille typewriting, braille shorthand, music, book binding, radio engineering etc. by the Training Centre for the Adult Blind. The institute manages a workshop where blind workers are engaged in caning chairs, manufacturing woollen and cotton textiles, making candles and engineering products. It has four teachers' training centres which offer a one-year diploma course through a common all-India examination. Research on several aspects of blindness is also carried out in the institute. Experiments in occupational and psychological research are conducted for evolving new methods of helping the blind. The Aids and Appliances Divisions is engaged in developing and fabricating aids for the visually handicapped which could be manufactured in the country itself. Factors influencing the work environment of the blind and the visually handicapped are examined by the Industrial Psychology Division.

The Institute has a central braille press which produce braille literature in Hindi and English. The United Nations Children's Fund (UNICEF) entrusted the press with the task of producing braille textbooks upto class VI for free distribution. The library of the institute circulates braille books free of charge to blind readers all over the country. It has now decided to make the material available on tapes to serve other disabled persons not able to read in print.

Model School for the Visually Handicapped

The school provides education to the Blind and partially seeing children upto secondary level. Both types of children are given education through media compatible with the nature of their limitations. Blind children are taught through Braille while partially sighted children make use of magnifying devices to read print. The children are provided free boarding, lodging, clothing, tuition and other facilities besides monthly pocket money.

The school is affiliated to the Central Board of Secondary Education for its 9th and 10th classes. The school has opened a pre-school unit.

The Institute has taken up research studies on case study of various disabling conditions and preparations of reports for complete set of management; effect of exercises in Physiotherapy treatment; innovative method of treatment in management of paraplegia/orthopaedic conditions; construction of indigenous activities of daily living use of simple methods in Occupational Therapy; develop simple method of treatment programmes in Occupational Therapy in the Zone of hand functions; and role of Electromyographic studies round the knee joint in different pathological conditions.

Workshops for Manufacture of Braille Appliances

Various aids and appliances like braille slate, arithmatic slate, plastic stylus, chess board, playing cards, pocket frame, folding stick, braille scale, etc. are produced at low cost in this workshop. The workshop has also produced during the period in collaboration with ALIMCO, Kanpur braille shorthand machines, which were being imported earlier.

The Institute's Braille Press is producing reading materials in braille for the blind on a large scale and braille books are supplied at highly subsidised rates to school children. The press took up printing of textbooks for the states of Bihar, Punjab, Haryana, Uttar Pradesh, Karnataka, Madhya Pradesh and Delhi.

The Library offers free lending services to the visually handicapped readers all over the country. It has 38,453 braille volumes and 4539 printing books. It also has a Talking Book Unit with 105 recorded books. A total of 65 new members were added to the library during the year raising total membership to 1890. The new recorded monthly journal namely 'Chayanika' has been circulated to 160 persons during the period.

Assessment and therapeutic services were also extended to the trainees and students referred for consultation at the Crisis Intervention Clinic of the Institute.

The Institute conducted long term as well as short term training programmes for various personnel engaged in the work for the blind in NIVH and its regional centres.

The Institute has a sheltered workshop and units for rural expansion programmes, management of newly blinded, home management, guidance and counselling, orientation and mobility services.

The courses run by NIVH are: Diploma in Teaching the Blind, Contact cum Correspondence Courses for Inservice Teachers of Blind, Diploma Course for Secondary Teachers of V.H., Training Course for Primary School teachers of V.H., Certificate Course Orientation and Mobility Instructors of the V.H. at different times. The other courses are: B.Sc. (Hons) in Physiotherapy, B.S. (hons) in Occupational Therapy, and the 2 years Diploma Course in Orthotics and Prosthetic.

National Institute for Orthopaedically Handicapped

The Institute was established at Kolkata in 1979 by the Government of India to:

— Conduct research on early detection, prevention, medical and physical rehabilitation of orthopaedically handicapped children and adults;
— Conduct education and training of orthopaedically handicapped children and adults, training of teachers; and
-- Plan economic rehabilitation of orthopaedically handicapped.

The National Institute in collaboration with Spastic Society of West Bengal have conducted a course to train special teachers. The schools that are being started in the National Institute will primarily act as a model in teaching the handicaped as well as training special teachers.

Alimco has located a limb fitting centre in the Institute premises. An orthotic and prosthetic unit is also functioning. The Physic therapy unit is also in operation.

The NIOH has taken up large number of research projects and studies. These include effect of exercises in physiotherapy treatment, occupational therapy, and several immature methods of treatment in the management of orthopaedic conditions.

Ali Yavar Jung National Institute for the Hearing Handicapped

The National Institute for the hearing handicap has been set up in Mumbai. The foundation stone was laid in December 25, 1978. The Institute is functioning since 1981. It has its regional centres in the country.

There is also a training centre for adult deaf which was established in 1962 at Hyderabad which continued to provide occupational training to deaf boys and girls in the area of sheet mental works, fitting, carpentry, electric wiremanship, cutting and tailoring, cutting and tailoring, welding, photography, turning. These students are drawn from all over the country. Recently the institute has made further studies by expanding education and training activities with latest audiological equipments to provide service facilities. Research programmes include early identification of hearing impaired. The courses run by AYJNIHH are: D.Ed. (Deaf), B.Ed. (Deaf), B.Sc. (AST), D.C.D.

National Institute of Rehabilitation Training and Research

National Institute of Rehabilitation Training and Research (NIRTAR) Cuttack came into existence when National Institute of

Prosphetic and Orthotic Training (NIPOT) a unit of Artificial Limbs Manufacturing Corporation of India (ALIMCO) established in 1975, was converted into an autonomous body on 22nd February, 1984 under Ministry of Welfare, Government of India.

Objectives

— To undertake, sponsor or co-ordinate the training of personnel such as Doctors, Engineers, Prsthetists, Orthotists, Prosthetic and Orthotic technicians, Physio-Therapists, Occupational Therapists, multi purpose rehabilitation therapists and such other personnel deemed necessary for the rehabilitation of the physically handicapped.

— To conduct, coordinate, sponsor or subsidise research into bio-medical engineering, both fundamental and applied, leading to the effective evaluation of mobility aids for the orthopaedically disabled persons or suitable surgical or medical procedures or development of new aids.

— To develop models of service delivery programmes for rehabilitation of the physically handicapped.

— To promote or distribute or subsidise the manufacture of prototypes and distribution of any or all aids designed to promote any aspects of the education and rehabilitation therapy of the physically handicapped.

— To undertake vocational training, placement and social, economic, educational and any form of rehabilitation and any activity to incidental to these.

— To undertake any other action in the area of rehabilitation of the physically handicapped.

A Regional Rehabilitation Training Centre is also attached to this Institute, besides a leprosy rehabilitation unit.

Rehabilitation camps are organised periodically in Rural and Tribal Areas to make the rehabilitation services available to the physically handicapped almost at their doorsteps.

Medical Services

Patients reporting at NIRTAR are registered at the Out Patient Department and examined by the Duty Medical Officer. They are advised and referred to other Departments as per the individual requirements of treatment and rehabilitation.

A well equipped Operation Theatre is available at NIRTAR for surgery of the Orthopaedically Handicapped people. Radiological Investigations are done at the X-ray Department. Pathological investigations are carried on in the Clinical Laboratory of the Institute Physiotherapy Department is well equipped with Hydrotherapy, Exercise Therapy, Electrotherapy and Heat Therapy. Physiotherapists by using the various physical modalities contribute towards the fullest functional restoration of handicapped. Occupational therapist provides treatment towards functional restoration, giving psychological support, training in use of Aid Appliances and Prevocations Training of the disabled on activities of daily living. Prosthetic and Orthotic appliances are fabricated using standard Alimco components and equipments in the prosthetic and orthotic workshop.

The institute runs several courses:

1. Diploma in Prosthetics /Orthotic Engineering.
2. Degree in Physiotherapy.
3. Degree in Occupational Therapy and

Short term orientation courses are run for:

- Rehabilitation for orthopaedic surgeons and physiotherapy medicine specialists,
- Physio-therapists,
- Occupational therapists,
- Psychologists and Employment Officer,
- Medical social workers/ teachers in integrated education vocational counsellors,
- Nurses in rehabilitation,
- Voluntary organisations, and
- Prosthetists and orthotists.

Thakur Hariprasad Institute of Research and Rehabilitation of the Mentally Handicapped

Thakur Hariprasad Institute of Research and Rehabilitation for the Mentally Handicapped, Hyderabad was established in the year 1968. It offers:

1. Special education programmes tailored to meet each student's special needs.

2. Modern Home like residential fort care mother settings.
3. Health care services.
4. Transitional services from school to work and other programmes.
5. Extensive Vocational and Rehabilitation Programmes.
6. Therapeutic Recreational Activities.
7. Special programmes for children and young with antism and behavioural programmes.

It has made significant contribution in the field of MR in India over the last decade. More specifically, THPI runs the courses such as:

1. ***Programmes:***
- Diploma in M.R.
- Diploma in Medical Pedagogy.
- Diploma in Development Therapy.
- Course for Paediatricians and Clinical Psychologists in Neuro-Kinsiological Diagnosis.
- Diploma in Vojta Therapy.
- Training for para-professionals etc.
- Need Based Training Programmes.
- Certificate course in Vocational Training.

2. ***Several specialised service wings:***
- Rehabilitation of children under judicial custody.
- Rural camps.
- Training of school teachers.
- Consultation services.
- Resource services.

3. ***In addition to general services:***
- Behaviour Modification.
- Speech Therapy.
- Occupational Therapy.
- Physiotherapy.
- Family Therapy.
- Home Guidance Clinic.
- Sibling Counselling.
- Need-based Interventions.

- Psycho-linguistic Therapy.
- Developmental Therapy.
- Vojta Therapy.
- Medical Pedagogy Therapy.
- Early Social Integration.
- Cognitive Therapy.

The Highlights

Manpower development is a basic requirement for expanding education of exceptional children. Teacher training facilities in the areas of teaching mentally retarded, visually handicapped, hearing handicapped, statistics, speech and hearing exist in the country and are continued to several voluntary and governmental organisations. Systematic breakthrough have been taken place after the National Institutes and various Regional Centres, university departments in special education have come up.

The All India Institute of Speech and Hearing at Mysore caters to the needs of speech and hearing handicapped by way of teacher training, and research functions. The NCERT has been pioneering and instrumental in bringing education of exceptional children into focus, preparation of modular packages for teachers, IED programme implementation and design and making of short term and one year MCT (Multi-category Training of Teachers) through its various regional institutes of education. Interest seems to be waning over the years.

The responsibility of rehabilitation council is to monitor various manpower development programmes including maintenance of a rehabilitation register. Graduate programmes in speech and hearing, masters level programme in speech and hearing, B.M.R., Diploma in Special Education MR, B.Ed., special education, MRW courses, prosthetics and Orthotic diploma courses, courses on All India basis on Occupational Therapy (BOT) and Physiotherapy (BPT) have been in operation.

The NIMH at Secunderabad basically covers care and habilitation programme in the area of for Mental Retardation running BMR and Diploma in special education (MR) courses, various research, development, extension programmes including running an experimental school in the campus for MR children called "Karavalamban Kendra'.

The NIVH at Dehradun, promotes research, teacher training, school education, Braille printing and library and documentation, vocational training in the area of visually handicapped.

The AYJNIHH located at Bombay deals with hearing handicapped, which runs training centres in the areas of deaf, occupational training, and extension programmes.

The NIRTAR and RRTC located at Olatpur, Orissa undertakes programmes of preparation of occupational and physiotherapists, MRWs, CBR programme workers, rehabilitation, and provide services to orthopaedically handicapped and allied health problems. It also runs diploma in orthotics and prosthotic engineering.

The THPI at Hyderabad is a voluntary organisation of repute in the area of rehabilitation, teacher training, extension programmes relating to mentally retarded. Its contribution to bring MR into a policy and national focus have been its major contribution besides services.

QUESTIONS

1. Briefly state the facilities of Teacher Training in the major areas of disability in India since independence.
2. What are the objectives of Teacher Training in Special Education?
3. State the contributions of the following in respect of Teacher Training in Special Education:
   (a) National Council of Educational Research and Training.
   (b) The Rehabilitation Council of India.
   (c) All India Institute of Speech and Hearing.
   (d) National Institute for the Mentally Handicapped.
   (e) National Institute for the Visually Handicapped.
   (f) Ali Yavar Jung Institute for the Hearing Handicapped.
   (g) National Institute of Rehabilitation Training and Research.
   (h) Thakur Hariprasad Institute of the Research and Rehabilitation for the Mentally Handicapped.

9

The Physically Challenged-1

We know that a disability consists of the objectively defined impairment of structure and function. For example, the loss of vision in one eye is a disability. The visual field of a one-eyed man is, no doubt, constricted. Again, the detection of the direction of a sound by a child who is deaf in one ear may be diminished. But these cannot be regarded as "handicaps". The 'handicap' arises from the cumulative effects of the disability and the personal and social consequences which have a detrimental effect on the person's functional level. So the distinction between 'disability' and 'handicap' is pertinent here. Again, all medically defined disabilities do not operate as handicaps. The disabilities of a blind man operate as a 'handicap' only when he competes with the normal sighted in activities involving sight.

Again different studies have shown that the extent to which any disability handicaps its possessor always depends upon circumstances. Some disabilities are there which do not operate really as a handicap. For example, colour blindness is a handicap for a navigating officer or a driver, but not for all. Similarly, a stammerer can be a successful scientist, but he may not be a good orator. By providing hearing aid for hard-of-hearing and self-propelled chairs for paraplegics, some disabilities can be mitigated.

Somehow the "handicap" is only partial. Otherwise the individual may be normal. It is observed that disability usually affects one organ-sense, region or system. But the rest remains unimpaired or even better than average. There is no evidence that the handicap does reduce all the power and abilities, but it does restrict their range. A mentally retarded child may have a good physique, but he is unable to use it to advantage. Similarly, a blind child may have strong legs, but is unable to make the utmost use of it. Some disabilities can also produce secondary handicaps. Evidence of this fact shows that a child with normal speech organs but with other severe defects, is likely to have speech defects.

The Definition

Three reasons are pertinent for which the term "Physically handicapped" has been defined in various ways:

(i) There is no clear-cut demarcation between the "able-bodied" and the "handicapped".

(ii) The terms "physically handicapped", "disabled" and "crippled" are used in an identical sense.

(iii) Some definitions of the above term have been cited here for various purposes and as such they have been based on various criteria.

Taking the dictionary meaning of the term, we can say that a physically handicapped person is defined as possessing a physical defect which reduces one's efficiency in performing one's personal and social obligations according to a socially determined standard.

Another definition reveals, "An individual who is afflicted with a physical impairment that, in any way, limits or inhibits his/her participation in normal activities may be referred to as physically handicapped".

Taking this seriously into consideration, the handicapped person may have many problems for adjustment. It must always be remembered that a physically handicapped person is not necessarily mentally deficient. The physically handicapped persons are generally divided as:

(a) The visually handicapped or Blind;

(b) Acoustically handicapped or Deaf;

(c) Speech handicapped or Mute;

(d) Orthopaedically handicapped or Crippled.

Physically handicapped persons have to adjust with their own disabilities as well as to their social circle. Actually they have to bear a double burden-social handicap and actual physical loss.

Visually Handicapped Children

Blindness is regarded as the most severe and traumatic physical handicap. Since more impressions are conveyed to the brain through the eyes, the visual anomalies may influence the life of the individual in physical, mental, social, vocational and educational aspects. In our society, the visually handicapped have always been the favoured group as compared to those with other types of handicaps. Priority was given to this group for making social and educational provision. Since special rights and privileges are being provided to them, they attract more public concern than any other categories.

The blind people have central visual acuity of 30/200 or less in the better eye with corrective glasses. A visual acuity of 20/200 means that the person is able to read from a distance of 20 feet, a line or words which a child with normal vision can read. The totally blind are born without any seeing capacity or must have gone blind by accident, operation etc. If the child is totally blind, he or she should be sent to the special school for the blind where he/she can learn through the Braille system. Again, the partially blind can be considered as those who have visual acuity between 20/200 and 20/70 or 50 in the better eye with the best corrective means.

Segregation of the partially sighted children should be made and large-print textbooks and similar other devices can be provided to teach them. Hygienic reading habits in the children should be developed.

In India, there are about 0.12 million visually handicapped children who fall in the age of 4-15 years: The National Commission of Teachers reports that "not more than 5 per cent of blind are estimated to be in about 800-1000 special schools. Most of these schools are located in the metropolitan cities and other urban centres. About 80 per cent of blind children generally live in rural India. But these children remain practically unserved by educational facilities."

The Identification: Priority should be given to identify the visually handicapped children as early as possible through periodic tests. Appropriate educational facilities can be provided after identifying these children. An annual test with Snellen chart is generally given to identify these types of children. This is a very simple test. It can be quickly administered by a nurse or a teacher. But this test has certain limitations. It is not also feasible to use this test. Thus identification of visually impaired children may be associated with some behavioural symptoms.

Identification Checklist for Visually Impaired

1. Complains about headache following close eye work;
2. Covers one eye and thrusts the hands forward;
3. Rubs eyes excessively;
4. Holds objects including books close to his eyes;
5. Blinks eyes frequently;
6. Asks other children to read aloud when taking notes from the blackboard;
7. The pupils of the eyes dilating;
8. Smaller eyelids/Red-rimmed eyelids;
9. Seems very sensitive to light;
10. Watering of eyes;
11. Takes false steps while walking;
12. Squint eyes;
13. Becomes inattentive during reading sessions.

Total blindness can easily be recognised and identified but a detailed examination is needed to recognise partially blind children. Total blindness can be detected when the child is about one year old. But this is not possible with the partially blind child. The detection for the latter ones is a much more difficult proposition. Such a child has little concept of "vision" and hence it is difficult for him to report about his visual problems.

The Problems: The visually handicapped children have many problems like behaviour problems, problems of learning, problems of their placement in society or problems of social adjustment. Some problems are discussed below:

Poor Intelligence: Research analyses reveal that visually impaired children have a poor I.Q. Since they have impairments in the exploration of their environments, they have impairments also in concept formation resulting in their poor performance in intelligence tests. Some intelligence tests are measured by degrees of information, knowledge or experience. But for blind children, this pattern of scoring is reduced to a very low level.

Academic Retardation: These children have poor academic achievements even if they use large types or Braille. They are noted to be retarded by at least one to two years and are found to be underachievers. Visual impairment is the main factor for slower acquisition of information by observation. These children have a slower reading rate and lack concreteness in instructional procedures.

Slower Speech Development: Totally blind children cannot learn the art of speech by imitation. They can only learn through what they hear and from occasional touch observation. Progress in speech development is not significant in comparison with normal children due to the above reason. Through research it has been discovered that acquisition of words may get hampered by blindness also.

Personality Disorder: We know that personality development includes both hereditary and environmental factors. It is a psychophysical organisation of the individual modified by his life experiences. For congenitally blind children, life experiences go in their own ways which are totally different from normal children. These differences affect their personality as a whole. Due to his handicap, he is more likely to experience nervous strain and the feeling of insecurity and frustration are common with them.

Problems in Social Adjustment: Normally these children are looked down on and ridiculed by normal children every now and then. They face both personal and social adjustment problems. Because of this, they feel inferior and ultimately this leads to maladjustment. There is a controversy among psychologists regarding the adjustment problems of these children. Some research workers feel that the blind children are maladjusted in school, but others refute it completely.

Partially Sighted Children

As it has been mentioned earlier, visually impaired children can broadly be divided into two types-(i) The partially sighted, and (ii) The blind.

As we have noted earlier, the blind are quite easily identified; but the partially sighted require a detailed examination. Total blindness is an obvious condition; it is easy to recognise and define; but partial blindness is rather difficult to recognise and define. Accordingly the definition varies. Thus we have "educational blindness", "legal blindness", "medical blindness", "occupational blindness" and so on.

With significant visual anomalies, children are often divided into two categories – (i) The blind, whose vision is so pronounced that they cannot be educated through visual methods and hence, have to be educated through channels other than vision, and (ii) The partially sighted, who are able to utilise vision in acquiring educational skills.

On the whole, partially sighted children are those children who have defective vision even after correction. They require to be provided with visual materials and special methods of instructions. One important factor which distinguishes partial sight from blindness is that while a partially visually handicapped child can utilise vision as an important channel of learning, the blind must rely on other approaches, primarily auditory and touch. So taking all these points into consideration, the differentiation between normal vision, partial sight and blindness is made theoretically on the basis of visual equity.

The Identification: Generally three methods are adopted to identify partially sighted children: (i) Ophthalmological examination, (ii) Visual screening, and (iii) Classroom observation.

The authentic method for identifying partially sighted children is ophthalmological examination. By this method, children have to be medically examined before going to school. Again, the medical check-up is also done after brief and specified intervals throughout their school life. If ophthalmological examination is not possible, visual screening may be undertaken by the District Health Officer. Parents should try to get their children examined before admitting them into school. Sometimes classroom observation is also conducive for identifying the partially sighted children. For this, the identification checklist discussed above may be taken into account.

Causes: All the causes of partially blind can be placed under three categories - (i) Pre-natal causes, (ii) Perinatal causes, and (iii) Post-natal causes.

Pre-natal period continues from the conception to birth. Research analyses indicate that use of strong drugs by pregnant mothers, maternal malnutrition and unhealthy living conditions are significant causes of partial blindness. Medical science also reveals that brain fever, brain tumour etc., are some of the important causes of visual impairment.

Some mishaps like instrumental delivery, use of anesthetic agents in delivery, premature delivery etc., also contribute a lot towards blindness.

The post-natal causes of visual impairment include malformation, accidents, infectious diseases, injuries, poisoning, general diseases, tumours and cancer. Research data reveal that a high percentage of blindness is usually attributed to pre-natal factors.

Educational Provisions

Emphasis was laid first on the education of the partially sighted children in Western countries like England and Scotland. Then it received attention in the United States. Unfortunately the number of such schools in India is insignificant. Vision impairment may be acquired at an early stage of life. If it is identified in time the children can be given special medical and educational assistance.

The following provisions can be made for those who are partially sighted:

Medical Care: If the teacher discovers a child who is partially blind, he may bring the case to the notice of the primary health centre or hospital for an eye check-up. His parents must be informed immediately, and warned to be aware of their child's health.

Special Class: Special classes should be introduced for the education of such children. It is true that the number of partially seeing children requiring special educational facilities is not wanting in our country. The District Educational Authority may decide whether special classes should be arranged or some other provision be made for these children. Different grades may also be introduced in a class. The school must be centrally located and good transportation facilities must be available. Hostel and boarding facilities must also be there, specially in rural areas.

Introducing Co-curricular Activities: The partially sighted children may develop some kind of inferiority complex which is dangerous for them. They are always compared with other normal children. If extra curricular activities are introduced, these may act as sources of satisfaction and arrest their self-demanding feeling. As a result these children can avoid developing a sense of inferiority complex.

Minimum Visual Tasks: Partially sighted children must be provided with minimum visual tasks. Maximum tasks which never put strain on their vision are recommended to these children. Delicate mathematical constructions, laboratory work and meticulous observations are strictly prohibited for them. These children may be given training for comprehending with minimum reading load.

Attitude of Parents and Teachers: Parents, teachers and friends must be sympathetic towards these children. They must show much affection and adjustiveness. They must keep in mind that these children should not feel inferior in anyway.

Classroom Arrangement: The teacher should be very alert on the following points in the classroom while dealing with these types of children:

(i) The teacher must see that in the class, these children should be front-benchers.

(ii) The teacher must write in bold letters on the blackboard which should be legible and unambiguous.

(iii) The teacher may speak what he writes on the blackboard.

(iv) Books with bold letters should be kept in the library to cater to the needs of these children.

(v) The District Rehabilitation Centres and hospitals may provide hand lens, magnifying glasses etc., to children whose correction is beyond the spectacles lens.

(vi) Books printed in large clear pencils with thick soft leads and unglazed paper should be provided to the children. Again, there must be sufficient light in their working place. Chalk boards, bulletin boards, charts, graphs, demonstration and other allied information are to be provided to these children.

(vii) A detailed time schedule for radio broadcast should be given to each student. They may also be encouraged to listen to those programmes. If the, situation warrants such facilities should be made available audio-cassettes may be used. For different curriculum arenas, State Institutes of Education and Technology, State Councils of Educational Research and Training (SCERT), National Council of Educational Research and Training (NCERT), and other organisations may be approached for cassettes.

Blind Children

Total blindness is easy to recognise. Basically it is detected in the child by the time he is a year old or even earlier. These children have to be educated through channels other than vision. A child who is born blind (congenital) depends upon hearing and touch for his knowledge while a child who becomes blind after birth may however retain his visual imagery and correlate what he hears or touches with it. The education of blind children is certainly tedious. Very often, the teachers become companions of the blind children. In the beginning, education of these children is directed at establishing contact with the world, viz., the kinesthetic, gustatory, cutaneous and olfactory senses and arousing a desire for learning. Recently special educational provisions for the blind and mentally retarded have been devised. Emphasis is placed on individualised instructions and classes consisting of not more than four children. These special instructions include learning of Braille, the extensive use of auditory, factual and kinesthetic experiences and special mobility training. Some educational provisions are being discussed below:

Residential School: Residential schools are very much essential for blind children. The school assists the children through the use of special methods and aids. Braille classes are very conducive for them. A blind child learns to adjust with the world in which he has to live as an adult. Braille classes supply only supplementary assistance as is necessary to enable the blind child to participate in regular classroom instruction. Besides this the primary aim of this kind of education is social adjustment.

Special Equipment: For blind children, the medium of education should be different. Since these children require education through touch and hearing, special attention should be given to practise on the regular typewriter. It permits written communication with vision. For teaching geography, relief maps and globes are to be used. Schools arrange excursions and study tours to acquaint children with their surroundings. The children must be provided with opportunities to visit museums and specially prepared educational models must be given to them for additional experience.

Besides all these above steps, since drawing and painting are impossible for these children, other creative activities like modelling can be given. Working with clay and plasticine also give them pleasure.

Staging of drama of fairy tales and dramatisation may increase the self-confidence of these children. In some affluent societies, it was found that the blind people are expert musicians. So special attention must be paid to provide the necessary facilities to those children who want to learn music.

Physical Education: Blind children are very much restricted so far as physical activities are concerned. But special attention must be paid towards gymnastics, corrective posture works such as sports, running, swimming, rowing, wrestling and all kinds of outdoor activities. Various types of handicrafts are also included in physical education. Priority should be given to household arts for girls.

Workshops: For vocational training and employment, sheltered workshops for the blind are certainly conducive. Previously, the vocational emphasis of these workshops was almost exclusively on things like brooms, rugs and brushes. But presently, the workshops are attached to various industrial concerns. In India, one workshop of this kind has been set up at Worli (Mumbai) and reports say that this one imparts good vocational training and provides employment to the blind.

Special Educational Principles: Educational experts for the blind may adopt the following principles to yield good results:

Concreteness:Care must be taken to make necessary arrangements to provide as many concrete experiences as possible. For blind children, hearing acts as a social contact medium. Again it is the source of receiving descriptive information. So actual knowledge of the objects and their spatial characteristics can only be gained from such observation.

Unified Instruction: Teaching experts should teach the blind children by a unit plan of instruction and not by unrelated interests in formal objects. It is true that these children gain many impressions which are discrete. But experienced teachers organise them.

Additional Stimulation: A teacher who deals with blind children in the classroom is completely different from other teachers in a general sense. It is necessary to provide opportunities for these children to gain new experiences. The additional stimulation can be provided to these children in two ways-(1) These children can be taken to have experiences like study tour, excursions, field trips and museum visits etc. (2) Experiences can be brought to them by radio programme etc. Of course, the effectiveness of this kind of additional stimulation depends upon the preparatory and follow-up work connected with them.

Self-activity: Self-activity is regarded as an essential part of his training. He must receive training and guidance. This will help him to develop and mature. It is difficult for him to cope with his environment and to enable him to live as a blind person in the world of seeing. So he must be encouraged to do as many things as possible for himself.

The above remedial measures for partially sighted and blind children can only be possible if educators, authorities and parents cooperate with each other.

Speech Handicapped Children

As we know, human interaction involves language. Communication is an integral feature of interaction between organisms. Many people know what language is, still the term language is frequently interchanged with 'speech'. Quite a wide range of speech patterns is considered normal. But when the speech of a person differs significantly from others so as to call attention to itself or to interfere with communication, it is diagnosed as a speech defect. The number of children suffering from speech defects is much more than that from any other type of handicaps. Of course, it is a very difficult problem to find a satisfactory place in which to allocate speech defectives in a classification of exceptional children. The difficulties are not psychological, rather these are physical, social and emotional. Since speech is considered as the chief avenue of social communication, they tend to have more psychological and emotional conflicts.

Speech Impairment: Many sources are responsible for speech difficulties. Therefore, they have many attendant by-products. For this reason, any concise definition becomes difficult. The following important definitions can be considered.

(a) From the point of view of the listener, any child who speaks so that attention is distracted from what is being said to the manner of its production may be considered to have defective speech.

—Jon Eisenson

(b) Speech is said to be abnormal when it deviates so far from the speech of other people, that it calls attention to itself, interferes with communication or causes discomfort or distress to the speaker or listener.

—Van Riper (1978)

(c) Speech may be considered defective when it is not easily audible to the listener. Speech is defective if it is vocally unpleasant. Finally, speech is defective if it is inappropriate to the individual in regard to his/her mental and chronological age, sex and physical development.

—Pinter, Eisenson, Stamton

From the above definitions, it is pertinent that a child's speech is defective when the amount of distraction is sufficient to make it difficult for him to communicate readily with a normal listener. The amount of distraction and the degree and significance of the defect may vary.

Again speech may be considered defective if the speaker is unduly self-conscious or apprehensive about objectively small deviations.

Type of Disorders: In general, the classification of speech disorders is based on etiology according to which it may be organic or functional.

Organic group comprises speech handicaps caused by palatal anomalies, dental irregularities, paralysis and tumours of the larynx, brain damage etc. Functional group represents failure to learn speech owing to general personality and emotional disturbances. But this dichotomy is not crystal clear. Rather some experts think that the classification of speech defects depends mainly on the purpose of classification. It may be classified according to the major symptoms such as articulation disorders, voice disorders, delayed speech, stammering and disturbances of rhythm.

Disorders of Articulation: These disorders include distortion, omission, addition or substitution of speech sounds. Again it is characterised by the mispronunciation of an entire word or words. This is a common speech defect and it accounts for 70 to 80 per cent of the diagnosed speech defects. In case of young children, this disorder may appear as immature speech.

Disorders of Voice (Phonation): Voice disorders are generally related to the variation in production or phonation of voice. It is characterised by marked deviations in loudness quality, pitch or intensity of sound. The chief defects of voice production are those concerned with nasality, either excessive or insufficient. The pitch is the psychological perception of the physical frequency of the produced voice. The variation of the pitch generally depends on many factors such as age, sex and structure of the vocal cords. When the pitch register is higher than it should be, it is termed as high-pitched voice.

Again when it is lower than it should be, it is termed as low-pitch; if the voice breaks as in emotional outbursts, it is termed as pitch break. The causes may be emotional, vocal abuse, overuse or infectious. However, this disorder is often seen more in adults than in children.

Delayed Speech: Statistics reveal that this disorder occurs with greater frequency than any other communication disorder. Different studies report that the sole cause of delayed speech is hearing loss, mental retardation, cerebral dysfunction, emotional disturbances and environmental deprivation. Very often, children do not speak at the usual age due to lack of motivation. Of course, there are many causes of delayed speech and the diagnosis and treatment involve services from a number of professionals.

Stuttering (Stammering): Stuttering is often considered as a disorder of rhythm. In many books, the discrimination between stuttering and stammering is found to be negligible. In stuttering, the child has hesitations in the flow of speech prolongations and repetitions of sounds, words or phrases frequently accompanied by facial grimaces, rapid eye blinking, irregularities of breathing and muscle tensions.

In stammering, the children are unable to produce any sound for a brief spell and then suddenly sounds come out in a torrent. Spasmatic movements and facial grimaces usually accompany efforts to articulate.

There have been two approaches for treatment of stammering - (a) Symptomatic treatment, and (b) Psychotherapy.

In symptomatic treatment, the patient seeks help for removal of the symptoms. He wants to stop stammering and speak fluently. But in the latter case, stuttering is believed to be a symptom of neurotic behaviour. Here the effort is made not only to remove the symptoms but to deal with the basic problems.

Disorders Associated with Cerebral Palsy: A good number of speech defects are found in the case of children suffering from Cerebral Palsy, particularly the spastics, athetoid and ataxic children. Some articulatory deviations are found in the speech of the spastic child whereas the athetoid child shows slurring in rhythm and constant change in pitch and inflection. On the other hand, the ataxic child talks with the same rhythm as shown in his gait and bodily movements. These children often lack the motivation to speak and they need to be highly motivated for speech therapy.

Besides all the disorders discussed above, disorders of cleft lip and palate are pre-natal in origin. Structural defects in cleft lip and palate may cause a number of speech deviations, mainly articulatory anomaly. Only through surgery can this defect be removed.

The Problems: Speech impaired children face many problems in daily life. Some of the important problems are being discussed below:

(a) For these children, maladjustment is very common. These children show aggressive tendencies, anxieties and fears. They usually perceive their parents as authoritarian figures.

(b) Speech impaired children are inferior to normal children so far as reading is concerned. They are underachievers in the school. Generally they do not conform to the general behaviour standard.

(c) Sometimes other children attempt to make fun of their defective speech and consequently the child withdraws himself from the social situation. By that, the socialisation process is also hampered. These children cannot become leaders in their concerned peer groups.

(d) Depending on the severity of the anomaly, the children can be more or less separated from the sole means of mental growth.

(e) Very often, children become conscious of their defects. They find difficulty in communicating with others. So they cannot take active part in games and group activities.

(f) A poor articulator is often poor in auditory discrimination. Pronunciation difficulties interfere with word recognition and spelling.

The Causes: The causes of speech impairment are many. Some causes are being discussed below:

Organic Causes: The organic causes of speech defects include palatal anomalies, dental irregularities, paralysis and tumours of the larynx, brain damage etc. In some cases, deformation of jaw and lips also result in lisping. The articulatory and vocal difficulties of the child with a cleft-palate can be attributed directly to this type and severity of the cleft.

Functional Causes: It is observed that many children, with normal speech mechanisms, have defects in articulation and/or of voice. Studies report that in some cases, imitation of an older sibling, a playmate or an adult may be the sole cause for his anomaly. It is true that children learn to articulate, vocalise and use language "by ear". They learn to speak in a fallacious manner, if they hear faulty vocabularies. Generally, speech faults are based on imitation of adult's behaviour.

Psychogenic Causes: Recent studies of speech defect reveal that many defects of speech are psychologenic. When the causes of speech defects are not organic or functional, they can be attributed to children's reactions to the environment, particularly to their parents. In his study, Wood reported that functional articulatory defects of children are definitely and significantly associated with maladjustment and undesirable traits on the part of the parents.

Psychological Causes: Speech defects also have emotional and psychological origin. Speech does not depend only on the efficacy of the speech organs but also on the personal maturity of the child, his attitude to himself, his relationship with others and the degree to which the home has stimulated and encouraged speech. Some psychologists are of the opinion that these defects are the outcome of disturbed feeling or emotions, faulty language habits arising from social pressures.

Loss of Hearing: Development of speech reception requires normal auditory system. If the child's hearing is impaired, the auditory input is distorted. Then speech reception skills may have some deviations or delay in development. Due to this faulty feedback system, this may affect speech production. Reports say that the degree of hearing loss has a direct bearing on the production of speech and language.

Social Influences: Language is a means of communication. This also develops in social context. In an impoverished environment, children lack stimulation. They do not get the chance to learn new words. For the language achievement of children, stimulating homes, schools and play pivotal roles. Children from higher professional groups show early speech development.

Cerebral Palsy: Children who are the victims of cerebral palsy often lack stimulation to speak and hence need to be highly motivated, for speech therapy, spastics, athetoid and ataxic children often have a good number of speech defects. Observation can easily reveal that a spastic child would show articulatory deviation and the athetoid child would show slurring in rhythm and constant change in pitch and infection.

Educational Provisions

The following educational provisions can be made for speech impaired children:

Speech Therapy: If a child needs speech or language therapy, then immediately an expert or a therapist should be consulted. Very often, the school does not have any facility for this purpose. In such cases, parents should be advised to contact the nearest speech and hearing centre. Generally the speech therapists help children in correcting and removing the disabilities in articulation. They also try to reduce stuttering as far as practicable. However, psychotherapists are consulted to treat the cases of stammering, but not the speech therapists. The reason is that some psychological factors are responsible for stammering.

Articulation Correction: Due to various reasons, very often, the parents are not in a position to obtain the required help for children. In such cases, the resource teacher should be able to help the children at school when he has time to spare. Simple correction of articulation may be performed by the teacher.

Speech Training Activities: Teaching experts can make a more direct contribution by giving the child practice in using the correct sound after it has been elicited by the speech therapist. Speech training activities may be done taking groups into consideration. The activities like rhymes, jingles and speech games are suggested in speech training activities.

Extra-curricular Activities: Besides the above activities, these children should be taken to visit places of interest, i.e., historical, social, cultural or geographical places such as museums, factories, workshops, dams or lakes, animal zoos etc., where they will be automatically stimulated to gather new experiences. There they would ask some questions and the answers given to them would help them to learn many new words. As a result, their vocabulary may be increased and they may be encouraged to read books, journals, magazines etc.

Role of Parents: In Western countries, parents are very much conscious of the speech defects of their children. They take care of their children properly, consult with the speech therapists or psychotherapists at brief intervals, try to be confident about their children's achievements. But in some developing countries like India, parents are not aware of the helping centres and about the progress of their children. Here they should be invovled in their child's training and made to keep a record of each activity of the child. They should be advised to go to the appropriate centres for help, if possible.

Role of Teacher: A teacher's role is very important for speech impaired children. It is the primary duty of a teacher to recognise the speech defects of children under him. As the society neglects these children, the love and sympathy of the teacher can contribute a lot to help improve the child's speech. A teacher can try to improve upon his deficiency in vocabulary. He has to listen carefully to what the child says. The child should not be compelled to talk. The teacher must see that these children are being allowed by other normal children to play and work together. This will give an opportunity to make social contacts and to develop self-discipline. Teachers must try to eliminate all conflicts, emotional reactions of fear and worry to the maximum level.

QUESTIONS

1. Who is a handicapped child? Discuss different types of handicaps.
2. Discuss various speech handicaps in children and their implication on behavioural development.
3. With examples, discuss the adjustment problems in children arising out of various handicaps.
4. Who is a crippled child? How can you educate a crippled child?
5. Who are visually handicapped children? Discuss some preventive measures to overcome the problems of visually handicapped children.
6. Discuss various principles and methods of educating the blind children.

10

The Physically Challenged-2

Aurally Handicapped Children

Hearing is the main sensory pathway through which speech and verbal communication develop. If a child hears imperfectly, he is likely to speak incorrectly. Again, hearing also influences learning and other aspects of maturation. Early detection of hearing impairment is important for the child's over-all development. If there is a defect in hearing mechanism there is also a problem in perception. Hearing impairment reduces our knowledge of the world around us. Again, it also adversely affects the child's performance in learning.

Children with auditory impairments may have difficulty in hearing in either one or both ears or have no power of hearing at all. "Hard of hearing", "deaf', "partially deaf", "deaf mute" and "partial hearing" are some terms recently used to denote hearing impairments. But any classification is doubtful to cover the multi-dimensional nature of the variable. Some of the important variables are the degree of hearing loss, age of the onset and type of hearing loss. Children with profound and severe hearing loss, who have to be educated through the sense-modality other than the ear, are referred to as "deaf children." Children who are born deaf are known as "congenitally deaf' while those born with normal hearing but later lose their hearing power, are referred to as "adventiously deaf".

There are some basic differences among "hearing impairment", "hearing disability" and "handicap". An impairment may be defined as a defect in the hearing due to hereditary and/or environmental factors. Children cannot use their hearing for ordinary purposes owing to this impairment. Thus, disability arises out of impairment. Because of this, children cannot enjoy the normal process of hearing sounds. This handicaps the children in hearing.

Besides all the terms described above, some experts have divided impairment into two sub-groups:

(i) Pre-lingual Deaf. A "Pre-lingual Deaf" child is one who is born with little or no hearing. His hearing impairment is marked before speech and language patterns are acquired.

(ii) Post-lingual Deaf. A "Post-lingual Deaf" child is one who becomes deaf due to environmental forces. His hearing impairment is marked after he has attained speech and language pattern.

But the medical professionals have classified all the hearing persons into five groups. These are shown in the following table (see table in the next page).

Recently a group of experts sub-divided the hearing impaired people into the following categories:

Conductive Hearing Loss: Conductive losses are common among the hearing impairments of children. These result in the reduction in the loudness of the sound. The main cause may be the pathological changes in the middle ear owing to congenital or acquired abnormalities of the ear. Though mild, still they are amenable to surgical or medical therapy. Prevention of the chronic infections of the ear will often greatly reduce the incidence of hearing defects.

Sensori-neural Hearing Loss: Sometimes abnormalities in the inner ear or the auditory nerve result in loss of hearing. But it is rarely curable through surgical therapy. Hearing aids for amplification of sound has little to do with this defect. Here the sound is conducted properly and the difficulty lies in analysing or perceiving it properly.

Showing Different Categories of Hearing Impaired People According to Medical People

Category loss in decibles	*Level of hearing*	*Educational Placement*	*Special Need*
Mild	20-30 dB	Required modification in sitting arrangements in IED (Integrated Education for Disabled).	Hearing aids.
Marginal	30-40 dB	Auditory training and speech therapies in IED.	Hearing aid speech therapy.
Moderate	40-60 dB	Amplification of auditory material and increased use of visual aids in IED.	Adaptation of instructional and methodologies. More visual cues.
Severe	60-75 dB	Special class and limited integration.	Special attention in learning and speech. Use of special techniques.
Profound	75 and Above	Special day school, difficult to integrate into academic	Intensive special instructor. areas.

The mode of therapy which can be introduced for children suffering from this defect is purely educational. Children with moderate defects may need hearing aids, auditory training, lip-reading and language training. But children with profound hearing defects may need special schooling.

Psychogenic Hearing Loss: In this case, the cause of the disorder is purely psychological. The child presents greatly exaggerated symptoms of hearing impairment. There may be ear infection which leads to the localisation of the psychic symptom. Sometimes, the child may unconsciously develop hearing loss as an escape from what according to him is an intolerable situation.

However, it becomes difficult to distinguish between organic defects and psychogenic losses. Only appropriate audiological techniques under careful observation can help to make a correct diagnosis.

Central Auditory Defects: These types of defects are extremely complex and their cause or pathogenesis is poorly understood. Such children seem to be aware of sound but are unable to discriminate its meaning. This causes severe communication problems. During early infancy, the percentage of such defects appears to be very high. Again, certain life saving drugs also appear to affect the auditory system. It is very difficult to manage such type of children because they require extensive and prolonged individual therapy.

The Characteristics

The hearing impaired children invite certain limitations. The nature and severity of these limitations depend upon the type and degree of the hearing impairment. Naturally these limitations cause certain changes in behaviour. The following are some important characteristics of the hearing impaired:

Socially Handicapped: Hearing impaired children are not well adjusted in the society. They find it very difficult to adjust with the environment. They develop certain personality disorders and slow temperan-trums, withdrawal or submissiveness etc. Communication difficulties are rampant with them. They, very often, fail to understand what other people say.

Problems in Personal and Social Development: The problems regarding personal and social development are very much pertinent for hearing impaired children. Language becomes a barrier for them for communicating with other children. This affects the socialisation process and plays a vital role in the personal and social development of children. The most significant aspect of these children is their increased dependence on others which leads to a sense of inferiority.

Personality Problems: Certain studies reveal that these children face some personality problems. Partial hearing difficulty may create more confrontation and personality problems than in the case of totally deaf children, because a partially deaf child gets more frustrated as he tries to reach the level of the normals and a totally deaf child seems reconciled to his fate.

Psychological Characteristics: Hearing impaired children have some behavioural problems. Children develop a sense of inferiority since they find themselves helpless in adapting to circumstances that require verbal communication. The child always compares himself/ herself with his/her normal siblings/peers and also judges the attitudes of society towards him/her. He/she observes that the attitude of the society towards him/her is not normal, but either overprotective or rejective. She feels that he/she is different from a normal child. This feeling hampers growth and development of the personality.

Linguistic Difficulties: Since language is an auditory vocal process the acquisition of language is very difficult for deaf children. It is found that the hearing impaired child is abnormally slow in its linguistic development. These children have to receive visually, what other children receive orally. They differ significantly from the normal children in so far as language development is concerned. The normal children learn language and the language is taught to the deaf. These children have a limited vocabulary, they lack comprehension of complex words and words with multiple meaning and concept. Again they feel difficulty in understanding complex structure of language and sometimes they have no language exposure.

Abnormal Emotional Behaviour: Very often, young hearing impaired children show abnormal emotional behaviour. This may throw tantrums to attract attention to himself or his needs. Lack of comprehension may invite tension and resistance. He is frequently obstinate and has a tendency to tease. He gets irritated when he cannot make himself understood.

The Causes: All the causes of hearing impairment can be categorised under four headings: (a) Hereditary and Non-hereditary (b) Congenital and Acquired (c) Pre-natal, Perinatal and Post-natal, and (d) Physiological and Psychological. For the benefit of all, we will discuss all the causes in a nutshell.

Sometimes hearing impairment is predetermined by the genetic structure of the individual. It may be present at birth or develop later in life. Some of these defects are acquired through disease, trauma or accident. There is a hereditary type of degenerative disability. Again there is a hereditary type of degenerative nerve deafness which may be present at birth or develop later in life. Overdose of strong drugs like streptomycin, quinine and L.S.D. are associated with hearing impairment. So mothers are restricted to take these drugs during pregnancy. Maternal malnutrition and unhealthy living conditions during pregnancy are some important causes also. Studies reveal that marriage among close blood relatives is another cause to produce hearing impaired children. Medical practitioners say that brain fever, the improper growth of brain or auditory system and brain tumour are some of the neurological causes of hearing impairment. The perinatal causes include full time delivery, followed by anoxia problems, use of forceps in delivery, instrumental delivery, premature delivery followed immediately by jaundice and use of anaesthetic agents in delivery. Whooping cough, typhoid fever, encephalitis and mumps are significant post-natal causes of hearing impairment. Besides all these factors, accidents, severe burns, toxic drugs, emotional depression and traumas also cause hearing defects. Abnormalities in the inner ear or the auditory nerve result in loss of hearing which is rarely amenable to surgery. Sometimes psychogenic deafness is confused with malingering in which the individual pretends to be unable to hear. But malingering can be detected by special audiological tests.

The Identification: Recently, due to the advancement in technology, the identification of hearing impairment has become easier. The following are some important techniques for identifying impaired children:

Development Scale: Developmental status may be taken into consideration to identify hearing impaired children. It is conducive for establishing the child's current status with regard to sensorimotor development. "Bayley Scales of Infant Development" is very helpful for this purpose. This scale provides a basis for early diagnosis and corrective action in case of retarded development.

Neuro-psychological Tests: Another important test is the assessment of neurological functions. Owing to cerebral dysfunction and brain damage, a good number of hearing impaired children have additional percepto-motor deficiencies. An expert clinician may be able to find certain signs in such children.

Medical Examination: By this technique, a physician takes the general medical history of a child. He investigates the functioning and dysfunctioning of various organs related to audition. The relationship between the auditory deformities and personality disorder is also sought.

Case Study: The case history is generally taken by a psychiatrist. The psychiatrist may collect the data from the child directly or from a close relative of the child. While collecting the data, the following points may be taken in to account:

(i) Identification of the child, i.e., name and address etc.
(ii) Statements of the present problem (symptoms etc.).
(iii) Health history (illness, serious disease, surgical operation etc.)
(iv) Developmental history.
(v) Family history.

Systematic Observation: This method is highly conducive and extremely useful for assessing the hearing impaired. The salient observable points of behaviour displayed by children who are to be identified are as follows:

(i) Frequent ear eggs are observable;
(ii) They turn heads on one side to hear better;
(iii) These children are unable to follow directions;
(iv) In the classroom, they always request to repeat instructions, questions etc.
(v) They focus specially on the speaker's lip;
(vi) They always hesitate to participate in group discussions;
(vii) They display restlessness, inattention and speech difficulty.

Educational Provisions

Since these children need some educational provisions, special arrangements can be made to meet their needs. Some educational facilities are being discussed below:

Use of Hearing-aid: The hearing aid is very necessary for hearing impaired children. For their training and education, it has been proved effective. But the hearing aid should be selected according to the degree of hearing loss. Since it is a delicate and complicated instrument, it must be handled with care. These children may be provided with hearing aids of both the individual and group type for their auditory training. Headphones and a low speaking system may be used to enable the children to have clear and stronger sound. But the individual child may use wearable hearing aids; this is particularly very useful for the deaf and partially deaf children.

Vocational Training: Emphasis was placed on vocational training by different experts in their studies on hearing impaired children. These children have the advantage in residential type of schools. They do well in athletics, extra-curricular activities and in their personal and social development.

Auditory Training: Perception of various speech sounds is possible through this training. Through this, the child distinguishes one voice from another. This type of training provides a thorough understanding of the principles of hearing rehabilitation, lip reading, speech development and testing of hearing educational diagnosis.

Nursery Education: Informal educational system like nursery education is quite beneficial for hearing impaired children. Necessary provisions and useful settings are generally found for the assessment of these children's need. Nursery education is helpful to increase self-confidence in children and moreover, it invites a clear-cut avenue for the child's successful integration into regular schools.

Classroom Arrangements: The hearing impaired children in the class should be front benchers. Accordingly, the seating arrangements should be made. Again, they must take their seats within close proximity of the teacher. The teacher may use a reasonable level of pitch while speaking. Speaking too fast must be strictly avoided. The lips of teachers should be visible to the children so that they may be able to supplement listening by lip-reading. Teachers may avoid moving when speaking. Interaction of friends and peers with these children should be encouraged. To supplement the general teaching input, visual aids may also be used.

Speech Reading: Speech reading is an art of understanding a speaker without hearing, just by watching the movements of lips and tongue and other facial expressions. Of course, teaching speech-reading is a very tedious job. It requires labour, patience and tact on the part of both parents and teachers. A teacher, in the classroom, should stand in front of the children and speak clearly, not by hiding his lips or face. Here the children learn not through hearing but from the signs and gestures, and expressions on the face and forehead. On the whole, they learn by watching lip movements and facial expressions.

Role of Parents: In different studies, priority was given to the role of parents for successful implementation of this programme. If parents want to share the responsibility of their children, the successful integration of hearing impaired children may be possible. The parents may take the following steps to encourage their children for this purpose.

(i) They should speak clearly while talking with their children.

(ii) They must try to speak to the deaf or partially deaf children as often as possible.

(iii) They must try to check on the working conditions of the hearing aid and the thickness of the ear mould.

Role of the School: Orientation for administrators, teaching and non-teaching staff of the school, head of the school and finally children become necessities for the successful integration of this programme. Efforts should be made to extend all possible help and cooperation, so that the children adjust themselves without any difficulty to the new circumstances. Accordingly teachers should adopt new methods to adjust with the new environment. Teachers must encourage such children to ask questions freely. Usually these children become easily fatigued. So they should not be engaged for a longer span of time. Teachers must organise the programmes according to children's needs and abilities. Unhealthy competitions should be avoided as far as possible. Above all, teachers should create a situation where there will be free participation among their classmates. Any rejection of the classmates should be strictly viewed by the teacher.

Orthopaedic Handicapped Children

The problems of orthopaedic children have been more than duly recognised these days. In the past, the orthopaedic handicap had been the main problem of individual families, their family doctors and orthopaedic surgeons. In the society, we come across several children who are crippled, deformed or physically handicapped. These children constitute a heterogeneous group, each requiring a special adaptation of physical help, aids and procedures in instruction.

But who is orthopaedically handicapped? There are many definitions of orthopaedically handicapped. One comprehensive definition is as follows:

Orthopaedically handicapped are those who suffer from a defect that is accompanied by one or another type of deformity that inhibits the normal exercise of his/her muscles, joints or bones.

The types of orthopaedically handicapped are mainly crippled, polio-stricken etc. Again the crippled can be sub-divided into two types—the mild and the severe. The mildly crippled child is one who has problems like congenital anomalies such as dislocated hips or joints. But the severely crippled is one who requires hospitalisation on either temporary or permanent basis. In case of temporarily hospitalised children, integration of regular school programmes is necessary. But in case of permanently hospitalised children, hospital bound programmes are needed.

The Identification: Identification of orthopaedically handicapped children is very easy in comparison with other disabilities like partial sightedness and hearing impairment etc. There are some children who have problems of a mild degree which may be overlooked. For these cases, identification can be made with the help of the following checklist on behavioural manifestations:

(i) These children have poor motor control and coordination.
(ii) They walk awkwardly or with a limb.
(iii) These children show signs of pain during physical exercise.
(iv) They fall frequently.

The Causes: The causative factors of all types of handicaps are many. But a thorough knowledge of some main causative factors is necessary for planning a programme for them. The sole factors are as follows:

Hereditary Causes: This anomaly passes down from generation to generation because of some sort of disturbance in the working of inherent gene mechanism. However, it may be noted that a particular condition may be hereditary and yet it may not manifest itself at birth or might not have appeared before the individual's immediate family.

Congenital Cause: Congenital defects are those that are present at birth. Common congenital defects include club foot, dislocation of hip, missing bones, bow leg, webbed fingers etc. These defects are possible due to infection, nutritional deficiency, x-rays, glandular disorder of the mother, maternal malnourishment etc.

Acquired Causes: Acquired defects include birth injury, accidents, nutrition' deficiency, defective bones or joints, viral infection, etc.

White House Conference has been a definition of the crippled child as follows:

The crippled child, in the orthopaedic sense, is a child that has a defect which causes a deformity or an interference with normal function of the bones, muscles or joints. His condition may be congenital or due to disease or accident. It may be aggravated by neglect or by ignorance.

From the above definition, it is obvious that crippling may be congenital or accidental or effect of diseases. But studies reveal that the crippled is usually intellectual normal.

Educational Provisions

Remarkable progress has been made during recent years for the education of the orthopaedic handicapped children. In the metropolitan cities of India, many schools have incorporated many unusual features including medical and therapeutic equipments to meet with the educational and physical needs of these children. However the schools may take the following steps to provide better facilities to these children.

(i) Vocational training should be given to these children as far as possible. School equipments must be adjusted to his/her deformity, e.g., table, chair etc., may be specially designed. The classrooms must be larger than those for regular pupils. The auditorium, dining room etc., must be within the reach of the orthopaedically handicapped children. The schools must have health and physiotherapy programmes regularly.

(ii) The role of parents and teachers is very important also. A teacher must help the child to accept his handicap to prevent the psychological crippling. Genuine efforts must be made to assist the children to the maximum extent possible to accept their handicaps, be self-reliant and adjust to their limitations. Again the family background of every crippled child must be collected by the teacher. Teachers should see that these children are provided with recreational facilities. Very often, the recreational needs of these children are ignored in the school because of their disability. For grading the children, the disability of children must be taken into account. Oral tests must be introduced for the children who face difficulties in writing the answers. If possible, they may be given extra time for this purpose. The teachers and experts, along with their parents, may take action to provide relevant aid for mobility of the limbs and functioning of the extremities. District rehabilitation centres provide such facilities. Hospitals and primary health centres may be contacted for this purpose.

QUESTIONS

1. Who are aurally handicapped children? Discuss the causes and preventive measures for the aurally handicapped.
2. Discuss the problems of speech impaired children. Suggest some educational measures for them.
3. Discuss the educational programmes for partially sighted and blind children.
4. Write short notes on the following: (a) Cerebral Palsy (b) Crippled Children (c) Speech Impairment.

11

Learning at Slow Pace

Slow Learner

Sometimes a large segment of school-going children present a serious problem to public schools because they have limited scope for achievement. These pupils have intelligence quotients between 76 and 89 and they constitute about 18 per cent of the total school population. Their ability to deal with abstract and symbolic materials, (i.e., language, number and concepts) is very limited and their reasoning in practical situations is inferior to that of average students. These pupils differ slightly from normal children in learning ability. Research works reveal that the attention span of slow learners is relatively short. They are also unable to deal with relatively complex games or school assignments. They need much external stimulation and encouragement to do simple type of work.

Slow learners constitute an appreciable fraction of our population. As Burt (1937) has rightly pointed out the term "backward" or "slow learner" is reserved for those children who are unable to cope with the work normally expected of their age group. Kirk (1962) took "rate of learning" , as the basis for identifying slow learners. According to him, the slow learners, gifted and the average children can be classified according to their "rate of learning". He also strictly refused to equate slow learners with mentally retarded because the former is capable of achieving a moderate degree of academic success even though at a slower rate than the average child. As an adult, a slow learner usually becomes self-supporting, independent and socially adjusted; but in the early stage, he adapts himself to regular class programmes which fit in with his slower learning ability.

Previously psychologists held that slow learning is directly related to intellectual ability. But recent studies in this regard revealed that heredity alone is not responsible for the backwardness of the child; but environment contributes significantly to the scholastic achievement of the child. The backward child is a slow learner and he finds it difficult to keep pace with the normal child in his school work. Taking only I.Q into consideration, we cannot call a child who is a slow learner, mentally retarded. On the whole, the only difference between a slow learner and the average child is his slower rate.

The Characteristics

Research has shown that specific reading disabilities (dyslexia) are seen in about 10-12 per cent of school-going children who are intellectually normal. They have a poor sense of self-esteem and some children show signs of mild depression. They have adequate vision but their reading ability is retarded. Usually this disability is more pronounced in boys than in girls. Very often, these children show signs of tension in habitual manipulation of body parts, and aggressive behaviour. These children can memorise well, often spell words or numbers without knowing what they are spelling or having a "number-sense".

These "slow learners" can be placed under three categories: Those who show signs of brain damage or neurological deficit like Aphasias (can see and read the words but cannot say what it means-can hear words but cannot give their meaning can hear and see words but cannot write). The use of unaffected sensory apparatus (Vision or Hearing) and hands in building up proper meaningful associations yield positive results in these cases. Reports reveal that some children have either been forced to change from their left-handedness to right-handedness or have a 'Split-literality' (Crossed-Eye-Hand Dominance), i.e., they have a dominant right-handedness with a left eyeness or difference in the perception and shape of the objects through their left and right eyes. This is popularly known as "Primary Reading Disability".

Again, secondary reading disability results from emotional disturbance and defects in educational methods employed. To overcome this difficulty remedial teaching with phonetic training has been recommended.

Taking the above facts into consideration, we can now bring out the characteristics of slow learners systematically:

(a) Slow learners have limited cognitive capacity. They fail to cope with learning situations and to reason abstractly. Rational thinking becomes practically impossible. They have the capacity to succeed in rote-learning. These children show interest in learning where relationships are clearly demonstrated. With regard to retentive memories they require more practice and revision in comparison with normal children.

(b) One of the pertinent characteristics of slow learners is poor memory. It occurs due to lack of concentration. It is impossible to say how much a child can learn and retain although he is motivated externally and internally. Experimental evidences reveal that very often the dull children can recall facts about their local cricket team as well as its players.

(c) Classroom situations include distraction and lack of concentration of slow learners. This typical behaviour is also associated with poor motivation. Again different studies also report that when the learning materials are presented through concrete situations, the slow learner's concentration and attention do not differ significantly from that of a normal child.

(d) Inability to express his ideas through language is another significant characteristic of a slow learner. A slow learner also lacks imagination and foresight. He faces difficulty to foresee consequences in the future.

(e) In developing societies, the slow learners invite social as well as educational problems. Of course, some dull children are very poor in scholastic achievements in the school. Their performance is not satisfactory. But some children who come from sophisticated homes show good performance because they get help and encouragement from home. This is only possible at the primary stage of education. But at the secondary stage, the frustrations and failures come from different sources. The children develop an attitude of resentment towards the authorities and create problems. This kind of attitude may lead to anti-social behaviour in the future.

Sandra's Checklist

A checklist containing 69 (sixty-nine) behaviour symptoms arranged under five characteristic patterns was primarily aimed at identifying specific problems of mild retardates who constitute a significant group of slow learners. A single characteristic pattern has no meaning at all. But a group of characteristics provides a clue to analyse certain learning problems of the child.

Characteristics of Cognitive Learning Problems

(i) The slow learners learn at a slower rate and they face difficulty in retaining what they have learned.

(ii) The slow learners prefer concrete learning to abstract learning.

(iii) Transfer of learning becomes impossible for slow learners.

(iv) They lack judgement and common sense and they are highly distractible.

(v) They gain from direct teaching and do not acquire skills incidentally.

(vi) A slow learner is an underachiever and has a very short span of attention.

Characteristics of Language and Language-related Problems

(i) Verbal expressions for slow learners are difficult.

(ii) Oral reading is more difficult than silent reading.

(iii) Slow learners face articulation problems.

(iv) Proper expression of thoughts becomes difficult for them.

Characteristics of Auditory Perceptual Problems

(i) Slow learners face trouble in writing from dictation. They usually leave common prefixes and suffixes while writing.

(ii) Slow learners fail to understand verbal directions. So they are unable to give proper reply, when a question is asked.

(iii) They prefer visually presented materials to orally presented materials.

(iv) Identification of different sounds becomes difficult for them. They also find difficulty in distinguishing between similar sounding words. (e.g.; Tap-Tip, Pen-Pin etc.)

(v) Slow learners usually give inappropriate answers to verbal questions. They also fail to learn the art of counting by memory.

Characteristics of Visual-motor Problems

(i) Slow learners are easily distracted by visual stimuli. They have awkward movements.

(ii) They find it difficult to discriminate between colour, size and shape relationship and are unable to recall to memory the objects that they see.

(iii) They have a very poor handwriting and face difficulties in motor work. Very often they complain about physical problems. Recognition of common objects becomes a problem for them.

(iv) Slow learners prefer part learning to whole learning and find oral learning tasks easier.

Characteristics of Social and Emotional Problems

(i) Slow learners do not have the stamina to sit in a class for long periods.

(ii) They are lovers of solitude and are not gregarious. They fail to make friends and are not at all sociable.

(iii) Slow learners become aggressive towards their friends and peers on trivial matters and they are afraid and self-conscious. They daydream in excess compared to normal children.

(iv) Nail-biting is another interesting characteristic of slow learners. Sometimes they also engage themselves in anti-social activities.

(v) Their mood changes frequently and their achievement is below expectancy.

(vi) They prefer not to work in a group and have inappropriate and excessive verbalisation.

The Causes

The causes of slow learning are many. Some important ones are discussed below:

Poverty: In a developing country like India, poverty is considered to be the primary cause of slow learning. Poverty affects children in two ways— (i) by impairing children's health, and (ii) by reducing their learning capacity. Again it brings rare opportunities to acquire general knowledge through enriched experience. In other words, a child from a sophisticated family has a variety of avenues to explore and he gets plenty of materials to meet his requirements. He gets educational toys and books which are conducive to acquire general knowledge to improve his educational background. On the contrary, a child from an impoverished family does not get enough opportunities to live a full life. However, poverty is not the sole cause of slow learning. We have to investigate into other causes to gain first hand knowledge about slow learners.

Intelligence of Family Members: Another potent factor of learning is the level of intelligence of parents as well as family members. It indirectly affects the slow learning of children. It is true that educated and intelligent parents can provide educational experiences and materials to their children according to their own intellectual level. But if the parents are not intelligent or sophisticated, they cannot take positive steps towards the upliftment of their children. Again, the economic condition of the family also plays a major role to permit the parents to spend a little amount of money on their children regularly. If their purse permits, then they become interested to purchase for their children some materials which have educational value. A sophisticated family which is economically sound can provide better opportunities for their children. Children coming from affluent families which have high socio-economic status are not usually slow learners. Research evidences also confirm this fact.

Emotional Factors: Emotional factors contribute a lot towards the slow learning of children. Psychologists confirmed this through their research analysis. When a child comes to the school, he brings his emotional world with him. Experiments have already established the fact that tensions and conflicts exercise a negative effect on learning of the child. So the tensions at home, the relationships between the siblings and parents themselves have an adverse effect on the child, not to mention the frustrations which he sustains from his family and from the external world. Research data revealed that in the democratic homes, children get less frustration than the autocratic homes. So, in a way, we can conclude that children from autocratic homes are usually slow learners.

Personal Factors: Besides all these above factors, there are some personal factors which are more or less responsible for slow learning. Personal factors include long illness or long absence from school and lack of confidence in self. It was found that children who lack self-confidence are usually slow learners.

The Identification

There is every possibility that in a classroom there must be some slow learners. These children consist of a group with mild handicaps. They come to school regularly but they are likely to become dropouts if their needs are not met. From the psychological point of view, it would be conducive for these children to be identified earlier. Then necessary steps can be taken to help them in their learning. Survey works reveal that it is somehow easier to identify more severely handicapped children than the mildly handicapped ones. A teaching expert is easily able to identify any deviation in classroom behaviour pertaining to learning difficulties of children. He has primary knowledge about the fact which spells out clearly that the slow learners require more time and more help to acquire the skills in comparison with the average children. These children also rely more on concrete learning rather than abstract learning. Psychologists and experts use various tools and techniques to identify slow learners. These are as follows:

Observation Technique: Observation of children's behaviour by the teacher as well as experts may help in identifying slow learners. This observation may be done under simple as well as controllable conditions. While observing children's behaviour, a strict watch can be kept for their reaction to various situations. A child's behaviour is not only observed in the classroom, but also on the playground, home and in the group etc. Observation may be done by just watching the child's behaviour directly and by moving along with the child. It should be kept in mind that for this technique, the observer should have the capacity for analysing and interpreting the information he gets from his observation. Observation technique is conducive for ascertaining the recreational, occupation and extracurricular interest of children.

Case Study Method: As we know, by this technique, the history of the child, his family, his early life and home environment are revealed. Through this method, psychologists also try to study the learning difficulties, adjustment problems and behavioural problems of a child. By finding out the causes of such abnormalities of children, psychologists as well as teaching experts are able to suggest the best possible remedial measures. Of course, this is a long drawn process and psychologists undergo a strain in interviewing such children, their relatives and parents at short or long intervals.

Medical Examination: Before confirmation, the developmental history from early childhood should be meticulously verified by a qualified medical expert or medical practitioner. Under strict physical and medical examination, the anomalies, disabilities and handicaps can be highlighted.

Scholastic Tests: Evaluation or deficiencies in school achievement can be possible through scholastic tests. These tests can throw light on areas like arithmetic, reading, spelling, composition, writing, language and comprehension. General and specific problems of children are singled out by the psychologists and educationists through scholastic tests, and causes of anomalies can also be evaluated properly.

Personality Test: Through personality tests, attempts can be made by psychologists to throw light on the emotional characteristics of children as well as temperamental traits. Evidence shows that there are certain personality traits which have direct relationship with specific backwardness. Persistence, sensitiveness, concentration, emotional stability, assertiveness etc., are some of these traits. Thematic Apperception Tests (TAT), Rorschach Ink Blot Test (RIBT), Word Association Test (WAT), Free Association Test and some psychoanalytical procedures are very much helpful to the psychologists here. Research analysis by W.P. Alexander have also revealed that teacher's assessment of children's traits for personality can be very profitably used for diagnostic and productive purposes.

Intelligence Test: Through the use of any standardised intelligence tests the intellectual level of children can be assessed. Both verbal intelligence tests and non-verbal tests can be used for this purpose. But psychologists prefer individual verbal tests to group verbal tests. An expert can get a true picture of the mental capacities of backward children by giving many intelligence tests. A single test is not sufficient to bring out the full picture of the mental capacities of a child. Psychologists use more than one standardised test to ascertain a particular anomaly.

Psychometric and Psychological Tests: For diagnostic purposes, psychologists use psychometric tests which are of a sensory nature. For better appraisal, analysis and evaluation of specific skills of backward children, these tests are primarily used. By these tests, psychologists try to discover the exact nature of errors made by the backward children. Again some other psychological tests may also be used to assess span of attention, auditory perception, steadiness, memory and reasoning powers.

Educational Programmes

One of the pertinent characteristics of slow learners is that they learn slowly and unevenly. Again, they are unable to cope satisfactorily with the usual educational standards of the ordinary school. However, with proper guidance and care they are capable of being educated. In adulthood, they become self-supporting, independent and socially adjusted. One defect, however, which is worth noting, is that most of the slow learners are not properly identified till they attend school.

Conscious efforts are being made to help the child after being identified. Psychologists specify that the remedy for slow learners lies mainly in their nature and the extent of the causes which produce it. Of course, each case is unique and requires specific remedial measures. Psychologists recommend the following remedial measures which may prove conducive to slow learners.

Elastic Curriculum: Educationists may take care in preparing the curriculum for slow learners which should be as flexible as possible to suit the requirements and needs of the individual students. Slow learners are generally interested in concrete perceptual experiences. So attention must be paid towards concrete aspects of work. Educationists should lay less emphasis on abstract and theoretical studies. Because slow learners do not grasp abstract things easily. Again emphasis must be placed on the use of visual and concrete aspects of work. Experiments on slow learners revealed that the learning of generalisation, abstractions and concept is difficult for these children. So teaching experts should strictly avoid these concepts. The crafts which are found to be conducive to these children include mental work, wood work, leather work, cane work, knitting, tailoring and other subjects of household economy.

Remedial Instruction: Generally, teaching experts provide remedial instruction for slow learners. Studies have shown that the remedial instruction proved profitable in case of specific slowness in a specific subject area. First, the deficiencies are determined and confirmed by the experts giving these children some diagnostic tests. Then the cooperation of specialists is sought to deal with specific slowness. The following points are taken into consideration for smooth working of a remedial programme.

(i) Gradation of teaching materials may be carefully done taking the capacity and requirements of children into consideration.

(ii) Short frequent lessons should be introduced instead of long lessons every week.

(iii) Experts should be aware of the fact that a friendly approach in remedial teaching is highly conducive.

(iv) To generate interest, social skills and confidence in slow learners, priority should be given to art, music and drama.

(v) Practice, drill and review should be given importance to by teachers while dealing with slow learners. Repetition and direction should also be emphasised.

Healthy Environment: An important aspect of remedial measures for slow learners is rich environment. The school atmosphere of children should be healthy and reasonably free. Sometimes poor environmental factors contribute a lot towards the slowness. These should be removed as early as possible. Again, there must be provision made for a variety of approaches to the various subjects. Very often, the slow learners suffer from emotional problems. So care must be taken to place them in protected environment.

Periodical Medical Check-up: Physical anomalies are: important contributory factors for slow learning. Poor health and other malfunctions also have similar effects. If a particular anomaly is detected and correctly recognised, then a slow learner may become a normal learner after treatment. So a special medical check-up should be arranged for every slow learner.

Non-promotion: Experimental facts of a group of psychologists are in favour of non-promotion of slow learners. These psychologists follow a policy that permits retention of a child in a class for the second year. But very often, it is found that when a child is not promoted and retained in the same class, he resorts to self punitive measures. For this reason, many educationists object to this idea of non-promotion. Rather, they lay emphasis on remedial instructions and understanding.

Motivation: Slow learners lack the experience of reinforcement in the home environment. Fear of failure and disinterest are pertinent in their daily school activities. So adequate and appropriate measures should be taken to improve their academic status. When a slight improvement is noticed some motivational techniques may be used to stimulate. Use of illustration, examples and aids may also be conducive for creating motivational atmosphere inside the class. A teaching expert should try to instil confidence in children and he must also make constant efforts to remove fear of failure.

Individual Attention: Treatment of slow learners should be given individual attention. The teaching experts may place emphasis on recognition of individual differences among students. They must also respect the individuality of the child through helpful environment. Again, teaching experts should be very kind and sympathetic towards their students. The teachers should allow the students to proceed at their own rate of learning. One of the best advantages of this method is that there is no failure since the children are assessed against their own success. Complete freedom is given to children to budget their own time to bring out their assignment forte.

Special Methods of Teaching: Educationists as well as psychologists have conducted many experiments to devise special methods of teaching for slow learners. Their results indicate that the slow learners require short and simple methods of instruction based on concrete experiences. Verbal instructions should be limited. Educational excursions to places of historical, geographical, scientific and cultural interest may be conducted. The use of pictures, models, charts, films and other audio-visual aids will also be profitable. Employment of project methods is helpful in imparting education. As the slow learner needs security, an atmosphere of assurance and love should be created. Direct experiences and concrete examples are of great help for children:

Home Visits by the Teachers: To make family environments sophisticated and healthy, the teachers should take an interest in visiting the homes of the parents and advise them accordingly. An unfavourable home environment and autocratic homes are important factors for slow learning. Teachers may suggest some remedial measures for slow learners to the parents relating to home environment.

Maintenance of Progress Record: Assessment of children's progress is essential for recommending their entry into a higher group. There should be a well planned regular evaluation of the progress of the children in all curricular or co-curricular aspects. Records of evaluation should be preserved properly. Progress charts and cumulative record cards may be of great help for them. These records are essential for individualised treatment. Condensed case history with assessments helps the teacher to provide better educational treatment for slow learners.

Attempts have been made here to chalk out the remedial measures and some guidelines for the teachers. But problems are not easy to surmount. A teacher may be the first diagnostician rather than an instructor. But educational psychologist, social workers and state authorities should take interest in discovering and rectifying the causes of slow learning. Then this anomaly can be obliterated and millions of slow learners will be provided with opportunities for developing their self and live happily in this world.

QUESTIONS

1. Who are slow learners? Discuss various educational programmes for slow learners recommended by educationists.
2. Bring-out the differences between a slew learner and a normal learner. Suggest some remedial measures for slow learners in the classroom situation.
3. Discuss the attempts that can be made to bring the slow learners back to a normal level of attainment.

4. Who is a slow learner? Discuss various characteristics of slow learners.
5. Briefly discuss various causes of slow learning.
6. Write short notes on the following:
   (a) Individualised Instruction
   (b) Remedial Instruction
   (c) Slow learning
   (d) School Readiness programme
   (e) Identification of slow learners
   (f) Educational Programmes for slow learners
   (g) Characteristics of slow learners suggested by Sandra
   (h) Causes of slow learning
7. Distinguish between:
   (a) Slow Learners and Normal Learners,
   (b) Individualised Instruction and Remedial Instruction.

12

The Mentally Retarded

Many terms are used to define mental retardation. In 1955, the term "Subnormal mind" was used by British Psychologists like Cyril Burt, Clark and Clark and by the WHO (World Health Organisation). In the recent revision (ICD-9), WHO has preferred the term "retardation". The American Psychiatric Association (APA) uses the term "mental deficiency". Commonly used terms that are synonymous with "mental deficiency" are feeble-mindedness, amentia and oligophrenia. The term "amentia" is generally used to differentiate individuals with low intelligence from individuals who are mentally ill (dementia). Oligophrenia is the accepted term in continental countries. But professionals working in this area use terms like "exceptional individuals" or "typical individuals". The popular term "feeblemindedness" is no longer used. The psychiatrists and contemporary psychologists use the term "mentally retarded" or "mental deficiency".

Everybody feels that there is no uniform method of defining the term "mental retardation". According to English law, mental retardation is a condition of arrested or incomplete development of the mind which takes place before the age of 18 years, whether arising from inherent causes or induced by disease or injury, (Mental Deficiency Act, 1929).

According to Tredgold (1937), "it is a state of incomplete mental development of such a kind and degree that the individual is not capable of adapting himself to the normal environment of his fellowmen in such a way as to maintain existence independently of supervision, control or external, support". The WHO (1954) referred to it as "incomplete or insufficient general development of mental capacities". The American Psychiatric Association (1968) has defined mental retardation as "Subnormal general intellectual functioning" which originates during the developmental period and is associated with impairment of either learning and social adjustment or maturation or both. "The American Association of Mental Deficiency (AAMD) refers to mental retardation as significantly sub-average in general intellectual functioning existing currently with deficits in adaptive behaviour and manifested during the developmental period". ICD-9 defines mental retardation as a condition of arrested or incomplete development of mind especially characterised by sub-normality of intelligence. A meticulous survey of all these above definitions of mental retardation reveals that the key concept underlying these definitions is intelligence. The most widely accepted definition of mental retardation is given by AAMD. It not only takes the intellectual ability into account but due consideration is given to adaptive ability also.

The Classification

In France, Esquiral (1838) distinguished clearly between psychotic and feebleminded patients. He revealed that there are different grades of idiocy depending upon their ability to use language. The first degree of idiocy, according to him, is marked by patient's use of words in short phrases. The patient is able to utter only nonsensical syllables or certain sounds in the second degree.

In the first decade of the twentieth century, the first attempt to classify mental retardation in terms of intelligence tests was made. Alfred Binet (1905) developed some tests to measure intelligence in terms of reasoning and problem solving rather than motor skills. He also devised the concepts of "Mental Age (MA)" and "Chronological Age (CA)" on the basis of which he could differentiate between bright children and dull ones.

Levels of Retardation

Previously the following classification was used by the psychologists and educationists.

I.Q. between 110 and above	—	Superior
90 to 110	—	Average
80 to 90	—	Dull/Normal
70 to 80	—	Borderline
Below 70	—	Feebleminded

The feebleminded were further classified as:

I.Q. from 50 to 70	—	Morons
25 to 50	—	Imbeciles
Below 25	—	Idiots

The terms like "moron", "imbecile" and "idiot" became derogatory terms later on. These terms were consequently changed by the American Association of Mental Deficiency in 1973. However, during the first decade of the twentieth century, attempts were made to bring out the levels of mental retardation on the basis of the degree of mental development expressed as equivalent to the actual or life age in terms of Intelligence Quotient (I.Q.). Later, it was felt that I.Q. alone does not provide an adequate measure of an individual's adaptive capacity. So the person's level of adaptive behaviour in terms of the degree to which he meets standards of personal independence and social responsibility expected of his age and cultural group were also taken into account. Keeping all these factors in the forefront, a new attempt was made to develop a different type of classification with new terminologies.

Classification Based on I.Q. Obtained from Binet Test

Mild Mental Retardation (I.Q. 68-52):

About 90 per cent of the mentally retarded individuals are found to belong to this category. Persons in this group are considered "educable". Intellectually they are equal to an 8.3 to 10.9 year-old child They show no organic pathology and require little supervision. With parental assistance and special training, they can be taught to be self-supporting.

Moderate Mental Retardation (I.Q. 51-36):

These people are otherwise known as trainable retardates. About 6 per cent of the mentally retardates belong to this category. Intellectually, these people are equal to a 5.7 to a 8.2 year old child. Even if they are able to speak, still the rate of learning is very slow. Physically they appear clumsy and suffer from motor in-coordination. Sometimes brain damage and neurological disorders are found in most of the moderate retardates. Though some of them require institutionalisation, they can manage to live safely under the protection of their family members. With parental help and adequate opportunities for training, they can manage to earn their own livelihood.

Severe Mental Retardation (I.Q. 35-20):

Severe retarded people represent more than three per cent of the retarded individuals. They are sometimes referred to as "dependent retarded". These persons suffer from severe retardation in motor and speech development. Sensory defects and motor handicaps are also common. The majority of them are permanently institutionalised and require constant care and attention. They face problems while learning simple tasks. Still they can perform simple occupational tasks under supervision.

Profound Mental Retardation (I.Q. Under 20):

This group represents one per cent of the mentally retarded people. They are popularly known as "life support" mental retardates. These persons are severely deficient in adaptive behaviour and unable to master simple tasks. They are completely unable to look after themselves. They cannot attend to their basic physical needs. Major deformities of the brain, head and body are often observed with these retarded individuals. A great percentage of profoundly retarded people die at a very early age. Retarded growth, pathology of central nervous system, mutism, deafness and convulsive seizures are common symptoms of these people. These people require constant supervision throughout their life.

The above classification of mental retardation has been made on the basis of I.Q. scores obtained by the Binet Test. But classifications based on the Wechsler Adult Intelligence Scale (WAIS) are slightly different. Here the individuals with I.Qs betwen two and three standard deviations below normal are labelled "mildly retarded", those with I.Qs. between three and four standard deviations below the mean as "moderately retarded", those with I.Qs between four and five standard deviations below the mean as "severely retarded" and those with five standard deviations below mean as "profoundly retarded".

Tredgold and Lewis proposed two systems of classification that have gained wide recognition.

Primary-Secondary

Tredgold tried to bring out a division of amentia which he has called "Primary" and "Secondary". According to him, all degrees of deficiency may occur in either form, but there is tendency for secondary aments to be less intelligent than primary aments. Primary amentia includes all cases where the mental deficiency is hereditary. Tredgold assumes that eighty per cent of mentally defectives are of this type.

On the contrary, secondary amentia includes all cases where there is no inherent germ impairment. Here the normal development is interfered with by adverse external factors acting after fertilisation. Secondary amentia is acquired rather than inherited. For example, a child may inherit genes having the potentiality of producing a perfectly normal brain, but he may become feebleminded as a consequence of cerebral damage occurring before and after birth. Twenty per cent of all aments are classified as secondary.

But some psychologists vehemently opposed this classification of Tredgold. They pointed out that in a large proportion of cases it is impossible to decide whether the mental deficiency is of hereditary or of an acquired nature.

Sub-cultural Pathological

Lewis has brought a division of mentally defectives and these are (i) sub-cultural and (ii) pathological. According to him, most feeble-minded individuals are of the sub-cultural type. They represent the low end of the intelligence scale of the general population. Pathological amentias do not represent the extreme end of normal variation. Again, sub-cultural aments for the most part resemble normal people in general appearance, but pathological aments exhibit anatomical and physical abnormalities. Studies revealed that subcultural aments are generally brighter. Heredity is considered to be the potent factor in the production of sub-cultural cases. Statistical analysis of Lewis has shown that aments of the pathological variety are found evenly distributed among all sections of the community but the subcultural group is concentrated on slum areas. This classification is somehow similar to that suggested by Tredgold.

General Characteristics

Limited Intelligence: Generally intelligence is defined as the ability to learn useful information and skills, adapt to new problems and conditions of life, profit, from past experiences, engage in abstract and creative thinking, employ critical judgement, avoid errors; surmount difficulties, and exercise foresight. The mentally retarded persons are markedly deficient in all these attributes. Their learning capacity is limited. Research works reveal that the teaching of mental defectives is a slow and tedious process. Learning depends more on rote memory than on understanding. The errors are repeated again and again. The brightest among the mentally retarded can be taught to read and write. The absence of intelligence is relative rather than absolute.

As revealed earlier, there is no sharp line of demarcation between the average and the mentally retarded persons. The difference is one of degree. Surveys based on thousands of individuals have shown that I.Q.'s ranging from 70 to 90 are classified as dull and individuals with I.Qs. under 70 are classified as mentally defective. These limits are purely arbitrary. The moot point, however, is that neither the mentally superior nor the mentally defective are special groups sharply separated from average.

Social Insufficiency: Mentally retarded children are incapable of adequate selfcare, self-support or self-management in society. These children also require an undue amount of assistance. Care is taken to feed and dress them until a late age. Association with younger children is very much pertinent. But adults are largely dependent upon others for their economic welfare. In a continuous study, the British Mental Deficiency Committee has found that only 14 per cent of males were almost self-supporting, 46 per cent were partially self-supporting and the remainder contributed nothing. The degree of self-support was even lower among female defectives. Later studies in this field reveal that adult defectives are incapable of handling personal and social affairs with ordinary prudence. If they are not guided properly, they engage themselves in socially undesirable behaviour. This type of behaviour includes stealing, general destructiveness and sex delinquencies.

Mentally retarded persons have little control over their impulses. Their sense of right and wrong is poorly developed. Moreover, their behaviour is determined by the immediate situation. They express their sexual urges freely when stimulated. These social reactions may be controlled with proper supervision.

Emphasis has been placed on the socio-economic aspects of amentia by English writers. The 1929 Wood report (37, p. 10) defined mental deficiency as "a condition of incomplete development of the mind to such a degree or kind as to render the individual incapable of adjusting himself to his social environment in a reasonably efficient and harmonious manner and to necessitate external care, supervision or control".

A special test has been devised by Doll (1935) for measuring social development. This is popularly known as Vineland Social Maturity Scale. The items of this test involve concepts like self-help in eating and dressing, locomotion, occupation, communication, self-direction and socialisation. These are arranged in age sequence from birth to maturity. By determining a person's level of performance on the test, it is possible to obtain his social age. Dividing the social age by the chronologic age gives a social quotient or SQ, which may be used to supplement the I.Q., in arriving at a diagnosis of mental retardation.

SA
SQ = -------------- (i)
CA

Where as

SQ = Social Quotient
SA = Social Age
CA = Chronological Age

Drives and Emotions: With the degree of mental retardation, the development of drives and emotions vary. Even the basic self-preservation drives are absent with some of the lowest grades. External manifestations of hunger or thirst are not prominent and the individuals make no attempt to avoid injurious stimuli. Their inferior emotional life is very prominent. Biological drives are well developed at the intermediate level but the affective life is mainly limited to the simpler emotions of pleasures, fear, anger and surprise. Most of the studies on mental retardation reveal that these people rarely experience complex sentiments involving honour, social righteousness and duty.

Personality: We know that no two individuals, in this world, have the same personality. But in case of mentally retarded people, individual differences appear to be less prominent than among the general population. Among the retardates, it is rare to find individuals who might be described as dynamic, charming, forceful, vicious, obnoxious or outstanding. Many persons are colourless and tractable individuals. A group of defectives can easily be influenced. They also tend to be submissive. The defectives are either stable, apathetic, or unstable and excitable.

Organismic Inferiority: Mentally retarded persons suffer from general structural and functional inferiority of the entire organism. They learn to talk and walk at a much later age. Defective speech and shuffling gait are two very prominent characteristics of these individuals. In comparison to normal persons, their sensory discrimination is less acute. The defectives are relatively insensitive to pain and their auditory and visual defects are common. Normal performance is very rare among mental defectives and they fall short of normal performance on tests of mechanical ability.

Clinical Types

Simple: Generally 60 to 70 per cent of mental defectives display no distinguishing physical characteristics. No doubt, they are undersized and have a larger number of physical defects. Their brain studies reveal no specific abnormalities. Among them two-thirds are morons and the remainder are mainly imbeciles. Unfavourable environmental surroundings and limited education are two prominent causes of this type. But psychologists think that besides these causes, the basic cause of simple type is heredity. Different studies reveal that most mental defectives are the offsprings of dull parents. It was found that the brothers and sisters of mental defectives usually have I.Qs. ranging from 80 to 95.

Mongolism (Downs Syndrome): Mongolism or Down's syndrome is caused by chromosomal aberrations. It was first described by Langdon

Down in 1886. It has been so named because persons so afflicted frequently have almond-shaped slanting eyes. The disease occurs among Negroes as well as Whites. Oriental children also suffer from this syndrome.

A number of physical features are often found among children with Down's syndrome. The physical anomalies include slanting eyes, flat face and nose, large and deeply fissured tongue, irregular and misshapen teeth, small skull, protruding belly, underdeveloped genitalia and disproportionately small legs and arms. The height of an adult mongoloid does not exceed four feet. Generally Mongols appear to be alert, lively and bright. They are affectionate, good natured and tractable. About two-thirds of Mongols are imbeciles and the remaining one-third are idiots. Mongoloid children perform better in a family where there is emotional warmth rather than in institutions. With proper guidance and encouragement, mongoloids can perform simple household work.

Microcephaly: Microcephaly (small-headedness) refers to an arrest in the development of the brain at the fourth or fifth month of foetal life. Microcephalies are mental defectives having tiny heads. Less than one per cent of the mental defectives are of this type. The cause of this defect is the impaired development of the brain and a consequent failure of the cranium to attain normal size.

The most pertinent characteristic of the microcephalic is his small head. The circumference of this head rarely exceeds 17 inches. The cause of microcephaly is not definitely known. Research works indicate that mothers, who, for therapeutic purposes, are subjected to pelvic X-ray radiation during pregnancy are likely to give birth to microcephalics. Tredgold reported that most cases of microcephaly are the result of pathological variation of the germ cell.

Hydrocephaly: The accumulation of an abnormal amount of cerebrospinal fluid within the cranium causes damage to the brain tissues and enlargement of the cranium. The resulting large cranium is technically known as hydrocephalus. There is every possibility that the fluid may be collected in the ventricle spaces within the brain or in the subarachnoid space outside the brain. The former is called inner hydrocephalus, the latter, external hydrocephalus. External hydrocephalus is not associated with mental retardation. But inner hydrocephalus is related to mental deficiency and the persons suffering from inner hydrocephalus may possess normal intelligence. However, hydrocephaly accounts for about one percent of mentally retarded cases. Paralysis of limbs and legs is a prominent symptom of hydrocephaly. Attempts to treat the disease by surgical operations invited doubtful results.

Cretinism (Thyroid Deficiency): This disorder is due to endocrine imbalance. It is generally referred to as hyperthyroidism. This is mainly due to the decrease or absence of the thyroid hormone, thyroxin. Sometimes the thyroid gland fails to develop properly or it undergoes degeneration or injury during infancy. Most cases of cretinism result from lack of iodine in the diet. Thyroid deficiency may also occur as the result of birth injuries or in connection with infectious diseases such as measles, whooping cough or diptheria. Generally cretins are malformed dwarfs with a bloated appearance. Emotionally they are dull and apathetic.

Traumatic Amentia: One of the potent factors of mental retardation is brain injury. There is every possibility of cerebral damage before, during or after birth. Most cases occur due to intracranial lesions and hemorrhages occurring during birth. Severe head injuries occurring before or after birth occasionally result in mental retardation. The accidental situations of pregnant women and head injury experienced by the neonate during infancy are some of the factors which cause mental retardation.

Factors at Work

Mainly two factors are responsible for mental retardation. These are categorised under two headings: (i) Organic, and (ii) Environmental. These factors are otherwise known as cultural and familial. Organic factors include genetic factors and the factors caused by various infection and trauma. Again social and psychological factors come under the environmental causes. Organic factors account solely for moderate and severe retardation cases, while the environmental factors account for mild and moderate retardation.

Different studies and research works reveal how genetic, physical, social and psychological factors are associated with mental retardation. Studies of Linford Rees (1970) and David Stafford Clark (1964) reported that at least 5 per cent of the babies born turn out to be retarded at the time of birth. Again Gibson (1963) reported that about 3 per cent of the children aged between 6 and 16 years are mentally retarded.

Genetic Factors: Retardation is determined at the moment of conception in genetic conditions. In this, there are two types, namely; those caused by pairing of two defective recessive genes and those caused by chromosomal aberrations.

(i) Mongolism or Down's syndrome is caused by chromosomal aberrations. It was Langdon Down who first discovered this syndrome in 1886. Reports say that about 10 per cent of moderately and severely retarded children suffer from Down's syndrome. Research works reveal that aged mothers generally give birth to mongoloid children. Medical examination through testing whether the child in the foetus is mongoloid or not are now possible. As a result, medical termination of the foetus is possible.

(ii) "Klinefelter's Syndrome" is another kind of chromosomal abnormality in which an extra chromosome is found to be defective.

Metabolic Disorder: Statistics of mental retardates reveal that about 1 in 20,000 births suffers from PKU (Phenylketonuria). Phenylketonuria is a rare metabolic disorder. Schild (1972) reveals that about 1 in a 100 in institutions suffer from this type of disorder. PKU was first discovered by Folling (1934). Here the enzyme responsible for the metabolism of the biochemical phenylalanine is not present at birth.

Maternal Infection: Reports revealed that about 5 per cent of pregnant women have some viral infection which invite dangerous effects during the first three months (Hellman and Pritchard, 1971). Mothers who contact rubella or German measles during the first three months of pregnancy may produce children who show symptoms of disorder and retardation. Some symptoms of deafness, cataract and malformation of the heart are also seen. Medical examination reports that a variety of pre-natal infectious conditions may also lead to mental retardation of the child. These conditions include cytomegalia, a body disease in which a maternal virus infects the foetus and toxoplasmosis, which is an infection due to a protozoan. Of course in both the conditions, the infection may be latent in the mother but transmitted to the foetus. Toxoplasmosis is a disease that can cause severe neurological damage to the developing foetus.

Mental Retardation Associated with Intoxication: The cause of mental retardation can be associated with intoxications due to carbon monoxide, lead, arsenic, quinine and other substances. Permanent brain damage and mental retardation are found due to post-natal accidental poisoning of infants and children. Toxic condition during the first few days following birth may cause kernicterus which is another brain disorder. The term "Kernicterus" refers to the yellow staining of certain nuclear masses of the brain including the basal ganglia and the hypothalamic nuclei. This pigment is identified as "bilirubin".

Mental Retardation Associated with Trauma: Physical damage due to pre-natal injuries or during birth may cause mental retardation. Exposition to large amounts of irradiation of a pregnant woman causes retardation also. Here the foetus may be adversely affected. The type of damage depends upon the developmental stage of the foetus. Reports of medical examination reveal that when the uterus is irradiated during the first three months of pregnancy, the incidence of mental retardation is reported to be significantly high.

Besides the above factors, respiratory difficulties after birth, convulsions and inability to make normal sucking movements are some of the causes of mental retardation.

Haemorrhage of the brain at the time of birth is also a potent factor for mental retardation. In normal births, the risk approaches to zero; but in cases of abnormal positioning of foetus, breech extraction or the use of forceps increases the possibility of bleeding in the brain of the child. There is every possibility that these children are ten times more likely to be retarded than a child born normally.

Some psychiatrists reveal in their research reports that premature birth is an important cause of mental retardation. Again, cerebral palsy, motor disability associated with organic brain damage is associated with mental retardation. The main symptom here is motor in-coordination.

Mental Retardation Associated with Tumours: Studies in the mental hospitals confirm that a tumour in the brain may cause hydrocephalus, i.e., accumulation of an abnormal amount of cerebrospinal fluid in the cranium. Neurofibromatosis is a condition characterised by skin patches of a dark brown colour. Different sizes of patches are generally found. Skin tumours are present. In some cases, there is normal intelligence, while in others mental retardation is significant. Epiloia is another disease transmitted by a dominant gene with variable expression. Numerous nodules and tumours throughout the brain are found. A butterfly-shaped rash develops on the face and spreads over a wider area. The condition may be accompanied by the development of convulsions and retarded mental development. Microcephaly refers to an arrest in the development of the brain at the 4th or 5th month of foetal life. It is mainly caused by an abnormal growth of cells that form the supporting structure of the brain tissue. This disease is characterised by enlargement of the skull, increase in the size and weight of the skull, visual impairment, convulsions etc.

Retardation Associated with Environmental and Psychological Causes: A combination of genetic and environmental factors is responsible for familial type of mental retardation. Early emotional deprivation and disturbed parent-child relationships are some of the potent factors associated with mental retardation of this type. Emotionally disturbed children are considered to be oversensitive to psychological stress and vitamin deficiency is likely to cause over susceptibility to infection.

Several small-scale surveys report that the familial type of retarded children are found in low socio-economic families. In all these cases, the parents' intellectual and educational levels are low. Heber (1970) pointed out that the latter factor is responsible for mental retardation. These kinds of mental retardates have a family background characterised by poverty with no facilities for gratification of physiological needs. In addition to these, the parents' intellectual level is low. As a result, lack of social, emotional and motivational support for the child is found. Study of Benda et al., (1963) has revealed that by eradicating or reducing poverty, the incidence of mental retardation can be considerably reduced.

Problems of Adjustment

Special psychological difficulties for retardates are found in day-to-day life. These are as follows:

(a) Mild depression, feelings of worthlessness and helplessness are experienced.

(b) As a retardate grows older, he becomes lonely and unable to adjust in society. Evidence points towards the frustration of psychological and social needs which predispose some retardates to feel angry and rebellious.

(c) Parents of such children develop a guilt complex Parental overprotection is a glaring example. Sometimes they do not encourage self-help; rather they continue to dress and feed the child up to an advanced age. As a result, this type of behaviour encourages a dependent style of interaction in the child. Mainly overprotection and denial of the parents invite adjustment difficulties of such type of children.

Prevention, Remedy and Care

As it has been suggested, prevention is preferred to treatment and rehabilitation in case of mentally retarded children. It is possible to prevent metabolic disorders such as phenylketonuria (PKU) and cretinism if treatment begins in the early periods of life. Statistical analysis reveals that there is a correlation between the mother's age and mongolism. So programmes of public education can be introduced to encourage parents to have children before the age of forty. Again, through public education, retardation caused by toxic agents may be prevented.

Compensatory Education: Generally compensatory education aims at preventing developmental defects that interfere with educational progress in the disadvantaged pre-school child. In Western countries like USA, many institutions of this type are found. "Project Head Start" is this type of institution which started in Milwaukee, USA. This project was proved successful in USA. Mainly it demonstrates the effectiveness of early and comprehensive intervention in the prevention of cultural familial retardation. The above project aims at selecting children of mentally retarded parents with an I.Q. of 70. This gives the children some structured programme of sensory and language stimulation that emphasises achievement motivation, problem-solving skills and interpersonal relations, which is imparted to the children daily, and the mothers of these children receive training in the understanding and managing of the retarded children in their homes.

Special Education: We know that a retardate learns at a slow pace. So structured curricular materials and techniques are necessary for educating retarded children. Recently individual centred programmes have been tried out at the Institute of Defectology in Moscow, USSR. At this centre, the retarded child is identified within six months after its birth. From the 6th month till the onset of puberty, individual programmes from multidisciplinary points of view are devised and implemented for children. It gives a healing touch to the children with the onset of puberty.

It is true that such kind of individual-based programmes are not found in India and neither does it appear possible in the near future. But an attempt can be made to work out programmes involving small groups.

Day Care Centre: When the children are too young or too retarded to be included in other community programmes, their needs can be met by "Day care centres".

Sheltered Workshop: As its name indicates, a sheltered workshop provides an opportunity for mentally retarded persons to develop their work skills to a point where they can get a job. In developed countries like USA or USSR, many sheltered workshops are found. In our country, the Department of Social Welfare provides grants to the states to improve services for vocational rehabilitation of the mentally retarded. Many private organisations avail themselves of this opportunity. Still they are all inadequate to meet the needs of the society.

Parent Counselling: In our society, the parents of mentally retarded children face some special problems. They bother about their children's physical and emotional problems. Also social adjustments of these children place heavy demands in the society. As the children grow older, problems regarding physical health, schooling and placement crop up. Keeping all these problems in the forefront, psychologists suggest parent counselling services. Home training services with community-sponsored educational training programmes must be provided to the mentally retarded children who live at home.

Education of the Mentally Retarded

It is true that the mentally retarded child fails to make progress at school. But it is difficult to know why they fail to do so. Researchers put all mentally retarded children in four groups-(i) the slow learner, (ii) the educable mentally retarded, (iii) the trainable mentally retarded, and

(iv) totally dependent mentally retarded. Very often, the slow learner and the educable mentally retarded remain undetected in the classroom. Here we will discuss only the provisions for educable mentally retarded and trainable mentally retarded.

Provision for the Educable

We have evidential proof that educable mentally retarded children tend to fail in an ordinary school. However they are capable of making progress in normal schools. So the schools must provide such curriculum and methodology of teaching that will enable them to overcome their difficulties easily. The teacher must give priority in helping the mentally retarded child to become self-sufficient and an accepted adult member of the community in which he lives. The special methods which are generally adopted in teaching the educable mentally retarded are as follows:

Individualisation: While we consider the special methods for educating the educable mentally retarded, obviously the dominant theme which comes to mind is the "individualisation of education." This term does not mean that the children receive individual instructions with small classes, but it implies that each child is allowed to proceed at his own pace of learning according to his own unique growth pattern. Of course, these children need opportunities for group participation, so that correct social attitudes may be developed.

Learning by Doing: For educating the educable mentally retarded children, the implication of the "principle of learning by doing" cannot be ignored. Here the basic principle of special education is that the children should learn by doing. Top priority is given to activity methods which lay emphasis on learning through experience. Generally the defect of the mentally handicapped child lies in the area of relational and abstract thought. So he faces difficulties in learning where the method of communication is largely verbal. These children learn better through such materials which appeal most to their senses.

Need for Learning Readiness: The concepts of maturation and willingness to learn should be given due importance while introducing academic work to the mentally handicapped. These children have the ability to learn to read, but they should be prepared through appropriate readiness programmes. It is advisable to wait until the child is intellectually and, psychologically ready to accept the challenge.

Graded Curriculums: It is true that these children learn more slowly than average children. So the necessity of careful gradation of these subjects becomes a must. Here the teachers face difficulties for gradation of students and for preparing the study materials for slow learners. No doubt it is a tough task for teachers, still, not impossible to accomplish.

Repetition: Mentally handicapped children have a poor memory. For them, teaching method must provide for a considerable amount of repetition if learned material is to be retained. However, there is no justification for rote learning. The children should understand the materials clearly before facing any retention test. The memory span of these children can be increased by making them interested and motivated. Research has shown that the memory span of these children increases, if the learning materials have meaningful associations.

Periods of Short Duration: Mentally retarded children have limited power of concentration. For this reason, formal teaching periods should be kept fairly short. It is of importance to note as to how long a child can concentrate when the subject is stimulating.

Concrete Problems: It is true that mentally retarded children show lack of imagination and foresight. As a result, they have difficulty in transferring the learning experience of one situation to a similar but new one. For them, real life problems should be introduced whenever possible so that immediate application of learning can take place.

Projects: "Introduction of Projects" or "Centres of Interest" is a significant approach for teaching mentally retarded children. Research is on to know how this can be done without serious disruption of the basic subject programme. The teachers should not introduce the topics around which centres of interest grow and develop. But it should arise naturally out of classroom situations where the manifestation of further information is clear. Here the point of origin may be a short story, a poem, a song, a film or a picture in a magazine or newspaper. Undue importance should not be given to the source, but the teacher must know how to present it through careful planning and guidance.

Trainable Children

The trainable mentally retarded children have I.Q. in the range of 25-55. These children are much more retarded than educable mentally retarded children. So their educational structure and curriculum are different. These children are mainly taught to take cáre of themselves and to do simple occupational jobs. Though physical anomalies like seizures, lack of control over elimination etc., are very much prominent, regular schooling is difficult for these children. The primary objectives of TMR education are to teach these much more retarded children how to do their daily work without the help of anybody. These daily works include washing, dressing themselves, eating properly, doing simple jobs and toilet training etc. Recent reports reveal that in many cases, TMR education has proved a failure because they learn nothing more than what they would have learnt at home (Dunn, 1973).

Here, less emphasis is given to the teaching of academic subjects and more time is devoted to the development of sensori motor, self-care and daily living skills. A more definite timetable is necessary with short periods of activity. However, with the above objectives in mind, the curriculum should cover the following:

Self-care: The curriculum should include a programme of simple habit training. This enables the children to develop skills of self-help in respect of their daily practical needs. Methods which are adopted for this purpose should relate to the real life experiences and everyday needs of the children.

Social Training: Priority should be given to group activities such as games, simple dramatic work and story-tellings etc. By this, the gregariousness and affiliation may be increased. The children become generally active and cooperative. .

Sesory Training: Special emphasis must be laid on instructions by which the children will be able to make the fullest use of their senses.

Language Development: They must be provided with some aids through which they can have better speech development and proper understanding of verbal concepts.

Craft Work and Music: For developing the feeling of self-confidence in TMR children, the curriculum should include simple crafts training programmes like weaving, rug making, basketing etc. By having this, economic self-sufficiency can be reached.

Research reports say that music is sometimes found as a means of releasing energy and provides a form of expression which the mentally retarded children enjoy. So this should find a place in the curriculum.

Besides all these above factors, emphasis is put on the group work. However individual study of each child is necessary for chalking out individual programmes related to different aspects of personality growth.

Individual-centred programmes are now being conducted at the Institute of Defectology in Moscow, USSR to educate the mentally retardates. Primarily the child is diagnosed as retarded by the age of six months. The time span from that age till the onset of puberty is very important for these children. During this span, individual programmes, from the multidisciplinary points of view, are prepared and implemented. It is observed that with the onset of puberty, the retardation is overcome It is true that this programme is quite difficult and time consuming. It is also costly to manage individual based programmes. In a developing country like India, it is quite unthinkable, however, attempts should be made on an experimental basis to view the outcome.

Some psychologists have opined recently for normalisation of education for retarded children. Of course, their argument is in support of EMR children. According to them, special education for mildly retarded children may only develop a complex in them insofar as they are inferior to and different from others. They argue that mildly retarded children should be taught in regular classrooms instead of placing them in separate groups. The most prominent supporter of normalisation of education of EMR children, is Dunn who says that the past and present practices of special education are morally and educationally wrong.

Further researches of Robinson and Robinson (1976) also supported normalisation of education of mentally retarded. They are of the opinion that a special classroom is an isolating experience. They are also of the view that EMR children are better able to succeed socially and academically if they are exposed to models other than their own. Meticulous observation confirmed that retarded children placed in regular classrooms may be less disturbed than those forced to remain in special classes. One of the reasons is that it is reality-oriented. Mentally retarded children help other children to understand and accept them. As a result, the retarded child gets better scope for emotional security and adjustment. However, recently modern education for the EMR child involves a combination of special and regular classes.

Some Suggestions for Parents

Very often parents fail to understand their children, and prefer to keep the mentally retarded children at home. But they have to develop a right and positive attitude for bringing them up. If parents suspect that a particular child is mentally retarded, they should get him medically checked up first. If possible, they should take the child to the guidance or psychological centre to ascertain the degree of mental retardation. After confirmation, they must face the problem courageously and with determination. They should not blame anybody or curse their fate for their child. The parents should know that the child needs basic security and he can have it through love and affection. Sometimes certain neighbours are so unsympathetic that they become responsible for increasing the stress on the family. But they should be a little cautious in dealing with such type of children. In some developed countries, baby sitters are prepared to deal with all possible dispositions of the mentally retarded children and they relieve the parents to go out together occasionally. But for a developing country like India, it is only a dream. The family members of mentally retarded child must see that their child is not bullied or teased by other children.

QUESTIONS

1. What is Mental Retardation? Discuss causes thereof.
2. Discuss the provisions for educable mentally handicapped children.
3. Enumerate important causes of mental retardation. How can the mentally retarded be classified?
4. Point out the processes to develop curriculum for the trainable mentally handicapped.
5. What is mental retardation? Discuss its clinical types.
6. Discuss the general characteristics of mentally retarded children.
7. Point out the adjustment problems of mentally retarded children.

13

Juvenile Delinquency

Who is a juvenile delinquent? The answer is too controversial. No systematic effort seems to have been made in this country to evolve a precise concept of juvenile delinquency. For finding out a legal definition, emphasis is laid on the criminal and not on the crime. A juvenile delinquent is a child or a young person who is under the age specified by law for the time being in force at the place concerned. The legal definition of juvenile deliquency varies from country to country and state to state. In many European countries, a minor is legally considered a delinquent only if his breach of Penal Code is an offence for the whole population. On the other hand, in the USA, the charges on which a minor appears before a court cover a wide range of behaviour. such as truancy from school, consistent disobedience of parents. consumption of alcohol, smoking in public, etc. On the whole, juvenile delinquency is a legal term which denotes acts of varying degrees of social consequences from mere naughtiness to major assault punishable by law.

A child is said to be a juvenile delinquent when he starts stealing, assaulting, indulging in sex offences and develops symptoms like pathological lying and truancy. These offences are said to be criminal actions when committed by a person beyond the age handled by juvenile courts. Cyril Burt, in his book revealed, “A child is said to be regarded technically as a delinquent, when his anti-social tendencies appear so grave that he becomes or ought to become the subject of official action.”

In India, the meaning of the term is something different. Here the legal tendency is to consider young offenders ranging from the age of seven to twenty-one years as juveniles and the Indian Penal Code uses the expression, "Juvenile Offence" rather than the term "Delinquency". According to Reformatory School Act, first passed in India in 1876 and later codified in 1897, a "youthful offender" means any boy who has been convicted of any offence punishable with transportation or imprisonment and who, at the time of such conviction, was under the age of fifteen years. The Act provides for the establishment and maintenance of Reformatory Schools which impart industrial training to such youthful offenders. In some states of our country, special courts known as "juvenile courts", have been established to deal with youthful offenders. Very often, delinquency has something to do with misbehaviour. But these are two different terms, not synonymous. All misbehaviours are not delinquent. Both the quality of the behaviour and the degree of social deviation are factors in judging an act to be delinquent, trivial or psychopathological.

We have discussed the legal definition of "juvenile delinquency" till now. Coming to the viewpoints of psychologists, we can better say that delinquency is not a unique form of behaviour as laymen think. No sharp differentiation can be made between delinquents and non-delinquents. Suppose a 11-year-old boy steals some food from a shop because he is hungry. So to avoid starvation, he has committed a mistake. From the legal point of view, he is viewed as a juvenile delinquent, but psychologists cannot take the boy's behaviour as anything but anti-social. Only he can be called a delinquent, if he develops a habit of stealing in all situations and is predisposed to harm the society.

The legal definition does not reveal any picture of the delinquent's personality or the causes of his behaviour. Lawmakers are not concerned so much with delinquency as with delinquents and naturally their definition of delinquency has been mostly incomplete and misleading. Psychologists say that a delinquent is one whose attitude towards society is such that will eventually lead to a violation of the law. According to Bandura and Walters (1959), delinquency is aggression. They have tried to relate delinquency to the frustration of dependency needs which cause aggression. In many studies, psychologists came up with differences between the psychological make-up of the delinquent and non-delinquent. The difference was quantitative rather than qualitative. They consider delinquency to be an unfortunate expression of the personality and emphasise that the various indices of maladjustment shown by the delinquents have one or more personal meanings behind them.

Delinquency may mean to the offender an attempt to:

(i) escape or take flight from a tense, unpleasant situation;
(ii) obtain social recognition;
(iii) provide excitement and thrill;
(iv) take revenge against parents and others;
(v) deny dependence to others;
(vi) seek punishment in order to shake off the sense of conscious to unconscious feeling of guilt.

It seems that the legal definition of delinquency is incomplete. It assumes that the delinquent child is characterised by greater emotional instability than the normal child. The term "emotional instability" may imply the manifestation of a great number of symptoms in the behaviour of an individual. The instability of emotion itself is the result of frustrated or unfulfilled needs of that individual. The dynamic energy for human behaviour comes from basic needs of the individual and these needs are closely connected with emotions.

Taking the above point into consideration, delinquency may be considered as an outlet or as an ego defence for the tension caused by frustration of one or several of the needs present in the individual. Due to their intrinsic nature, the nation's laws cannot be applied to every individual.

Before the age of 14, a boy is not considered capable of having sexual relations according to English law. In one case, the court had to return a verdict other than "not guilty" for a boy little over his teens, who had raped a small girl, thereby causing her death. Considered from the psychologist's point of view, the enforcement of law by the police brings an arbitrary element into the concept of juvenile delinquency. It is realised that a country with efficient police network will have a higher delinquency rate than a country where police network is fallacious. Truly speaking, the social position and influence of parents play major roles to refer a boy to a juvenile court in any country.

The foregoing discussion proves that juveniles do not fall into one simple homogeneous psychiatric or psychological category. The distinction between the delinquents and the non-delinquents is based on factors which have quantitative differences.

No one can deny the relationship that exists between delinquency and psychological or psychiatric factors. Some individuals in a group follow the rules and taboos while others do not. The latter do not form a psychologically homogeneous group. But psychology can help to explain their behaviour. Although the majority of juvenile delinquents are found among this group, not all of them are delinquents. Again, all delinquents are not maladjusted. Delinquent behaviour can be adaptive, meeting the special circumstances in which a group finds itself, although such behaviour clashes with the generally accepted laws of the society to which the group belongs. This observation is made from a psychiatrical, and thereby to a certain extent from a psychological point of view.

The concept of delinquency is artificial in nature. This nature varies according to the laws in force or the ways in which they are applied. It becomes very difficult to establish statistical comparisons between one country and another or one period and another. Research works reveal that this is a major obstacle to research and is a possible source of serious error.

Different studies during the war report that there was a statistical increase of delinquent behaviour between 1942 and 1945. Still there is doubt whether these figures really prove an actual increase or not. There is every possibility that the statistical increase is chiefly due to the increase of minor offences, of which many seem to have been committed under the influence of temporary adverse social circumstances. Again, those juvenile "pseudo-delinquents" are relatively easily re-educated by normal methods.

From the above discussion, we can easily conclude that the term "delinquency" is a legal term used in courts and not in medical diagnosis. A delinquent can be apprehended only in terms of what the laws of that country recognises as a cognisable offence. Different societies and even different social classes of the same society punish deviant behaviour differently. It is, therefore, futile to find a definition of delinquency that is universal. Delinquency should be recognised as a psycho-biosocial phenomenon.

Nowadays, psychiatry has recognised two types of reactions that are different both in terms of prognosis and management:

Dyssocial Reaction: Under this type of reaction, the children are brought up in a normal or immoral home or social environment. Their behaviour is in conformity with that small community although they are unacceptable to the society at large, for example, the children of gypsies, migrant or criminal tribes. Children's personality development is influenced by distorted values of a special subculture. Here the children are capable of establishing enduring emotional attachments and loyalties.

Psychopathic Reaction: The children in the second category have poor ego development and even poorer development of super ego. They are incapable of forming stable emotional relationships. They have no insight or foresight and they cannot profit from past experiences. They show poor control and seek gratification of immediate desires. Most of them are refractory to all forms of punishment. These children tend to use other human beings as "pawns" or "toys."

The second group of cases have a constitutional or genetic defect. There are some behavioural disturbances of children that are also seen in adult psychopaths like truancy, alcoholism, drug addiction, stealing, burglary and sexual promiscuity. In 1951, the International Union of Child Welfare especially recommended the following categories of offences (by children) for investigation: Stealing from home, persistent telling of lies, wandering from home, cruelty to animals and other children, repeated truancy, setting fire and sexual offences etc. Of these, setting fire and sexual offences are not so commonly reported in India.

There may be very thin line of demarcation between deviance and delinquency because if effective interventions do not occur at appropriate stages, there is every likelihood of a deviant turning into a delinquent. So the value system of any society, as reflected in its legal norms, continues to serve as the basis for identifying juvenile delinquents. Taking this view into consideration, a juvenile delinquent is one who falls within the age group of 7-16 years (18 years in case of girls) and indulges in any act that is prohibited by the Indian Penal

Code or Local or Special Acts relating to arms, gambling, explosives etc.

Extent and Dimensions

Adequate and appropriate social agencies are not available to supply correct data of the deviant activities of juveniles in our country. So we have to depend on the police records. Even at the police level, the earliest attempts to provide a national picture on crime and delinquency, were initiated in 1953. Therefore a national picture for the earlier period is not easily available. Modes and methods of adult criminality provide a reference for juvenile delinquency. The incidence of delinquency has been rated variously from 3 to 7 per cent of the childhood population. The boys outnumber girls on one Swiss study by 5:1 and according to some Indian clinicians by 2:1. The important source from which the statistics on crime and juvenile delinquency can be taken is Crime in India (Government of India, 1980). A meticulous examination of the figures reveals that except in 1973, in the case of girls and in 1976 in the case of boys, the involvement of juveniles in delinquency acts has been progressively increasing.

Socio-economic Background

Juvenile delinquency is not unique to a particular class, caste or socio—economic group, but official data reveals that the phenomenon is more pronounced in the lower socio-economic groups. The monthly income of the parents of delinquents is below Rs. 1,000.

Near about 70 per cent juveniles are educated up to the primary level; 20 per cent of delinquents reach the middle standard and 3 per cent are educated beyond matriculation. The higher rate of juvenile delinquency in the lower socio-economic groups could be because no effective intervention could be worked out by parents or others to keep these juveniles away from norm-violating consequences.

It is wise to evaluate a juvenile in the context of the socio-cultural milieu to which he/she belongs, rather than to judge him/her against the cultural norms of the larger society. There is every probability that the cultural milieu of some juveniles itself may be below the general cultural norms of society and a minor act of juvenile deviance may not be noticed by the members of that group. On the contrary, when this child is evaluated against conventional cultural norms of a society, he/she is identified as a deviant or delinquent.

The Causes: Delinquency is a phenomenon of multiple causation. It is the result of various factors interacting with each other. It is the end product of multiple causation. "Some are hereditary and others are environmental or psychological." Research evidences reveal that two factors are responsible for the causes of the juvenile delinquent: (a) Primary Factors, and (b) Secondary Factors. Again primary factors can be categorised under two heads, i.e., Biological and Psychological. The family, school and society come under secondary factors.

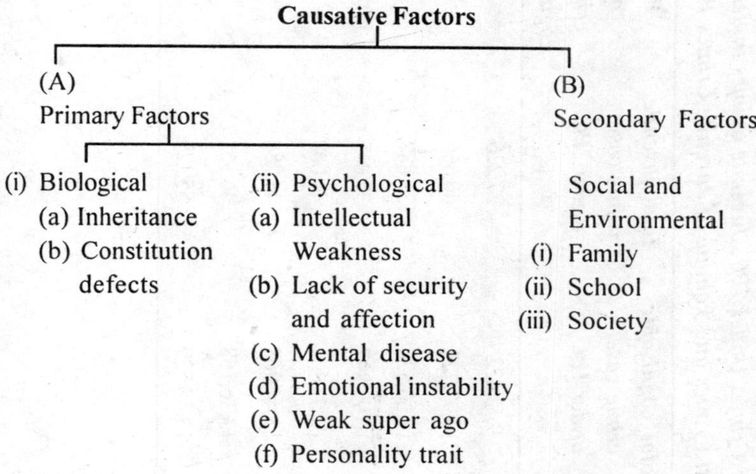

Primary Factors

Biological: The inheritance and constitutional defects constitute the biological factors of delinquency. Biological factors are otherwise known as somatic and constitutional. Biological factors are few and have evoked heated controversies. Identical twins rather than non-identical twins have shown a higher incidence of delinquency-thus lending further support to the genetic basis of delinquency (Kanz, Rosanoff & Handy). Dugdale confirmed that heredity does play some part in bringing about certain tendencies of delinquency.

Total Cognisable Crimes Under IPC, Juvenile Crimes under IPC, Proportion of Juvenile Crimes to Total Crimes and Volume of Juvenile Crimes Per One Lakh of Population

Year	*Population in millions (Estimated mid-year)*	*Total cognisable crime case under IPC*	*Total juvenile crime cases under IPC*	*Percentage of juvenile crimes to total cognisable crimes*	*Volume of juvenile crimes per lakh of population*
1970	534.3	9,55,422	27,226	2.8	5.1
1974	588.3	11,92,277	40,666	3.4	6.9
1975	600.8	11,60,520	39,888	3.4	6.6
1976	613.3	10,93,897	37,015	3.4	6.0
1977	625.8	12,67,004	44,008	3.5	7.0
1978	638.4	13,44,968	44,284	3.3	6.9
1979	651.0	13,36,168	46,351	3.5	7.1
1980	663.6	13,68,529	55,129	4.0	8.3

Juveniles Apprehended (By Sex)

	Figures in Thousands	
Year	***Girls***	***Boys***
1971	5.4	97.9
1972	7.2	120.9
1973	5.6	122.2
1974	8.5	132.1
1975	9.3	132.6
1976	9.4	124.6
1977	10.4	138.5
1978	9.7	151.2
1979	9.7	160.3
1980	9.5	178.1

Juveniles Apprehended (By Age Group)
(1971-1980)

	Figures in Thousands		
Year	***7-12 years***	***12-16 years***	***16-21 years***
1971	5.5	12.7	85.1
1972	10.5	17.1	100.6
1973	10.0	16.5	101.3
1974	8.9	19.6	112.1
1975	14.8	23.1	104.0
1976	19.7	24.1	90.2
1977	11.95	18.9	112.4
1978	10.53	18.3	112.4
1979	10.53	18.3	140.1
1980	10.45	20.0	157.1

Juveniles Dealt with During 1970-1980 (in per cent)

Total number of Juveniles	*1970*	*1971*	*1972*	*1973*	*1974*	*1975*	*1976*	*1978*	*1979*	*1980*
	90249	*83548*	*97921*	*114783*	*114839*	*123019*	*120910*	*135303*	*143802*	*125093*
Sent to Courts	100%	100%	100%	100%	100%	100%				
Restored to guardians	110.8	5:8	4.9	6.9	5.2	10.9	12.2	6.9	5.5	4.5
On probation	3.4	2.2	2.5	1.9	1.9	2.4	2.3	3.3	2.4	5.0
To reformatories and borstal To Schools	1.2	1.1	0.8	0.9	0.8	0.9	1.0	1.9	0.5	6.0
To Schools and institutions	1.5	2.2	1.2	2.4	1.1	1.4	2.5	1.2	1.0	0.4
Pending disposal	30.3	30.5	26.5	40.9	40.7	38.0	27.9	44.7	47.6	48.0
Otherwise disposed of	41.8	36.9	45.1	31.6	36.1	32.1	27.9	25.6	23.7	27.2
To adult institutions	10.0	1.4	0.8	1.5	0.3	0.6	1.0	1.0	0.8	0.7
Imprisoned	-	19.9	18.2	13.9	13.9	13.7	25.8	15.4	18.5	13.1

Constitutional defects like inborn mental deficiency, endocrine imbalances, deafness, blindness, organic psychoses and brain injuries are some important causes of delinquency. The physical deformities may give rise to inferiority complex which ultimately leads to aggressive behaviour. This aggression becomes an ego defence against the dependent and insecure tendencies. Studies report that premature puberty and early arousal of sexual impulses lead to sex offences in the adolescence period.

Psychological: The psychological causes of delinquency mainly centre around the development of ego and super ego. In a delinquent, the early parent-child relationship is defective. Again, the ego or the self is very weak in a delinquent. It is mostly guided by momentary pleasure. The weakness of ego is enhanced due to lack of sublimation in intellectual or social activities. The super ego being weak gives no support to ego. It is obvious that if a delinquent finds no checking force outside and inside, he is naturally driven to committing the offence. Of course when the super ego is strong, it does not approve the free and direct gratification. When the super ego becomes weak, the "id" gets a fair chance to be manifested. When the super ego becomes weak to check the upsurge of suppressed and repressed impulses, the id gets the opportunities for overt expression in a concealed and distorted form of neurotic symptoms. Very tactfully, the theory reveals that the weakness of the "ego" is accentuated by the weakness of the super ego. When the delinquent finds no check from outside and within himself (i.e., weak ego), he is compelled to commit delinquent acts.

Intellectual Weakness: Children with low intelligence are found to be delinquents. These children mostly lack understanding, foresight, judgement and the ability to see cause-and-effect relationship. Researchers like Garing and Goddard established the fact that the sole cause of delinquency is low intelligence. But Merrill had objected vehemently and concluded that low level of intelligence cannot be taken to be the cause of crime. In most of the studies, scholars reported that the delinquents have been found to fall within the range of average or just below average intelligence.

Lack of Security: Lack of security and affection of parents are considered as important causes of delinquency. Gregory reported that the highest rates of delinquency were observed in boys who were living only with their mother. Often gross neglect in child rearing is seen with the result that the child is unable to reconcile the conflicting demands of "reality principle" and "pleasure principle".

Sidney Copel points out that very often the personality of the delinquent's mother is found to be very unstable and her marked changes in moods and mercurial outbursts of temper do not permit the growing child to experience feelings of object constancy. Karpman revealed that the relationship with the mother is often tenuous and inconsistent, so the child's energies tend to be deflected back upon himself and he also becomes predisposed to a narcissistic fixation.

It is seen that some delinquent acts are nothing but reflection of deep-seated psychoneurotic tendencies. These are an inferiority complex (generated by physical or social handicaps) or sadism or masochism (provoked by tyrannical, alcoholic or psychopathic parents).

Emotional Instability: Emotional instability is a potent cause of delinquency. In his research findings, Burt has pointed out that the main causative factor responsible for a child's delinquency is innate emotional instability and disturbance. Control of intelligence in case of delinquents is practically impossible due to emotional instability. In an extensive research project, Bronner and Healy have confirmed that about 93 per cent of delinquents exhibited symptoms of emotional instability and imbalance.

Mental Diseases: In their studies criminologists have shown that there is a definite relationship between the mental diseases and crime. Some psychiatrists have emphasised that psychopathic children are produced in families where there is complete absence of affection, love and control. Psychopathic children are very unsociable, irritable, quarrelsome, obstinate and self-centred.

Some delinquents are found to develop compulsive behaviour seeking relief through magic and ritual like fire-setting, wanton destruction etc. Early cases of childhood schizophrenia may so blunt the emotional responsiveness that super ego development may remain stunted and delinquent behaviour may follow.

Personality Trait: Personality characteristics like irresponsibility, homicidal tendency, revolt, lack of control, suspicion, sadism, extrovert behaviour, emotional and social maladjustment etc., in juvenile delinquents are higher than normal children. In many comparative studies, particularly immaturity in sentiment and lack of emotional balance among delinquents were found to be about eight times more than in normal children. Delinquent children are found to be interested in dangerous nature of works when compared with normal children.

Secondary Factors

Family: A distorted family is a potent factor for juvenile delinquency. A large number of studies conducted so far, revealed that about 50 per cent of juvenile delinquents belonged to broken families. A broken family is that in which the existing family ties have been destroyed and there is no mutual intimate relationship between the members of the family.

In these type of families, children are not looked after properly and brought up carefully. There is no healthy relationship between husband and wife, parent and children and brothers and sisters. Very often, the home seems to be very much dominated by parents with their strict discipline. This leads to emotional insecurity which give birth to the feeling of inadequacy and inferiority. Lack of affection of parents may lead to theft and incorrigible behaviour in children. In such circumstance, children can easily become delinquents.

Again in some homes, it is found that the children are left in the hands of servants because both parents are working. In such cases, parents develop a guilty feeling and become lenient to their wards. Children get a lot of pocket money and this leniency paves the way indirectly towards a sort of negligence of what the child is doing. School performance of these children is very poor and they become habitual truants. There are some parents who quarrel in the house in front of their children. This has a sort of fearful effect on the tender mind of the child. Gradually such children become timid, rebellious and arrogant. Slowly this paves the way for delinquency.

Sometimes it may so happen that in the family, if the father is strict, the mother protects the child. If the mother wants to bring the child to task, the father interferes and favours the child. In such families, the child becomes very shrewd and knows how to bully whom and when. If both the parents are strict, grandparents pamper them.

In some vicious homes, the relationship is very defective. The husband is unable to make any adjustment towards his wife or one of the parents may be completely ineffectual. The child gets emotional shocks in these circumstances.

Nowadays, parents' divorce has a tremendous impact on children. Here the child is compelled to stay with one of the parents. Truly the child is deprived of parental love. It may so happen that both the parents take the child into their confidence. In such cases, the child becomes aware of many facts at the infant stage itself. In certain families, much favouritism is seen towards a particular child and rejection towards a particular child. Here in case of rejection, the child develops a feeling that he is unwanted by the parents. The poor child becomes neglected and a prey to some gang and finally becomes a delinquent.

It is seen that poverty leads to all kinds of abnormality. Parents in slum areas leave their children on the road and they are exposed to all types of vices. Due to unemployment and poverty, the mother goes to work to supplement the family income, leaving the child in the hands of fate. The children live in overcrowded rooms. They see many things which they are not expected to see at all in the early age.

It is common sense that when the children are not able to fulfil their desires, they have recourse to immoral and illegal acts. Dr. Haikerwal has rightly pointed out that hunger and starvation lead them to tread the easy and devilish path of crime. Various studies depict that a higher percentage of delinquents come from the lower strata of socio-economic conditions. When the children go to school without taking food, naturally they resort to stealing or other immoral acts. Considering the above facts, it can be concluded that poverty is the potent factor in breeding juvenile delinquency.

There is every possibility that the personalities of children are influenced by their brothers and sisters. For boys, this may be of little importance because they remain outside for a longer period of time; but for girls, it is very important since they remain at home and are not exposed to external influences. If the senior children of the family display criminal tendencies, the younger ones are bound to be influenced by those tendencies.

Children may have recourse to give vent to their pent-up emotions if the home fails to provide recreational activities for them.

School: Uncongenial school environment is also sometimes responsible for delinquency. Lack of healthy recreations and wholesome leisure time activities in the school are the most unfavourable school conditions which only add to the causes of juvenile delinquency. If the school is located amidst a crowded market, near a cinema hall or in an industrial area, then children are generally tempted to engage in acts of delinquency. Sometimes, when the child is disliked or ridiculed by the teacher for his poor achievement, he develops a challenging attitude. It is found that some teachers have their favourites and they give them too much latitude. This type of behaviour of the teacher creates hatred against the teacher and the favourites. The ultimate result is grouping among children.

Defective examination system is also responsible for maladjustment among school children. Examinations have no more motivational effect. On the contrary, they develop a fear complex in most of the students. Just before the day of the examination students try their best to cram the subjects; but in spite of that when they get poor marks in the examination they become desperate and aggressive.

The unfavourable school conditions also include teachers who often indulge in slurring, taunting and passing remarks. The inflexibility of curriculum, paucity of adequate curricular activities and pervasive atmosphere of severe competition deflate the ego-building capacities of children who are scholastically backward and slow learners.

For all the above reasons, a child is not attracted towards the school. He considers the teachers as monsters. They do not want to learn anything. Instead, they go on day-dreaming waiting for last bell of the school.

Society: Rapid industrialisation, a high degree of social and geographical mobility and creation of migratory population in urban slums are some of the sociological determinants of delinquent behaviour. All these lead to a state of normlessness (anomie) and lack of social control. Very often, the boundaries between home and environment become ambiguous by lack of privacy in the under-privileged areas. Special "subcultures" are formed due to the presence of these factors. This offers a forum for compensating "Status deprivation" (Cohen), lack of identity, unjust distribution of wealth etc. Cloward and Ohlin pointed out that "ostentatious" display of wealth and power, and the lack of opportunities must inevitably uncover "illegitimate opportunities" (organised crimes) or seek solace in "retreatist" behaviour (drug, alcohol etc.).

Here, in this atmosphere, the only way to thrive is to grow up as a tough aggressive fellow, alert in sensing "trouble" and in taking "right" chances. The group gives the feeling of security, belongingness and the collective image of a "tough achiever". The stage is all set for deliquency. For the occurrence of the offence, only some coincidences, some lust for adventure and excitement are all that is needed. One thing is obvious here that this sociological viewpoint fails to explain delinquency, found in children of the upper social strata.

Studies also reveal that the presence of a prostitute's house, gambling dens, dance etc., may further contribute to sex delinquency and anti-social acts. Conflicts between classes, company of other delinquents and the maladjusted children also result in delinquency.

In India, in quite a number of studies, various factors are presumed to be directly associated with the causal process of delinquent behaviour. The more common factors studied in relation to delinquency are religious and caste background of the subjects, marital status of the subjects, economic, educational and occupational status of the subjects, parental plans regarding schooling and their expectations from subjects, recreational modes of the subjects, physical structure of homes and marital facilities at home; type of family joint or single-number of members in the family, number of siblings, nature of family intact or broken, position of the subject in the family vis-a-vis other siblings, subjects' relation on vertical and horizontal planes, predilection of the subject towards a particular member of the family, behavioural modes of parents and the subjects, modes of discipline at home, reactions of the subjects towards parents, religiosity in the family and faith of subject in religion, social mobility-vertical or horizontal of the family of the subjects, immorality at home, the presence of undesirable persons in the home, mother's employment, etc.

Some scholars also lay emphasis on the association at the level of the neighbourhood and peer group. The influences operating during the stage of schooling that promote discipline/truancy/running away/ vagrancy have been investigated by a few scholars. A few investigators studied the influence of other community institutions to which a child is exposed during the period of growth, including the mass-media (Shukla, 82).

Some research scholars have indicated that a single factor does not contribute to delinquency but when factors like the status of a family, type of neighbourhood, poverty, a broken home, lower socio-economic status, lower educational status, relations on horizontal and vertical planes in the family, peer group associations and availability of models for delinquency learning combine and bring a score of nine or more, only then would a juvenile take to delinquency.

An Overview

Some eminent scholars reveal that causative factors are really hypotheses, attempting to account for the deviant behaviour in the individual case. William Healy, in his research on "delinquency", set the pattern for this approach and discovered that, in contrast to their many, general theories of criminal behaviour, delinquency in individual cases is a product of multiple causative factors. He has discovered 3.5 factors per case.

After a long period of time, Cyril Burt has found 9.5 factors per case using essentially similar case history methods of factor determination. But Freudians and Neo-Freudian clinicians challenged the role of multiple causation of delinquency, rather they laid stress on some deep motivations.

Delinquency behaviour is a part of a dynamic process and it can be understood only in relation to the sequence of experience of which it is a part. So when we deal with juvenile delinquency, we must view it in terms of both the conditions of the individual person or the social environment in which he lives.

As we have discussed earlier, environmental factors, within the home and outside the home are primary elements in the etiology of delinquency. But evidence indicated that the delinquents' behaviour is not the product of these factors exclusively. It is associated with community influences also, which are administered by the outside forces of the neighbourhood. For causing an upheaval in the behaviour of the child, community institutions and agencies are of great importance. The nature of these factors and of their varying conditions differ from one child to another.

Youthful Offenders

The attitude relating to youth oscillates between the two extremes of condemnation and commendation. Youthful age often has negative connotations. Owing to popular beliefs and not based on volatile and aggressive reactions of youth in most situations, they are generally considered to spell trouble. Adults show different types of sentiments towards the youth. These are scepticism, doubt, fear, prejudice etc. Accordingly, they evaluate their own children and those of others also.

The achievements of youth in the freedom struggle, natural disasters, sports, education, social work etc., are recalled with fervour. Their participation in NCC, NSS, Scouts and Guides etc., is obvious. Their motives in nation building, social reconstruction, idealism and morality are noteworthy.

In spite of this their inflammable nature, aggressive postures, intolerant responses, restive gestures etc., are looked down upon by the adults. But the concept of crime and youth are diffused. Literature of psychology revealed that the youth suffer from an identity crisis; they suffer from stress and strain. The youth invariably lack coordination between the heart and the mind.

Prevention

Throughout the world, there has been an increasing awakening of public interest in the problems of socially handicapped, exploited and victimised juveniles. Social workers, psychologists and sociologists feel the urgent need to promote the physical, mental, cultural and emotional growth of juvenile delinquents. The modern psychological investigation points to the fact that a child needs love, security and opportunity for self-expression. Deprivation of any of these may prevent or divert the flow of life-energy and cause mental illness. A delinquent is an ordinary boy or girl who is a product of his environment.

In a broad sense, juvenile delinquency has reference to anti-social acts of children and young people under a particular age. Every day, statistics reveal the increasing number of delinquents from different states and areas. The existing educational, industrial and social systems demand attention at the very root of the problem. Mere suppression of force by law would not obliterate it. The circumstances which lead to a delinquent act must be studied thoroughly. Psychologists today, more or less, agreed that delinquency is nothing but an outstanding sample of the common childish naughtiness. According to Cyril Burt, "Crime may be rare, but naughtiness is universal and the problem of character training should be the concern of all."

A general concept of juvenile delinquency ignores completely the dynamic aspect of its motivation and the recognition that certain kinds of delinquent behaviour are simply modes of self-expression. Meticulous investigation, in this regard, emphasises the sociological aspect of the problems of delinquency and ascribes the cause of poverty, lack of parental control, broken homes and undesirable associations to be primarily and directly responsible. But emphasis has not been placed on the complexity of the inner environment with its conflicts and other inner psychological forces within the inadequately formed personality. Delinquency is acquired. It is the result of the interaction of all the forces of the personality, including the feeling-tone and the realm of thought.

Treatment

By psychotherapy, the treatment of delinquents can be possible. The therapists first try to know the various psychological and root causes of delinquency. Then they apply various psychological methods and techniques for removing them. Here the child actively takes part in analysing his behaviour. The psychotherapist may adopt the following methods for treatment:

Re-education: The scientific approach which is very much conducive for treating juveniles is re-education. This technique reforms the offender, re-educates him and rehabilitates him. The objectives also include the change of behaviour and attitude of the offender. By that he will look upon the world as a fully potential friend. Social adaptatbility under better conditions is possible through this technique.

Mental Catharsis: Catharsis means the avoidance of undue repression. It provides opportunity to the child to express his pent up and suppressed emotional feelings by means of free expression. Page has rightly pointed out that catharsis consists simply in eliminating troubles, worries and conflicts. Here the therapist has to hear the delinquent's outpouring patiently and without imposing any comments of his own. Through this method, the delinquent is encouraged to realise the cause of his own problems. Play therapy, finger painting and psycho-drama are some of the important techniques which are used by the therapists to treat juveniles.

Persuasion: Through this procedure, the patient's symptoms, actions and reactions are analysed, many logical and common sense facts are suggested and the delinquent is encouraged to make efforts to improve and get well. The therapist may persuade the delinquent not to get involved in delinquency in future. But this persuasion should be logical and appealing.

One major drawback of this procedure is that it is limited to the conscious level, whereas the delinquents whose problems lie in the unconscious, cannot benefit from this technique.

Suggestion: Suggestion is nothing but the implantation of an idea and it is a successful appeal to the subliminal self. It is true that children are more suggestive than adults. Positive suggestions may strengthen the super-ego of juveniles. Basically this technique implies the influence of one person upon the other and it is a process of communication from one personality to another. It is one of the oldest techniques of mental treatment and is used to supplement other methods off cure.

Change in Environment: Different studies on delinquency reveal that changes in human and material environment of the delinquent can help in removing many of the symptoms of the delinquency in him. Nobody is a born delinquent. Rather delinquents are the products of environmental influences. Psychotherapists suggest that the delinquents may be shifted to better environments like foster-homes.

Various Factors

Research analysers indicate that delinquency is acquired and it is the product of various socio-economic and environmental factors. Truly speaking, treatment of delinquency is a very limited concept. If prevention is to be effective, there must be early detection of maladjustment in children. Remedies must be found for any cause present in the family or society, and which leads to delinquency must be eliminated. The following are some important preventive measures for delinquency acts:

Family System and Well-adjusted Homes: Rapid urbanisation and scientific advancement have resulted in weakening the family affecting the vitally important husband-wife and parent-child relationships. The consequential social change has an adverse effect on unified life in a family. In our tradition-loving society, the family is the sole agency for handing down the cultural heritage. The behaviour of the individual is regulated by social control groups to which he belongs. In big cities, people keep oneself to oneself. They have no group security. Though physical health is good, many people have anxiety states, often with hysterical features and reactive depression, attributed to boredom, social isolation and a false set of values.

No doubt, the adult world is governed by human emotions such as breaking down the homes and the intricate network of human relationships which result in clashes and alliances among individuals, groups and nations. Research works reveal that for a large proportion of persons suffering from such disorders the maladjustment is traceable to childhood and that juvenile delinquency and adult crime are intimately related. Therefore more attention should be paid to the emotional life of a child.

Another powerful operative factor is the break-up of the joint-family system. Since the older traditions are on their way out, new traditions are fast replacing the old ones. They invite a change in family life. Simultaneously, the old values of character and personality need to be revived by constant efforts in order to bring harmony between the old and the new. One potent factor affecting harmony in family life is the understanding between man and woman.

In man-woman relationship, three factors such as ascendancy, submission and equality have operated from time to time. The idea that man and woman are complementary to each other has also not been accepted in toto. In our male dominated society, the female is considered less intelligent but more emotional. A harmonious family life remains to be a dream, if man-woman relationship is not reconstituted or better understanding is not fostered.

If we consider these facts minutely, the causes of delinquency become more complex and variable. Still a well-adjusted home provides a solid band of affection between the parents and their children.

Improvement of family life is considered to be an important preventive measure. Young parents should be educated for adequate motherhood and fatherhood. They must know how to deal with their children. Working women should find time to remain with their children as long as they can within the course of the day.

Parents should not quarrel in front of their children and they must observe the norms of good conduct. They should be impartial and just to all the children. Besides that the parent must be aware of the interests of their children. The children should be made to realise that the parents are always there to help them whenever they face any problem.

Again, parents must remember that children acquire disobedience, obstinacy, quarrelsome behaviours as they grow up. These are not inborn qualities. Children's nature, interest, habits etc., are dependent on the treatment which they receive from their parents. Thus, it is necessary to see and observe these habits and their reasons. Besides that, parents should have complete knowledge about the upbringing of their children. They may receive some training from child guidance centres. The pocket money of the child should not be always given. He may develop some bad habits, if he gets it frequently. A strict vigil should be kept on the friends of the child. It is very important to note what type of friends the child has. The parents should call the friends of their child to their homes and should try to get information about their habits, interests etc.

Another important fact is that the attitude of the parents towards the sex element of children should be psychological and proper. The immoral and unwanted behaviour of other members of the family should be stopped at the earliest. Parents must isolate these family members who exercise bad influence on the children.

Adequate Schooling: Adequate schooling can contribute a great deal towards the prevention and control of delinquency by playing a more responsible role. Personality development of children is largely influenced by the schooling. That is why, in many affluent societies, attempts are being made to make the school an extensive of home with the same atmosphere of informality and freedom.

First, the school needs trained teachers with high moral character. They must be prepared to solve the problems of the students psychologically. In the school, education must be imparted according to the child's interests and abilities. Besides this, the school must have library and recreational facilities. Children must be encouraged to read. They are to be motivated by the teachers. Further, a coordination between homes and schools should be maintained. Teachers and parents should inform each other about the problems of the child.

Recreational Activities: Research reports show that the recreational activities play an important role in preventing delinquency. In rural areas, the lack of healthy recreation and of a community centre may induce youths to make their gathering place with gambles, prostitutes and other dubious acquaintances. Poor children living in slums do not have facilities for any healthy recreation. In most cases, it is necessary to take the child away from its unhealthy surroundings. It is wise to institute active guidance, allowing the child to establish new emotional bonds with healthy people. Improper use of leisure time is another sole cause of delinquency in children. Properly organised and supervised play and recreation can not only prevent delinquency among children but also improve their physical and mental health. Organised recreation has therapeutic values. The provision of adequate broad-based recreation services may make a substantial measurable contribution to the diminution of the problem of juvenile delinquency.

Role of State and Social Agencies: The state and the social agencies can play important roles in preventing delinquency. First, the state and agencies must establish good schools where the children can receive proper education. Poor parents and impoverished families should be taken care of by the state. The censor board must work strictly on films and motion pictures. The movies having open sexual acts and violence must be strictly censored. Orphan children and illegitimate children should be facilitated with homely environment. They should not feel that they are unwanted in this world.

Role of Police: In our state, the duty of the police is to control violation of the law and to enforce regulations. So the activity of the police is both preventive and protective. The juvenile poses special problems for the police because of the generally held view that the anti-social acts of children should be treated as behaviour problems rather than as crimes.

Truly speaking, the control of delinquency is a precautionary measure. In controlling delinquency, the police department has a pivotal role to play as a law-enforcement agency. In some metropolitan cities, statistics reveal that the police have been of considerable help to juveniles in distress and difficulty. It is not the number but the quality of the police which is essential for the control of delinquency. All agencies working for the prevention of delinquency should work in liaison with the police which is necessary for the control of delinquency.

As statistics reveal, the incidence of juvenile delinquency in some metropolitan cities is high. So the routine duty commitments of normal police were so heavy that they were not able to play this role effectively without the creation of specialised units; at least for the high delinquency areas. Such specialised units should consist of carefully chosen and specially trained personnel including women police. At the state headquarters, there may be a central agency which can be called the Juvenile Aid Bureau to direct and see the functioning of the various units at the district level. This unit may collect the data for evaluation and research activities. This Juvenile Aid Bureau may provide direct help and services to individual children.

Creation of Social Responsibilities in Children: For impoverished families, it is almost impossible for the parents to take care of the health of their children, because of their low income. Many children are thus exposed to the hazards of dangerous disease. But there are certain other factors which are as important as health. The young and tender minds of the children should be protected from the unhealthy atmosphere as they are more prone to bad company than good.

Very often the teachers as well as parents pay no heed to their children being exposed to unhealthy atmosphere. Consequently they become uncontrollable even before they reach the age of twenty.

Parents must understand that these qualities instil morality and spiritual strength which help them to lead a purposeful life and share greater responsibility which strengthens their will power to fight against all odds when they face the stress and strain of life. These qualities make them conscious of the social circumstances and their responsibilities towards its betterment. Indirectly it prevents them from remaining idle or becoming destructive elements in society. So parents and teachers must plan in a dynamic way to inculcate these qualities in children. Cooperation among the teachers, parents and social organisations and between teachers and parents as well as coordinated work among individuals are the essentials for the success of the programme.

While making programmes the following points should be taken into consideration:

(i) Children must be taught the essentials of social life, the role they have to play in their struggle for existence, and the responsibility they have to shoulder in the future.

(ii) They must be kept aloof from the social prejudices, superstitions, unnecessary quarrels, misunderstandings, political pollutions and other evil factors which will weaken their philosophical, psychological and mental make-up.

(iii) Children must be taught to show an adaptive and receptive mentality to modern science and technology.

(iv) Good children should not be mixed with the bad until the bad are set right and then only should they be allowed to mix with the good ones.

(v) Television serials, films and motion pictures stressing the above qualities and other social facts of life should be produced by social organisations, educational institutions and the Government and other private film producers. This type of film or serials should be screened in all educational institutions from time to time.

While taking precautions the parents should keep in mind that they have to conform to the small family norm. If they have only two children, they can look after them and make something of them in life and if they have more than two, then the task may be more tedious to make every one of them useful citizens. The more children parents produce, the more social and economic problems they have to face and consequently peace and happiness in life will be a far off dream for them.

According to the studies done by Desai (1972, 74) the socio-economic status has an important bearing on fertility. The experimenter collected data on family structure, education and fertility preferences of 136 mothers in the Ellis Bridge area of Ahmedabad city. Proportionate and consistent differences were found in fertility behaviour of high status and low status women.

Juvenile Court

The Juvenile court was first instituted by the Bombay Act of 1924. Generally it is the court for young criminals. The main idea behind it is that the delinquent is not allowed to mix with other criminals. In this court, hearings are not conducted openly. Even the court is presided over by a juvenile judge.

A juvenile finds himself in the remand home before his trial. Sometimes even after his trial. A remand home is a sort of waiting room for the young criminals. Keeping the juvenile in remand homes serves two purposes:

(i) He is segregated from other criminals and

(ii) He is available for trial, whenever he is wanted.

Before the hearing is held, some probationary officers are appointed to study the young criminals and their environment. They study the situations before the case comes for hearing or after the case has been disposed off. A probationary officer is a counsellor as well as a friend to the young offender who also is placed on probation. Then the young criminal is committed for his hearing of the case in an institution called a certified school. A young criminal has to remain in a certified school till he completes 18 years of age. If he behaves well, he may be let off earlier.

Since the approach to delinquency is mostly penal and administrative, every local authority of the country has to provide "Remand Homes" within its area to receive children waiting for their trial.

QUESTIONS

1. Define "Juvenile Deliquency". Who are the youthful offenders?

2. Suggest some preventive measures for the young delinquents.
3. Who is a juvenile delinquent? Discuss the "extent" and "dimensions" of juvenile delinquency.
4. Critically evaluate different causes of juvenile delinquency.
5. How can you treat a delinquent? Discuss some preventive measures of delinquency.
6. Discuss the role of teachers and parents in educating delinquents.
7. Write short notes on:
   (a) Youthful Offenders
   (b) Juvenile Court
   (c) Remand Home
   (d) Psychotherapy and Treatment of Delinquency.

14

The Socially Disadvantaged

The very term "deprivation" is multi-dimensional and seems to be a variation of "social disadvantage". But it is not necessarily confined to low socio-economic homes. Deprivation may be the cause of low achievement due to inadequate schooling facilities and parental indifference towards child rearing in more sophisticated homes. The ecology of both family and institution contributes a lot to educational deficiencies of the deprived. Priority has been given by psychologists in recent times for an ecological model for a better understanding of the concept of deprivation (Robinson, 1976, Panda, 1977).

Sinha (1976) revealed that deprivation, in ecological terms, consists of two-tier concentric layers – (i) The upper and more visible layer contains home, school, peer group etc., each providing three dimensions: Physical space and materials, Social roles and relationships and activities, and (ii) The supporting or the surrounding layer is provided by geographic and physical environment and the institutional setting of the general services and amenities. Of course, this scheme provides a better conceptualisation of various kinds of deprivation.

Again, cultural deprivation refers to a complex set of conditions which create intellectual deficiency in a child. These conditions include unstimulated environment, lack of verbal interaction with adults, poor sensory experience and other deleterious environmental factors associated with poverty.

However the term "deprived" or "disadvantaged" or "culturally different" was used to indicate who are marked by the following three general characteristics during their school careers:

(1) Progressive decline in intellectual functioning
(2) Cumulative academic achievement deficits
(3) Premature school termination or higher dropout rate.

The Characteristics

Studies on cultural deprivation came from research works on early experience and sensory deprivation in comparative psychology. Towards the last part of the third decade of the twentieth century, Hebb (1949) demonstrated that animals reared in restricted environment have shown deficiency in sensory and perceptual development. In 1961, Hunt extended this implication to humans and placed emphasis on early experience in scholastic attainments. Later studies of Haywood and Tapp (1966) concluded that an enriched early environment increases intelligence and the impoverished environment lowers the intelligence level.

Studies conducted by educationists reveal that high caste and Scheduled Caste students differ significantly in academic achievement. The lower achievement of the disadvantaged children can be attributed to at least five causes—(i) Malnutrition, (ii) Genetic factors, (iii) Lack of stimulating early experience, (iv) Social motivations, and (v) Cultural values. Again the cognitive style or strategy adopted by a group may account for the lower performance of the disadvantaged children (Panda, 1970).

Studies of Jensen (1971) revealed that children from low Socio-Economic Status (SES) use associative learning strategies and evidences are found to suggest that low SES children use sequential processing rather than simultaneous processing (Das, and Singha, 1975). The researchers in this area (Das and Singha, 1975) have suggested a general orientation for explaining performance deficiency in low SES children.

Keeping this nature of learning process aside, the gap between a culturally disadvantaged child and a normal child begins to grow with age and exposure to classroom learning. A wide gap was found between the Blacks and middle class Whites when achievement tests and verbal ability were taken into account. Actually it is not stimulation but the quality of stimulation that is important. The verbal milieu in which the middle class children grow up corresponds much more closely to school learning situation. Middle class children have a superior quality of both verbal and non-verbal stimulation at home. Again the stimulations are very distinct and the reinforcement system is of a delayed kind.

Of course, social and cultural disadvantage is not crystal clear in India. All low income group children are not necessarily at a disadvantage. The children of higher SES have a culture superior to those of the low caste Harijans who are given the same low socio-economic status. The distance between Brahmins and Harijans has widened due to the cumulative effects. There are empirical findings which support the. cultural effects of high caste home.

Das and Singha (1975) tried to answer some of the issues here. They conclude that the rich high caste parents showed significantly greater interest in the child's educational progress. They had knowledge of the child's educational progress, showed higher aspiration for the children and also made preparations for the child's education. But no difference in personality was observed although the authors expected that low caste children would compare better. It was also observed that in word reading speed, rich and orthodox Brahmins were superior to low caste and poor Brahmin children (Panda, Das, 1970).

A marked difference was felt among the students of different socio-economic groups so far as intellectual capacity was concerned. It is true that better economic conditions, education and occupational status of the parents were the most significant contributory factor for the intellectual development of the children. Researchers place emphasis on stimulating environment in early life for intellectual growth of children.

Studies reveal that in progressive matrices and figure copying tests, the low caste children did not lag too far behind the high caste. The cross modal coding revealed the superior performance of rich high caste children over the poor low caste, but the immediate groups were not significantly lower than the poor low caste. In Short Term Memory (STM) experiments, the same results were also obtained. The least disadvantaged children performed best in a majority of cognitive tasks. Again, the disadvantage of belonging to a culturally deprived home is greatly compensated.

Jachuck and Mohanty (1974) have undertaken a research project to study the effect of low SES belongingness on non-verbal reasoning and verbal ability as two forms of basic cognitive skills. Greater difference was noticed between the SES groups at the higher age level than at the lower suggesting the cumulative deficiency hypothesis or progressive retardation over age. Another pertinent fact is that the effects of class and caste remained confounded in this study and these variables are crucial in our context for observing the effects of cultural deprivation.

In 1970, Das, Jachuck and Panda raised some questions relating to cultural deprivation and cognitive growth. Their points were:

(i) Is incompetence largely determined by the subculture to which a child belongs at birth?

(ii) Is it stamped in fortuitously because of his indelible identity with a certain caste and class?

(iii) Does this disadvantage affect the child's cognitive growth adversely?

Here the cultural milieu is the caste to which a child belongs. In this study, the children were drawn from the Municipal Schools of Bhubaneswar. The children of Brahmin caste constituted the high caste, and Harijans represented the low caste group as usual. Rich and poor classifications were done taking the parental income into consideration.

A child was considered to be poor if his parental income was less than Rs. 200 p.m. The children of the professionals were included in the high income group. Children (or subjects) belonging to rich Brahmins, rich Harijans, poor Brahmins and poor Harijans were in the age group of (9-12). They were given Raven's Progressive Matrices (RPM), Stroop test, a test for STM and a recognition test. All the tests were administered individually except RPM.

The scores of RPM were available for rich Brahmin, poor Brahmin, rich Harijan and poor Harijan. The mean scores for these groups were 22.22,19.30,19.38 and 17.22 respectively. This research reveals the hierarchy of rich Brahmins at the top, poor Harijans at the bottom. In reading speed, the Brahmins scored higher than Harijans regardless of economic status. In colour naming speed also, the rich were superior to the poor. But the study did not give any clear picture regarding the capacity of Harijans for recall or inefficient coding in STM task.

Two scores were pertinent for each subject—(i) Correct recognition for unimodal, and (ii) Crossmodal tasks. Harijans committed a large number of errors in writing auditory material.

In another experiment, Das (1973) has tried to bring out the relationship between cultural deprivation and cognitive competence using cross-cultural data. The subjects were Grade-IV children belonging to: (a) High and low SES White children and Canadian Indian children of low SES, (b) High and low SES Black children compared to their White counterpart, and (c) High and low caste (Brahmin-Harijan) all of whom were given the same battery of cognitive tests and personality tests. Assessment of parental aspiration was also taken into consideration while the study was in progress.

When the parental expectancy was considered, the high SES parents had the highest score and the low SES Canadian parents had the lowest score. But low SES White parents had similar aspirations to that of Canadian Indian parents.

Tests on personality assessment reveal that the Canadian Indian parents and children were more introvert than their White counterparts. RPM scores were lowest for Canadian Indian children, the high SES Whites topped the list and the low SES Whites secured the second position. Cross-modal coding scores followed the RPM pattern.

Rath and Das (1972) conducted a series of experiments to determine the extent to which culturally backward children were benefited from classroom learning in comparison with higher caste children. The investigators have taken three groups of children namely Brahmin, Scheduled Caste and Scheduled Tribe. There were 110 students in each sub-cultural group. A series of cognitive and academic achievement tests were administered. These tests included RPM, Auditory vigilance to measure attentional deficiency, Rotter's level of aspiration board, Stroop colour word interference test, verbal concept formation test based on Class-IV language book. Besides all these tests, teacher's ratings, parental expectancy, wastage and stagnation figures, school examination marks were obtained.

Peculiar results were obtained which challenge the ill-effects of cultural disadvantage. The tribal children did not differ from high caste Brahmin children in intelligence. They have also shown higher level of aspiration than Brahmin children. Scheduled Tribe students did not show attentional deficiencies, rather the two other groups were inferior to ST children. In the Stroop tests, the three groups did not differ in word, reading and colour naming. Interference was significant in Brahmin group which was presumably due to language and second signalling system. The Brahmin children were consistently better in concept acquisition and concept comprehension of all the three types of concepts, i.e., scientific, literary and abstract compared to ST/SC children. It was also found that comprehension scores of SC children were superior to those of ST children.

In drawing, ST students were best in comparison with Brahmin students. But Brahmin students were superior to all disadvantaged children in all school subjects. Scheduled Tribe children were relatively better than Scheduled Caste children except in Arithmetic. Regarding parental expectation, the parental education and aspiration levels of the Brahmin group were superior to the two disadvantaged groups. Teachers' rating of pupil achievement and behaviour favoured the Brahmins more than the disadvantaged groups. Truly speaking, the teachers expressed very low expectations from the SC and ST students. One obvious factor of this sort of anomaly might be the frustration of SC children as they remained in close proximity with Brahmin children. No doubt, the findings were quite encouraging. But the variation in economic status has not been taken into account while planning for the study. Further studies by Tripathy and Mishra (1975) provided evidence of the low deprived children doing better than the non-deprived group. They found that on six tests of cognitive functions and mental ability, the low deprived group did better than non-deprived group. Castewise analysis did not show any difference and the SCs and STs did well like other sophisticated children. In 1973, Rath also confirmed that on the basis of intelligence, there was no difference among children born to Brahmins, Scheduled Castes and Scheduled Tribes.

Supported by NCERT, Mehta (1969) conducted a series of experiments on the achievement motivation of tribal and non-tribal high school boys. The results corroborated the above statement. The result was that the tribals are higher-achievers than the non-tribals.

Eysenk (1975) conducted a very interesting experiment on Eskimos. He reported that Eskimos living in most primitive conditions did better than those who lived in closer contact with the Whites. The point at issue is, if environmental effects impair one's cognitive functioning, the Ss should not have done well. The question is—"Is it then an advantage to be brought up in a tribal or impoverished environment?" Or is it a methodological error rather than an understanding process through which social deprivation affects cognitive performance and other behaviours (Panda, 1974)?

Sinha (1973) in a study conducted by him reported that the general performance level of children at schools where children from low SES went, were significantly inferior to schools which admitted children from affluent families. In the test, certain perceptual cues were to be interpreted. It was seen that within the same type of school, Scheduled Caste children were inferior to their non-Scheduled Caste mates on tasks requiring simple perceptual skills. Recognition of vocabulary, vocabulary use, length of remarks and complexity of sentence forms in disadvantaged children are all significantly below norms. Disadvantaged children lack persistence in a school-related task and evince a lower sense of control over the environment than the advantaged children. The achievement discrepancy score is very significant in case of the disadvantaged group. Intellectual achievement responsibility is highly related to academic achievement and children of low SES do not have a sense of personal control. Investigations of Crandall, Katkovsky and Crandall (1965) revealed that Negro children and lower class White children are more externally oriented and their achievement index was too low compared to the advantaged Whites. Further studies by Panda and Lynch (1974) and Das and Panda (1977) obtained similar results.

Studies by Das and Panda (1977) reported that the Brahmin and Harijan children significantly differed in the style of information processing the Brahmin children were more analytic than the Harijan children. They had also more positive self-esteem compared to the Harijans and the difference increased with increasing educational levels.

Another empirical study on "Social Disadvantage, Intelligence and Academic achievement" was done by Prof. Singh. This study highlighted the role of caste, income and tribal background in contributing to cognitive programme.

Prof Singh has taken 600 school students as Ss for his study. The Ss were taken from Ranchi district of Bihar (now in Jharkhand). The subjects were administered Porteus Maze Test to measure intelligence and Language and Arithmetic test to measure Scholastic Achievement. The stratified random sample consisted of five main categories and these are:

(a) Hindu High Income Group (HHI)
(b) Hindu High Caste Low Income Group (HHCLI)
(c) Hindu Low Caste Income (HLCI)
(d) Tribal Hindu Low Income (THLI)
(e) Tribal Christian Low Income (TCLI)

Each sample had 120 Ss which were equally subdivided into rural-urban cases and having equal proportions of age groups and male-female cases. HHI was considered socially advantaged, HHCLI semi-advantaged and HLCI, THLI, TCLI as disadvantaged groups. It was found that the socially advantaged group had higher intelligence in rural sample and better scholastic achievement in both rural and urban samples. Again socially advantaged group had higher intelligence and scholastic achievements. Whiteman and Deutsch (1968) were of opinion that the children from a disadvantaged environment miss some experiences necessary for developing verbal, conceptual, attentional and learning skills requisite to school success. Due to this deficiency there is progressive alienation from school environment and it exposes many deficiencies of a disadvantaged child.

Different studies on disadvantaged children brought another factor to the forefront. It was found that a crucial handicap of socially disadvantaged children is language. Acquisition and use of language need the functioning of three psycholinguistic processes – (i) Receptive Process, (ii) Associative Process, and (iii) Expressive Process. Despite controversies in this regard, all researchers agree that the socially disadvantaged child possesses a linguistic system which is different from that of the socially advantaged child. Language difficulties may be the result of one or all or any combination of the following factors:

(a) A different linguistic environment.
(b) A different language acquisition device.
(c) A different set of psycholinguistic abilities.
(d) Economic, educational and place of residence variables.
(e) Poor and uneducated families.

Language experts felt that an inadequate linguistic environment makes a poor input into language acquisition device and hence retards language perception and production. The development of linguistic awareness and language learning are hampered in an environment where there is very little linguistic interaction.

Besides language difficulties, nutritional deficiency is another potent factor for socially disadvantaged children which is considered as the greatest deterrant to physical health. Studies report that malnourishment has a serious effect on physical anomalies and deficiencies on intellectual performance of low SES children. They are inferior to advantaged children in discrimination learning. According to Livingston, "Malnutrition gives rise to mental apathy, a shortened span of attention, reduced mental powers and increased drowsiness, etc."

In 1964, Birch and Belmont have found that malnutrition is the main cause for short height and stunted growth. Besides that it affects reading ability and auditory visual integration. According to Birch, malnutrition might have caused a structural deficiency in the central nervous system which affects later's intellectual achievement demanding complex integrative mechanism but there is no conclusive evidence of such a damage. In a workshop (Sweden, August, 1973), WHO felt that the complex relationship among nutrition, mental development and the importance of other concomitant or interfering phenomena such as social deprivation and repeated infections have expressed a greater need for assessment of the problem and its effects on intellectual performance.

Studies on the assessment of the effect of malnourishment on intellectual performance were also done by Dutta and Panda (1977). Another study was done to ascertain the concomitant effects, physical anomalies and deficiencies on intellectual performance of low SES children (Spark and Panda, 1971). The former's study was based on an Indian sample, but both the studies included children from lower SES group.

The purpose of the study by Spark and Panda (1977) was to investigate the correlates of cognitive performance and achievement in reading, language, arithmetic and intelligence. Measurement was carried out using WISC and California achievement tests alongwith detailed physical examination by the medical staff.

Results showed that nearly two-fifths of rural disadvantaged children were underachievers in schools. Boys had poor attendance in schools in comparison with girls. Again boys have greater emotional problems, social problems and orthopaedic problems than girls. Within the class, mean intelligence score and achievement scores measured by California Achievement test were lower in Negro students than those in White students. Within the deprived community, the girls appeared to be comparatively better than boys in intellectual performance.

Scheduled Castes and Scheduled Tribes

In India, Scheduled Castes and Scheduled Tribes constitute a special group of disadvantaged community. Articles 341 and 342 of the Indian Constitution deal with protection and safeguards of SCs and STs. These SCs-STs consist of 25 per cent of the total population of India. The all-India rates of SCs and STs were 21.38 per cent and 16.85 per cent respectively according to 1981 census. The progress of the education of women of these communities is significantly poor. The literacy rates of women of SC and ST were 10.93 per cent and 8.04 per cent as against 29.43 per cent of other population sectors. However, the progress of higher education in these communities is significantly low.

In Orissa, tribal communities constitute 23.18 per cent of the total population. After independence, steps have been taken for the educational and economic development of tribals. But the percentage of literacy is not satisfactory. Some positive steps are also being taken by the government of Orissa to establish colonies in plain areas for tribal people. One hundred and five colonies have so far been established by Dandakaranya projects and the government is trying to rehabilitate the tribals. Simultaneously various new schemes are being implemented by the government for the economic upliftment of the tribals. Work-oriented educational facilities have also been provided to the tribals. Besides government facilities, some voluntary organisations in India are also making efforts for the upliftment of the tnbals. One of the prominent organisations is "Thakar Bappa", which began its work in 1921. The primary objectives of this organisations are to discourage the tribals from drinking, to set up schools for them and to get themselves acquainted with different activities. Till now, the objectives are not yet achieved.

Information about the Growth of Enrolment among Scheduled Castes and Tribes in India

Level of Education	*Scheduled Castes*			*Scheduled Tribes*		
	(1960-61)	*(1969-70)*	*Rate of Increase annually at compound Rate*	*(1960-61)*	*(1969-70)*	*Rate of Increase annually at compound rate*
Pre-primary	6452	14611	9.6	4298	4599	9.3
Primary	3196538	5285944	5.8	1336723	2147443	5.4
Middle	920429	1808005	7.8	350252	704625	8.1
Secondary	532631	1235513	9.8	94480	287022	13.1
Others	2272	237359	-	-	168917	-
Total	4656040	8617502	7.1	1785733	3317606	7.1
Higher Education	38709	101307	11.3	7266	25999	15.2

Percentage or Enrolment of Scheduled Tribes to the Tribal Population in the Respective age Groups

Name of the States	***I-V (6-11)***	***VI-VIII (11-14)***	***IX-XI (14-17)***
Andhra Pradesh	47.0	4.9	8.6
Assam	100.0	40.0	18.0
Bihar	56.0	15.2	6.7
Gujarat	55.4	15.5	6.0
Haryana	-	-	-
Maharashtra	68.1	26.8	15.5
Nagaland	90.0	35.0	9.0
Orissa	36.8	12.80	11.70
Punjab	-	-	-
Rajasthan	28.5	8.1	3.0
West Bengal	-	-	-
A & N Islands	30.0	22.50	5.60
Delhi	85.20	62.10	-
Goa, Daman & Diu	87.0	19.50	5.4
Manipur	41.80	26.10	9.70
Tripura	49.40	13.50	5.40

Retention and Dropout Rate among General, SC and ST Children at Primary Stage

CLASS	*General Communities*		*SC Communities*		*ST Communities*	
	Retention Rate	*Dropout Rate*	*Retention Rate*	*Dropout Rate*	*Retention Rate*	*Dropout Rate*
I	100	-	100	-	100	-
II	78.83	21.27	74.61	25.39	63.38	36.62
III	87.75	12.25	76.78	23.22	58.42	41.58
IV	53.83	46.17	40.82	59.18	24.73	75.28
V	40.05	59.95	27.03	72.97	16.28	84.72

Educational Strategies

Priority was given to the National Education Policy (NEP, 1986) for concerted efforts towards the educational development of disadvantaged children. Instrumental strategies were adopted accordingly for educating the underprivileged, taking the objectives of instructions and their entering behaviour into account. Actually there is no difference in the way in which the underprivileged children learn. Their learning processes are subject to the same general principles of learning as are the learning processes of the average or the normal, the only difference being the rate, the sequence, the type of materials and presentation modes.

The NPE of 1986 also tried to ensure greater enrolment and retention of such children in schools and to decrease their dropout rates. Again, the parents of socially disadvantaged children who themselves are socially disadvantaged require special incentives to allow their children to attend the educational programmes. Most of the disadvantaged children add to the income of their family. So monetary compensations to parents along with free educational provisions should be given priority to any successful programme of education for the socially disadvantaged children.

The following objectives should be taken into consideration for enrichment programmes on remedial education:

(a) Socially disadvantaged children must be trained to achieve three objectives, viz., Knowledge, Skill and Attitude.

(b) Self-concept, level of aspiration and achievement motivation should be accelerated.

(c) Language training and analytical thinking must be included.

(d) These children must be trained to acquaint themselves with concrete life situations.

(e) They must be aware of their various creative talents and they must be trained to develop a sense of comparative living in them, so that they can easily participate with normal students.

Educational Provisions

Educational provisions have been made for the socially disadvantaged by the government. In the arena of intellectual and social competence, enrichment programmes were designed to develop and enlarge children's conceptual repertoire and communicative skills. Some measures are discussed below:

Establishment of Residential Schools: Steps should be taken to establish residential schools and Ashram schools for disadvantaged children like SCs and STs. Of course residential type of schools are made to suit the needs of Adivasis. Measures should be taken to make these institutions more homely. Recently the government has taken the initiative to solve the economic problems existing in these types of Ashram schools. The charges for education, clothing, boarding and medical care are being met by the government. But a meticulous examination reveals that the existing number of residential schools are inadequate in this regard. So recreational centres, guidance and counselling centres should be established to meet the immediate demand.

Financial Help for Disadvantaged Children: Poverty is a pertinent factor which is found to be a barrier in the path of progress of the disadvantaged children. Of course, the government has been giving financial aid to these students long since. On the basis of poverty-cum-merit, other backward classes are also given assistance. Pre-matric and post-matric scholarships are also being given now by the government to provide financial help. In some universities and institutions, payments for admissions and tuition fees are also exempted.

Appointment of Expert Teachers: A decision has been taken by the government to replace the untrained teachers by trained ones and to absorb the existing hands in suitable posts. In some cases, these untrained teachers were asked to have the requisite qualification within a short space of time. Again, there is a plan to give rewards to those teachers who specialise in braille, tribal dialect and hearing aid. Residential accommodation is being provided to teaching experts and administrators who work in hilly and tribal areas. It is true that incentives in terms of additional payment, accommodation etc., reduce the truancy of the teaching experts. Also steps are being taken by the government to hold in-service training programmes and refresher courses. In some areas, teachers are also being trained in tribal dialect and tribal culture.

Craft Education: Under government instructions, some useful crafts like carpentry, weaving and tailoring were introduced to suit the needs of SCs and STs which are a must for their economic development. But a proposal should be made to the government to introduce agriculture and spinning in boys' Ashram Schools and gardening in girls' Ashram Schools. Statistics reveal that the government has made craft education compulsory in some states and union territories.

Incentives to Indigent Families: It is generally found that the percentage of dropouts for SCs and STs students is high during the early school years. The reason is obvious. These students come from low SES strata. Their parents are needy and impoverished. According to the parents of these children, education is not a necessity, but a luxury.

But recently government has taken steps for more enrolment of these students. Priority is being given for the education of the weaker sections of the people and children. Incentives are being provided to indigent families, so that they would be able to send their children regularly to school.

Compensatory Pre-school Education: Research works reveal that the mental development of children generally takes place between 3 and 7 years. During this period every child must be kept in a very healthy environment. Otherwise, he will face some anomalies in future. Keeping this in mind, special attention must be paid to pre-school education of every child. As a result, they will benefit from primary education in future. The disadvantaged children have a poor vocabulary (which is a setback) to follow the state language. Pre-school period is considered to be the formative period of a child's life. Through compensatory pre-school education, a child can improve his vocabulary and language difficulties can ultimately be surmounted. But provisions should be made to supply free reading and writing materials.

Adjustment of School Hours and Vocations: Adjustment of school vacations and school hours becomes a necessity for these children to meet the socio-economic needs of the community. The percentage of dropouts and stagnation can be reduced to the minimum if school hours and vacations can be properly adjusted so that these children get ample opportunity to assist their parents. For example, in agricultural communities, the schools must have three hours' duration for teaching and vacations can be adjusted keping the sowing and harvesting periods of major crops in view. There must be holidays for local festivals and community functions.

Adult Education Programmes: Truly speaking, educated parents can get their children educated with little effort. So parents must be educated first to take care of the disadvantaged children. Reports say that in our country, a fairly good section of people belonging to SCs and STs are not educated. So measures are being taken to educate them through adult education programmes. Through this attempt, they will be able to understand the value of education and responsibility for the future generation. Of course, the government has taken the initiative to open Anganwadis, non-formal and adult education centres to help SCs and STs people.

Techniques of Evaluation: Steps may be taken to adopt new techniques of evaluation and continuous assessment of these types will be conducive. Due to the fallacious examination systems and evaluation, most of the disadvantaged children fail in the promotional examinations. To bring out modern and sophisticated evaluation techniques, the teachers must be provided with item banks. Considering the stagnation and dropouts, continuous and meticulous evaluation must be introduced to help these children as far as practicable. Extra coaching after school hours may be encouraged to help the weak students.

Follow-up Action: Students coming from Ashram schools or from residential type of schools, generally go for higher education or take up any job to earn their livelihood. Government has a plan to help these students by providing grants to settle down in life. But sometimes correct statistics are not available. So steps have to be taken to the names of these students from Ashram schools and adjust accordingly with the authorities.

These points listed above may be studied carefully and absorbed into the educational strategy for the education of the disadvantaged, so that they will not become victims of cumulative deprivation.

QUESTIONS

1. Who are the Socially Disadvantaged Children? Discuss their characteristics.

2. Discuss the causes of Socially Disadvantaged Children.
3. Briefly discuss the problems of Socially Disadvantaged Children.
4. What educational provisions can be made to educate the Socially Disadvantaged Group?
5. Who is a Socially Disadvantaged Child? Discuss the remedial measures for these children.
6. How can Socially Disadvantaged Children be helped at School?

15

The Gifted Ones

Children possessing a high intellectual level and special abilities and talents are regarded as gifted. Havighurst defines the talented or gifted child is one who shows consistently remarkable performance in any worthwhile line of endeavour. This particular definition of Havighurst includes those children who are talented in academic work as well as those who are talented in other fields.

Psychologists as well as educationists place much less emphasis on the gifted than on the normal and deficient children. This is true of Western countries, specially the USA, where education has made much advance in recognising the needs and difficulties of handicapped or deprived children. Obviously, the handicapped or deficient children attract greater attention from educationists and others because of the defect they suffer from or by their inability to keep pace with the normal children. In the classroom, the gifted children fail to attract the attention of the teacher because they can keep ahead of the average child in the class. So, for them, the need for special attention is not felt acutely. On the other hand, the handicapped children always demand attention of the teacher.

In psychology, there are no hard and fast lines to separate one group from another, since psychological characteristics are distributed in a continuum. So it is very difficult to bring out the exact frequencies of the gifted. Anyhow, psychologists have defined the "very superior" and the "gifted" groups in terms of intelligence quotients. The classifications made in this regard are not in complete agreement as to upper and lower limits. The following classification is in common use. The percentages are based upon the distribution of I.Qs of the 1937 Stanford-Binet Standardisation group.

I.Q.	***Per cent***
160 and above	0.03
150-159	0.2
140-149	1.1
130-139	3.1

The above data mean that on the average it is expected that only three pupils among 10,000 have I.Qs. of 160 or higher, one in 500 an I.Q. between 150 and 159, slightly more than one in 100, an I.Q. of 140-149 and slightly more than three in 100, with I.Qs. of 130-139 are gifted. If we classify as "gifted" those with I.Qs. of 140 and higher, than we may expect to find 1.33 per cent of the general school population in that category or somewhat more than 13 among 1000 students. If we add the "Very Superior" group, we have 4.33 per cent of the total or a number somewhat greater than forty among 1000 pupils.

History has it that concern for guidance and education of the gifted children existed in the ancient Greek and Roman periods. But the improvement is not pertinent until the latter part of the 19th century. After the publication of Galton's Hereditary Genius (1869) and Lombroso's The man of genius (1891), studies on gifted children came to the forefront. Previously, the genius and insanity were thought to be closely associated. In 1905, Binet has made an epoch-making deviation by bringing out I.Q. tests and in 1925, Terman brought out the famous longitudinal study of the genius. Then emphasis on the gifted became more prominent and we find, after 1950, there has been a renewal of interest in this domain.

But "Who is gifted"? Gifted are those children whose cognitive abilities place them in the upper level of population distribution. They constitute only 3 to 5 per cent of the population. The academically gifted has an I.Q. of 130 and above. They have superior cognitive ability, creativeness in thinking and production and superior talent in special areas. According to Guilford (1950), "the gifted are those students whose potential intellectual powers are at such a high ideational level in both productive and evaluative thinking that it can be reasonably assumed, that they could be the future problem solvers, innovators and evaluators of the culture if adequate educational experiences are provided."

The Characteristics

There is no doubt that an intellectually gifted child shows his talent by his remarkable performance in any undertaking worth his while. Such children are generally identified in schools by their teachers who are able to do this by observing their performance.

A number of misconceptions are found among laymen regarding the characteristics of very superior and gifted children. From the caricature and "folklore", people get the idea that they are physically small in stature and poorly developed. They also have a strong notion that the intellectually superior people are "qeer", "unstable", "one-sided" and socially-rejected persons. Most of them turn out to be average adults as far as intelligence and achievement are concerned.

However, none of the above notions are correct. For more than two decades, groups of exceptional children have been thoroughly screened. The following are their major characteristics revealed in these researches.

Physical Characteristics: Different studies on gifted children reveal that they have above-average physical development. These children are taller, heavier built and well developed. Their general health is above average and continues to be so into adulthood. Incidents of mortality and insanity are found to be low in case of gifted children. They have good coordination and control of the muscles. In a study, Baldwin conducted body measurements of 594 children of Terman's gifted group (in which I.Q. was in the range of 130 to 189). These children appeared to be physically superior to the group they were compared with. In 1925, Terman obtained the following details of gifted children:

(a) Gifted children have greater weight at birth.
(b) They walk and talk earlier.

(c) They have earlier pubescence.
(d) They are preconcious.
(e) They have better than average nutrition.
(f) The gifted children have more height, weight, strength of grip, shoulders, superior motoring ability, less defective hearing, mouth breathing, less stuttering etc.

Development and Intellectual Characteristics: Studies reveal that gifted children are found to have superior development in all respects. Their learning to talk, walk and even to read, is discernible early.

They are endowed with many qualities of personality and intellect. Case studies of intellectually gifted children have shown that they possess better standards than average children. Their reactions are quick and their progress is conspicuous. At an early age, they enter school and at school, they are much ahead of their class. Their activities in the classrooms are wide and varied. Their interests are also very diverse.

As reported by Kirk, gifted children are more interested in abstract subjects such as literature, debate etc. and less interested in procedure subjects like penmanship and manual training. They are found to be less sociable. Different research works reveal that on the social plane of play interest, the majority of gifted children fall in the lowest quartile as compared to average children. Kirk also has confirmed that the gifted children are rated above average on character and maturity tests. Most of the gifted children are found to be aware of their talent and their utilisation. Their cognitive processes are very rich. They form creative ideas easily, are able to sense gaps in problems and bridge the missing elements intellectually.

Personality Characteristics of Gifted Children: Different research works confirmed that there is positive and intimate relationship between giftedness and personality. No doubt, gifted children are more desired, better known, more ambitious and hardworking. Usually they have a strong desire to explore and create. They are able to sustain frustration better than anybody else.

Some psychologists have found that gifted children are impulsive and self-confident. They are very much interested in aesthetic expression and reflective thinking. They have a high degree of motivation. Normally, they are sensitive, resourceful, flexible and enthusiastic. Various studies on gifted children tell us that gifted or creative behaviour is seen as a continuation and substitute for the play of childhood. The creative thoughts are derived from the elaboration of the freely rising fantasies and ideas related to day-dreaming and childhood play. Gifted children accept freely rising ideas whereas non-creative persons suppress them.

Family Background and Social Characteristics: Generally, intellectual children come from parentage of the educated and professional class. They also belong to the higher occupational group. Their environment at home also provides a stimulating atmosphere. They are gregarious and sociable. Studies reveal that these children are very popular and they are much sought after by the elder children. Besides all the above characteristics, they have a good sense of humour.

Some experimentalists also opined that these children are shy and lovers of seclusion. They segregate themselves from the group. Very few children have interest in the opposite sex.

These children are socially more mature than other children of their age. Usually they are rated higher by their teachers on the social and emotional plane. They always prefer games which require reasoning and judgement. These children play games that are favoured by children older than them. They are neither eccentric nor unpopular.

Learning and Education: These children learn to walk and talk earlier than the average ones. Their vocabulary is very good. They possess a wide vocabulary which they use to accelerate their language development. They also have a retentive memory. They are superior in their achievements in school subjects. Unevenness is rarely noticed in their achievement because they work hard and devotedly. Near about fifty per cent of gifted children have learned to read before entering school. After entering school, they develop a keen interest in more abstract school subjects. They rank well above their individual grades.

The Identification

Parents, teachers, psychologists and social workers can help in identifying gifted children at a very early stage. Of course, it is a problem that has attracted the attention of the psychologists and educationists all over the world. They have opined that it is very difficult to assess giftedness with the help of a single tool or test. In this connection, we can note that Tolman's model for identifying gifted children was both simple and powerful. Both group tests and individual tests were employed by him for assessing giftedness in children.

According to him, children in the top 1 or 2 or 3 per cent in I.Q. were gifted children. Later, he emphasised the fact that common intelligence tests represent a rather narrow band of intellectual tasks. Such tests are best for recognition or recall type of problems. Therefore he concluded that the full range of giftedness in children cannot be measured by intelligence tests only. It was further proved that children who score high on intelligence tests may not necessarily also be highly creative.

Coming to a different line of thought, Thurstone revealed, "To be extremely intelligent is not the same as to be gifted in creative work. This may be taken as a hypothesis. It is commonly observed in universities that those students who have high intelligence, judged by available criteria, are not necessarily the only ones who produced the most original ideas. All of us probably know a few men who are creative and highly intelligent, but this combination is not the rule."

Generally intelligence tests and creativity tests are given for identifying giftedness in children. Tests of creativity involve the ability to deal with verbal and numerical symbol systems. Besides these tests, scholastic achievement tests have been made to study the giftedness. But one of the drawbacks of this test is that it is not comprehensive or valid enough to assess creativity.

Efforts have been made to study giftedness by different psychologists. Getzels has described the following measures of creativity and giftedness:

(i) Word Association Test (WAT): The test presents words to the subject. Each word has multiple meanings. Here the subject is asked to write as many meanings as he knows for each word.

(ii) Uses of Objects: The subject has to write as many different uses for each object as he possibly can.

(iii) Hidden Shapes: The subject has to identify the complex figures in which the single figure appears.

(iv) Fables: Here the subjects are provided with the same fables whose last lines are blank. The subjects are required to fill in these blanks to form a suitable ending.

(v) Make-up Problems: Here the subjects are instructed to use the information given to make up as many problems as they can within a limited time span.

Kough and De Haon have developed a procedure for discovering special abilities and disabilities. Their works were also considered to identify giftedness. The above authors have given different criteria to identify special abilities and talents among gifted children. The criteria fall under three areas.

(i) Intellectual ability.
(ii) Mechanical skills.
(iii) Physical skills.

Willy has enumerated the following procedures for identifying giftedness:

(a) Accuracy and use of vocabulary.
(b) Language proficiency.
(c) Quick, keen observation and retention of information about things.
(d) Early interest in calendars, in telling time and in clocks.
(e) Quality of concentration.
(f) The early development of ability to read.

To recapitulate, we can say that there are several methods for identifying gifted children and a systematic procedure includes the following points:

(a) (i) In the first step, group of intelligence can be conducive for screening.
 (ii) Besides the group test, a standardised achievement test can be used to identify giftedness in children.
(b) Class marks and different records of student's achievement in the school may also give some indications.
(c) A teacher can provide indications of giftedness by observation. But some experimenters doubt the teacher's competency in this regard.

Careful observation should be made regarding the identification of the gifted and no single test should be used in this context.

Gallagher (1949) has discussed the limitations of various techniques generally used to identify gifted children:

(a) He said that intelligence tests are very expensive and time consuming.
(b) Again, group intelligence tests are good for screening. But one major drawback is that students having motivational and emotional problems are rarely identified and so are subjects having reading difficulties.
(c) Administration of achievement test batteries fails to identify underachieving gifted children.
(d) Children having hostile abilities towards schools are rarely identified as gifted by observation. Students having motivational as well as emotional problems also fall in this category.

On the whole, many tests are now available to recognise the gifted as early as possible. Objective tests of intelligence are needed to identify the bright students and these tests are in rampant use for the recognition of the gifted to a fair degree of uncertainty.

Educating the Gifted

History reveals the fact that in Plato's republic, there were plans for special education for all the different walks of life. This ideal Republic was the first plan to formulate explicitly the idea of special classes for scholars, artisans, warriors and labourers. We also get a similar indication in the origin of caste system in India. The entire society was divided into few groups with particular specialisations. Brahmins were supposed to be the intellectuals in the society, Kshatriyas-warriors, Vaisyas-businessmen and Sudras, servants of the above three classes. Under these plans, some kind of screening was also implied. Talented children were to be sorted out and given the kind of training best suited to them. This was done to save human wastage and to make the best use of human resources. In our old system of education, we get ample evidence of special education.

Literature states that individuals who have been specially talented were individually coached by either their parents or tutors. Organisation of a special class or special school for the gifted is of much later origin. In 1862, the earliest recognition of the gifted in USA was indicated in the form of promotion plans in the city of St. Louis. This plan suggested that promotions should be given after every six months to start with, then at intervals of three months and still later promotion after every five weeks. It was presumed that frequent promotions would provide a chance for the gifted to get recognition for their talent. Experiments were done in New Jersey in 1886 with the different groupings within a class. Children were classified in different groups according to their abilities and talents. Each group was allowed to advance as rapidly as it could. Results revealed that this provided the opportunity for each student to achieve his maximum target of ability and potentiality. In Europe, the Cambridge plan was originated in 1891 and it was spread over the section of school extending from fourth to ninth grade.

But in India, we do not find any school planned with this specific purpose. Of course, some provisions are marked in public schools and in some boarding schools. These schools are originally meant for the students coming from the upper socio-economic status families and sometimes children from Royal families. Children for these schools are selected indirectly. The fees and expenses of these schools are significantly higher. So a few parents are able to send their children to these type of schools. Once the child is admitted to the school, he has to follow an enriched curriculum than he would in an average school. One major drawback with this type of selection is that every child in this school is not gifted. But the school provides educational facilities for the gifted ones.

Nowadays, in India, attention is being paid to the education of the gifted by State and Central authorities. By providing merit scholarships, it is possible to spot the gifted children who can be placed in these public schools at Government cost. Through this procedure many scholars emerge from middle class families.

Generally gifted children, when allowed to attend regular classes, face a lot of problems of their own. An average class and its programme are planned for children of average ability. By admitting gifted children into this class, they are denied the opportunity they need for full development of their talents. Their education is restricted. The teacher finds himself placed in a very awkward position as to how to satisfy both the talented and the average children.

In the classroom, the average child develops a feeling of backwardness and inferiority. This often leads to frustration due to a continuous sense of failure experienced by the child. He sees that the gifted ones occupy the highest positions while he is unable to do so.

In our educational system, very often we allow double promotions which places the bright children in a senior class. It is done with the anticipation that the child will be able to find a challenge in the work of a senior class and utilise his talents. But we forget that when a child is given an accelerated promotion, he is placed out of his own group with respect to physical, social and emotional development. But it is found that when a talented child is placed with children who are higher in the developmental continuum, he may find himself out of step in other activities and interests. So it is suggested that the child should be provided with an enriched programme while he is allowed to share the experiences of children of his own level of development.

Again, it is customary in our schools to entrust more work to the gifted children. But this is a wrong step which should be realised by our teachers. It must be kept in mind that being overloaded with a mediocre type of work is not enrichment for a talented child. The work that is not challenging to him or the routine type of work may invite monotony for the gifted child. An intelligent child always wants to accomplish difficult tasks which pose a challenge to him and which he can complete independently. He derives satisfaction from the urge to investigate for himself. Enrichment includes the avoidance of repetition and drill. Backward children gain from the drill but it is monotonous for the gifted ones. Drill tends to irritate the talented children affecting their output seriously.

There is every possibility of the gifted children developing bad social habits due to lack of enrichment of educational programmes. They feel, very often, that the tasks given to them are not interesting and far from satisfying. So they engage themselves in loafing and indulging in anti-social activities for excitement. Sometimes, they invite disciplinary problems in the classroom. These problems become acute when they understand that the teacher usually plans work for an average child. Suppose a teacher anticipates that a particular task will take 30 minutes to be completed by an average child. He plans it accordingly. But when the task is given, a talented child would finish it within 20 minutes. So he gets some extra time on his hands. Then he plans to utilise it in an interesting way. But this act of the talented child may not be appreciated by the teacher. He may get disturbed by that and the classroom discipline may be affected. The talented children engage themselves in such activities because they have surplus energy and time on hand which they must spend. As a result, a conflict with the social discipline is pertinent.

Sometimes the planned curriculum is so arranged that it would miss some of the aspects of the developments of a child. A gifted child needs opportunities for an all round development of his personality. Enrichment of the educational programme, if aimed entirely on the academic side, will undoubtedly ignore the development of the social, aesthetic or emotional aspects of personality. A problem is still pertinent here. We know that each child maintains a different rate of growth and development. In the same age group, one may develop one aspect earlier and faster than others. There may be others who are slower in their general rate of growth. An ideal programme meets the demands of all these individuals so that every possibility is there that individual attention is paid to every child. The programme must be suitable for individual needs, demands and nature of development.

Programmes for bright children usually take one of these three principle forms: (i) Enrichment, (ii) Acceleration, and (iii) Grouping in special classes. We have discussed the first two points in detail with their advantages and disadvantages. We now discuss the points "for" and "against" special classes. Enrichment is basically a teaching procedure whether it is applied to a regular class or to a special class. But acceleration and grouping are essentially administrative techniques. Each may be used alone or in amalgamation with one or both of the other types.

Special classes and schools are universally accepted by psychologists and educationists for the education of gifted children. William Stern calls these classes as "elite-classes". Investigations revealed that it has yielded satisfactory results. Still the situation is not so simple as it is thought to be. There is a very interesting controversy about the desirability of special education for the gifted. There are some valid points raised on either side of the issue. Some of the points advanced in favour of special classes are:

(1) The work of an average child done in a class is a handicap to the talented child. Here he is restrained. But in a special class,

gifted children are provided with the opportunity to work according to their superior ability. In the average class, not only the superior child moves at a slower pace, but he also does not get the benefit of superior teaching. A very pertinent fact is that through mutual stimulation, a group of gifted children have the advantage of progressing and developing more rapidly.

(2) If a gifted child is placed in an average class, he will develop some careless habits. The tasks given to him are too easy to solve and sometimes he refuses to work them out. Very often such children become maladjusted and anti-social. But a special class offers opportunities to the talented ones for challenging work and develop their potentialities to the maximum.

(3) Where special classes are not available, the gifted children are often permitted double promotions. With this, they are compelled to mix with more mature and older children. But while doing so, one thing must be kept in mind that a superior child may not necessarily be superior in sociability and other aspects of development. Again, some adjustment problems are also found. The child may be superior in intelligence as far as his studies go, but that does not mean that when be, is put in an absolutely new group, he may not face the problem of social adjustment. However, he can overcome this difficulty if he is placed in a special class. He has the scope for passing grades at the normal rate and the opportunity to move with his own group.

(4) Very often, talented children suffer from social maladjustment. They get plenty of time in the average class because the tasks given to them are lighter and easy. They can solve it much quicker than the anticipated time span, leaving them with time to spare till the average students finish the job. In the meantime, their alert mind is diverted to seek other outlets. Research evidences reveal that many delinquents have proved to be children of superior ability, but they left school to avoid the monotony and boredom of the average curriculum.

(5) The empirical works in this area revealed that special classes also provide opportunities to develop leadership in various

arenas. In the group, there may be children specially gifted in painting, poetry, mathematics, literature and other branches of knowledge. More developed and well planned programmes become conducive for their talent and future leaders in these particular fields emerge.

(6) Henry Goddard (1933) has rightly pointed out that gifted children "are made of finer stuff than the majority". These children are more sensitive, alert and quick in their thinking. If proper stimulation is not provided, they create problems in the class. When put together with the average group, it becomes a problem for the teacher. Treatment and handling of the two types of children become extremely difficult.

These are the plus points in favour of special education given to special classes for the gifted children, so that they may get ample opportunity to develop their talents and potentialities. But a group of psychologists and educationists strongly refuted the isolation of these children from regular schools. They have their reasons too. We take these reasons as criticisms of the movement.

(a) The potent criticism against the movement is that it is highly undemocratic. "Equal opportunity of Education" should be provided to one and all. We support this point strongly.

(b) Very often, psychologists point out that if the gifted children are taken away from regular classes, they tend to develop conceit. Again, they become conscious of their superior ability and fail to develop modesty as a personality trait.

(c) Special classes give rise to a kind of intellectual aristocracy. The isolation of gifted children and formation of special groups give rise to ideas of superiority.

(d) When gifted children are separated, an average child tends to lose. When working with the gifted, an average child gets a chance to learn many things, and becomes highly motivated. Withdrawal of the gifted deprives the average child of rich stimulation.

(e) Some educationists feel that such programmes deprive the society of superior leadership. While working with the average children, the gifted gets a chance to act as a leader and gets training in leadership. Thus, the society is provided with future leaders.

(f) The most important criticism levelled against special education is the high cost of such programmes. Particularly in a developing country like India, this point is of special importance. Some critics argue that when there is not enough money for the education of the average child, such expensive programmes for the gifted is a little undemocratic.

Guidance for the Gifted

Psychologists point out that parents also play an equally important role in the proper development of the gifted children. It is very important for the parents to provide the right environment for gifted children, so that they may find scope to make good use of their intelligence. Sometimes their fundamental needs are overlooked. But parents should take note of it. The children must feel that they are wanted by their parent and their parents enjoy their company.

Again, gifted children need recognition. Sincere praise from their parents, teachers and friends makes them feel that they are liked. If they are denied recognition, they escape into daydreaming. Gifted children must feel that they are protected in case of need and the parents should encourage them in gaining new experiences. Every parent must think that the child seeks understanding and sympathy of his parents in his search for further learning. Parents should keep themselves well informed about many facts, so that they can answer the child's questions readily and correctly. As the child grows older, he should be encouraged to read and to find out the answers to his questions himself.

Generally children learn through observation. Gifted children are keen observers. They usually learn from examples set by their parents. These children learn good manners, correct speech habits, courtesy, neatness, honesty, punctuality at a very early stage.

Another potent factor is motivation. The motive of the gifted child should be satisfied. For them, curiosity is a strong urge. A gifted child is always eager to know "Why", "How", "When" and "Where" etc. and answering the child's questions will not only provide him the knowledge but satisfy his curiosity too.

Many parents overestimate the talent of their children. They usually insist on the child achieving things much beyond his actual capacity. Again, some parents select a certain vocation for their children without consulting a vocational counsellor. To force a child into a particular vocation is highly undesirable. Psychologists advise that no selection of a vocation should be made for a bright child before he finishes his high school. If parents have any problems in handling gifted children, they should consult with Child Psychologists or Guidance Counsellors immediately.

Coming to the role of a teacher, the teacher for bright children must be a flexible person and dynamic. He should allow the children to make new discoveries. The teacher must be a source of inspiration, encouragement and opportunity for them to test their potentialities, to explore more avenues. Bright children always need inspired guidance. Top priority should be given to productive learning and effective living.

Creativity requires sensitivity and independence. Both parents and teachers should help gifted children to discover their potentialities. They should keep them free in gathering, assembling, comparing and exchanging ideas. Parents and teachers must try to reduce the gap of emotional distance between themselves and gifted children. It is possible by participation and understanding.

Besides all these factors, it is generally agreed that education of superior and gifted pupils should emphasize certain other intellectual objectives, in addition to the acquisition of necessary and desirable information and skills. These other objectives include: (i) analytic perception, (ii) the methods of problem-solving, (iii) employing analysis, (iv) synthesis, (v) conceptual thinking, (vi) scientific objectivity, (vii) independent study methods, (viii) encouragement of originality and creative effort, and (ix) encouragement of special interests.

QUESTIONS

1. Who are gifted children? Discuss various methods for identifying gifted children.
2. Briefly discuss the needs and problems of gifted children.
3. Point out various characteristics of the gifted children.

4. "Creativity is the highest expression of giftedness". Elucidate.
5. Discuss various programmes for educating gifted children.
6. How can you plan the education of a gifted child?
7. Why are special classes needed for educating the gifted?
8. Define "giftedness". How can the curriculum be enriched for the education of the gifted?
9. Discuss the advantages and disadvantages of special classes.
10. Write short notes on the following:
    a. Homogeneous grouping.
    b. Special classes.
    c. Enrichment programmes.
    d. Personality traits.
    e. Identifying gifted children.

16

The Researches

Here, we bring into focus certain areas where research in India can be conducted to the vantage of modifying, enriching and applying different educational measures. These are:

- Conceptual Issues in Special Education.
- Service Delivery System and its Efficacy.
- Curriculum and Instructions.
- Management of Educational Environment.
- Strategy of Research in Special Education.
- Research in Piagetian Framework.
- Assessment Research and Identification of Disabled.
- Recent Development of Research Focus in India.

Research and developmental activities in the Education of Exceptional Children have emerged in recent years as areas of concern for educational researchers. Whatever research has been done in different areas of disability is more of an organizational and institutional nature. It is, therefore, a piecemeal academic exercise neither reflecting a view-point based on our socio-cultural ethos nor leading to any viable practical application. Excepting biomedical researchers in mental retardation, researches have predominantly been in the areas of attention, learning and memory, but often dealing with tasks that have less relevance in the classroom setting. A few researches cover the ground in the area of applied behaviour analysis and behaviour modification.

Researches in the area of speech and language disability are rather more rigorous but are confined to a particular institute and more in the line of therapeutic frame. Research in the true sense has not reached an appreciable degree of acceptance so far as assessment of educability and remediation programmes are concerned in the area of visual, auditory and orthopaedic impairments. The Journal of Mental Retardation, Journal of the Institute of Speech and Hearing, Indian Journal of Disability and Rehabilitation are almost extinct after pious beginning and headway. Disability and Impairments continues with larger input from medical field than from educational sector. The Fourth Survey of Research and the Fifth Survey of Research in Education are eloquent testimony. This then is the picture when we are thinking of research and development in special education in India. There are various constraints responsible for such a backdrop. Lack of trained personnel, lack of institutional support, late recognition of the idea that disabled children within the mild or educable range can be trained and several other socio-cultural constraints. This situation has slightly changed but is not very conducive to extensive and intensive studies and developmental activities in the area, primarily because of lack of organised effort by the specialists in the respective areas of disability. There is hardly any interaction and dissemination forum for research. Of course since the 1980's, National Institutes in the major areas of disability (Blind, Deaf, Orthopaedically handicapped, Mentally Retarded) and Institutes for Speech and Hearing, B.M. Institutes of Mental Health, etc. have been focussing attention on research and research based and/or related developmental activities. This is a significant step in this direction. In addition, University Departments of Education at Jamia Millia, Banaras, SNDT, R.K. Mission Institute at Coimbatore and Andhra University, etc. have opened up Special Education Departments. Finally, NCERT, through Regional Colleges of Education and its unit at Headquarters has taken up the challenge of starting systematic research, teacher training and development of instructional material in four major areas of disability. Staff has been trained in and outside the country. It is, therefore against this backdrop we must plan our research which will provide continuity and comprehensive data based understanding of the process in which the disabled child can gainfully be helped to learn within the limits of their educability, feasibility and practical application.

Especially, it will also be able to give a picture of education and training of disability in India, based on collaborative national level research wherever the approach is narmotive and at institutional and individual level where the need is specific. Keeping these broad goals and background, a perspective of research has been given with some hints of research areas and topics of interest in general.

Conceptual Issues

Although in the working group report for the education of the disabled, some nine categories of disabilities have been identified for care, training and education in a phased manner according to the magnitude of incidence, yet there is a need for status studies relating to incidence, service institutions, education and training institutions, in terms of physical facilities and resource specialists in each area of disability and their major classification and referral practices in vogue. Such status studies are necessary for programme planning and research understanding. Experience in observing the identification produces in several institutions reveal that there is no uniformity in assessment and diagnostic procedure. Often it is by intuition, observation of morphology, use of one available test or uses of several tests co-jointly but in redundant combinations. This is not to say that all that is existing is not worthy of doing but there must be a systematic research effort to develop what is called Learning Potential Assessment Device which would take into account assessment of cognitive competence and adaptive behaviour appropriate to the age levels based on performance measures and observations of daily living skills. In the socio-cultural context in which disabled children find themselves in India, this is a dire necessity. Any western, or pick and choose method of assessment of disability will be doing more harm than good. The LPAD can be used in all subcultures in our society. The next major thrust in this section should be an understanding of the Psycho-educational Characteristics of the Disabled (i.e., the cognitive, affective, socio-emotional, information processing nature, physical and motor activities, perceptual style, etc.) on a normative basis against which deviance can be identified and categorised. Such norms are of primary importance for placement of children in a special category and managing special services for them. At present such norms are conspicuously absent in our literature.

Another area of concern is the content analysis of school curriculum in each of the major categories of disabled in vogue in our country with a view to developing an uniform curriculum. The existing disparities are so great that no one system will be adequate for all categories of disabled children who are currently receiving education and training in different institutions, voluntary or governmental. Such is the case of teacher training curriculum of the disabled. Only recently the special education unit in the NCERT has taken up the stand and has arrived at a common teacher training curriculum in the areas of visually handicapped, hearing handicapped, mental retardation, orthopaedically handicapped with a composite course structure. However, the viability of these attempts needs to be examined in relation to objectives of training. The Rehabilitation Council of India has also standardised curriculum for as many as 34 courses in the area of disability.

Since language disability has not been spelt out at the moment as a separate area of disability, one cannot deny that language is the medicine for any cognitive, affective or skill learning that takes place. Language deficit is one of the major deficiencies in the disabled. The differential communicative competence and language competence should be studied through development of Language Assessment Kit for the disabled which will eventually help in developing language intervention programmes for different groups of disabled children.

Service Delivery System

It is a fact that deviance is a sociological concept although disability has organic and psycho educational base. More than to disabled children is done by using labels, developing negative expectancy, providing poor observational learning situations to achieve self-fulfilling prophency. Some of these are more prominent in a developing society like ours, where pragmatism and progressivism rarely enter into the domain of disability. Rather there is a strong sense of fatalism while thinking of educating the disabled. Against this background certain research problems do emerge. These are: How to parents, community members, teachers, perceive the disabled varying in socio-psychological and physical dimensions? How do other children look at the disabled children in an integrated school setting? How do peers act as models for learning among disabled? Such studies will lead us to examine further by empirical means whether integrated setting in our culture is more helpful to the disabled than the special educational arrangements? What are constraints and resources in making integrated education scheme effective? How can parents and community be changed so that they accept retarded and other disabled children and make referrals for education and provide necessary facilities at home? To what extent resource room planning is effective or a cost ineffective programme? Whether homebound instruction or out of school hours remedial teaching is a good alternative? How far the government and voluntary organisations compare with each other in terms of efficacy in respect to each area of disability? Such opinions if at all they exist are mere speculations. Research findings will give direction to developmental planning.

How can peer modelling be more effective by making certain cues salient for the disabled? For all these viewpoints research can only offer meaningful conclusions, conducted on a fairly large scale or using intensive case studied of disabled children and their capabilities as a function of the service delivery system and the parameters of an effective delivery system can till then be differed.

Curriculum and Instruction

Curriculum and instructional procedures can be clubbed as one major area of research concern in the area of disabled. More specifically, first, reading readiness programmes need be developed for each area of disability and level within a given disability area. The existing curriculum for normal children have to be watered down to the level of disabled child and only curriculum research could take such a step with regard to arithmetic, reading, language, social skills, etc. and determine empirically the efficacy of a particular method (s) of teaching these curriculum. Through research we should develop the disability specific instructional technique. Such researches are necessary because the western studies prescribe so many varieties of teaching approach and aids that one really needs to know, which one is more effective than others. Systematic and coordinated research work have been a felt need because ours is not a country of affluence but a growing and developing one. In order to make design of curriculum and methods of instruction effective for the disabled, research in these areas are imperative.

Management of Educational Environment

It has been already stated that disability is often caused by environmental factors and more so precipitated by the environment in which one lives. This brings into focus the place of a disabled child in home, in school, and in society. The home also has different variations like the delivery systems in school and community. A child who is disabled is perceived and managed in a poor home much more differently than if he is born in a well-to-do home. What is more important in this context therefore is the prevailing attitudes, stereotypes, prejudices and expectancies about the disabled. Before any systematic intervention or educational programme is undertaken, it is necessary to assess the pre-existing status in this regard or else even the best programme is not going to make any difference. Same is true of classroom climate and management of peer attitudes for a better adjustment. Hence, it is necessary to assess attitudes through research, bring changes in attitudes for a better adjustment through intervention, and dissemination of right kind of information about the disabled among the people and parents, develop such material for dissemination. All these aims at providing the disabled the least restrictive environment conducive for their optimal growth and adjustment to living.

The relative merits of isolation and mainstreaming would be another research direction in order to examine the long-term impact that the disabled have upon society and family. What should be the ideal teacher behaviours and parental interaction for these children? What should be the environmental circumstances that should foster development of cognitive-perceptual motor functioning, e.g., tactual, spatial, auditory, mobility, adjustment of the visually impaired, etc. the same logic applies to other areas of disability too. What kind of functional environment will promote learning and adjustment, verbal impact etc.? Parental responsiveness, model behaviours, acceptance of disability as mere difference or not a defect, parental/community participation in care and training many such issues would arise. Research can only show whether they are of trivial, tangential nature or have relevance for developmental programmes of the disabled.

Further, on the predispositional side, biomedical research is imperative to identify and prevent parental influences accounting for incidence of disability and the biochemical screening after birth, dietary habits, etc. that would go a long way in reducing its occurrence in society. Western countries have come up with many answers of which several are universal but others are culture specific, e.g., an expectant mother and women in general in India do not smoke or drink, do not expose herself to too much of radiation but there may be other factors i.e., malnutrition, ignorance about infectious diseases, etc. Hence, investigation would be necessary in this regard to identify culture specific influences which act as predispositions for creating disability slowly but surely.

Strategy of Research

It has been stated in the beginning that disability is a complex phenomenon. It has multi dimensions and multi casualty. Hence, in pursuing any systematic research in this area there is a need of collaborative effort among institutions, individuals having expertise in the specific areas of concern, for any fruitful result and development of the disabled. Partnership in research, participation and involvement should be the model as any individualistic orientation is likely to lead toward piecemeal, restricted and trivial and academic research. The former method is suggestive enough to accelerate research which has been neglected for so long.

Research strategy may take both cross-sectional and longitudinal studies approach. We may rely more on clinical case studies and observation but certainly normative studies are necessary. But no matter what method or strategy we follow our aim should be to understand casual, evaluative, and functional variables in the education and training of the disabled, with focus on studies on post school adjustment in family and society, the ultimate goals of any education and rehabilitation programme. Research in this area would thus provide not only a continuity in thinking, consistency in results but will prepare a sound empirical base in the area of special education which mass media can use of for the benefit of all, and more so for the disabled.

Research in Piagetian Framework

Jean Piaget, Switzerland's noted genetic epistemologist, proposed a developmental and constructive model of human cognition from birth to adolescence based on biological processes. Although his theory has been applied to regular education for several decades, fewer efforts have been made to apply his work to exceptional populations (Wachs and Furth, 1980). One reason for this apparent lack of interest is Piaget's derivation of theoretical principles from observations of essentially normal children, with the consequent assumption of lack of applicability to handicapped individuals. A second obstacle has been an assumed lack of it between more holistic instructional goals and strategies compatible with Piagetian theory and the specific step-by-step goals and methods typically prescribed for handicapped learners. Nevertheless, Piaget's cognitive-development theory provides a useful means of understanding and teaching children with special needs.

Attempts have been made in recent years to apply Piagetian research to special education children. Piaget described development of structure in terms of sensori motor, pre-operational, concrete and formal operational stages, through interaction with environment.

The sensori motor stages (birth to 2 years) describes the infant and prelinguistic child. The infant manifests cognition through actions on objects, such as giggling the crib to set a mobile in motion. The pre-operational stage (2 to 7 years) is characterized by use of language, symbolic behaviour, and lack of conservational logic. The 2-year old child demonstrates symbolic behaviours by pretending that a broom is a horse and "riding" it. The pre-operational child has not yet acquired the structures necessary for conservation: the ability to recognise that matter is conserved despite superficial changes in shape or form. For example, when 3 year old is presented two identical balls of clay one of which is subsequently rolled into a cigar shape, the child perceives the remaining ball and cigar as being unequal in size. When asked which is large (or "has more"), the child may attend only to length and select the cigar, or only to width, and choose the ball. The child does not consider the two dimensions simultaneously. Children in the stage of concrete operation (6 to 11 years) have acquired the rules of conservation as well as an understanding of relational concepts. The fourth stage, formal operations (12 and above) describes children who can use abstract rules in problem solving and conceptualize hypothetical terms.

Piaget's theory postulates that although children vary in the age at which they reach a given stage, all follow the same sequence. Piaget's constructionist model has been used to explain social cognition, or children's logical understanding of themselves and other individual in interaction. Children's development of social cognition parallels their intellectual development, progressing through a sequence of stages from egocentric to socio-centric thought. The infant is egocentric, or centered around the self. As children mature and gain experience with the environment, they become decentered. They learn that his self is separate from the other people, that other people have thoughts and feelings, and that other people's thought and feelings may differ from their own.

Three stages characterize children's development of moral judgement; objectives morality, subjective morality, and interpretation of the act. Children in the stage of objective morality base their judgements of good and bad behaviour on objective criteria such as the amount of damage incurred, for example, when someone breaks a lamp while trying to clean the table. In subjective morality, good or bad intentions become a prime criterion for judging behaviour. At the highest level, children simultaneously consider intent and outcome and develop a sense of moral responsibility for the own actions.

Much of the research on Piagets theory has addressed the invariance of the sequence of stages, the impact of specific training on development, especially on acquisition of conservation; the relationship of social cognition to cognitive development, and the relationship between social cognition and social behaviour.

The instructional principles that follow are directed at the teaching of concepts, generalizations, and thinking processes rather than at increasing the level of cognitive development.

— Because children's thinking is qualitatively different at the various stages of development, teaching objectives should be matched to children's level of development.

— Learning is the acquisition of higher order structures transformed from and built on previous structures. Thus. learning involves the acquisition of broad general rules or frameworks rather than particular, isolated facts. A such, learning proceeds through understanding rather than through incorporation of rote responses.

— Children are internally motivated by a desire for achieving equilibrium. Thus, learning is facilitated by the presentation of optimally challenging tasks and discrepant events that predispose the child to disequilibrium.

— Children learn best through interacting with and manipulating environmental stimuli.

— Group interactions may present children with ideas that challenge their own, leading to disequilibrium, reorganisation, and new structures.

These principles have been translated into more specific guidelines for teaching learning-disabled-students. Whether these guidelines are appropriate for other special needs children need to be researched in depth.

Teaching methods consistent with Piagetian principles and guidelines include cooperative learning, hypothesis testing, discovery learning, inquiry and other approaches that encourage inductive thinking. Cooperative learning is an instructional strategy whereby students work together in small groups to complete academic tasks. Potential benefits include gains in a academic achievement, basic skill development, problem solving, and socialization. More research is needed on the efficacy of cooperative learning with exceptional students particularly when learning does not take place in .certain groups of disabled children to an optimal or mastery level.

As a group, the educable mentally handicapped children demonstrated greater achievement in language and arithmetic with inductive approaches than matched peers in the control condition. These results suggest that inductive methods may constitute a viable addition to traditional approaches to instruction with mildly handicapped learners. While more researches is needed to validate the efficacy of such approaches for special populations, the approaches have theoretical merit and provide alternatives to traditional deductive methods.

Piaget's theory of cognitive development has had specific application to mild and severe/profound mental retardation, learning disabilities, gifted and other categories (Piaget, 1977).

Although the developmental approach as applied to mental retardation has received serious criticism, research has neither disproved the developmental approach nor proved the deficit position, and probably never will. The application of Piagetian instructional methods with the mildly retarded merits serious investigation and offers an exciting alternative to teachers wishing to broaden their instructional repertoire. Most important is application of Piagetian approaches to instruction may provide variety and challenge to the children themselves.

In general, the research suggests that learning disabled (LD) children demonstrate performance inferior to that of non-disabled (NLD) children on tasks designed to measure cognitive development and social cognition. A developmental delay in LD children's attainment of concrete operations compared with non-disabled (NLD) controls over a 3-year period has been obtained.

In conclusion, the available research on cognitive development of exceptional learners suggests, for the most part, that exceptional individuals progress through the same sequence of stages described by Piaget for normal children, although they vary in rate of development and level ultimately attained. Application of Piagetian theory to practice suggest use of strategies that engages children in active problem solving appropriate to their current level of development. Additional research is required to demonstrate the efficacy of Piagetian-derived instructional strategies for handicapped and gifted learners. Such strategies have potential as additions to the instructional repertoire of special education teachers.

Assessment of Research

Intelligence as sole criterion of determining school placement, institutional commitment and legal incompetence has been controversial. Primarily this is due to (a) Intelligence is reflected- as global intelligence, culture transcedent, and unmodifiable, (b) Instead of socially valued attributes, it is constitutional ability for competent participation in society, (c) Differences in preparative experience for the tests are reflected in the differences in group mean IQ, hence, does not fulfil cultural neutrality requirement. There is a need to measure associative, cognitive perceptual abilities rather than on overall intelligence. In addition to, testing of intelligence and evidence of physical, neurological, or psychological impairments, there are cognitive, perceptual, discriminative, adaptive and emotional functions and client's history are called for inferential generalisations.

The focus of testing behavioural deficits must centre around knowledge of how the child is actually performing within the structure of the community/ system. Children are not to be identified as disabled if they are able to function within a sufficient level of social invisibility. They must be able to perform certain tasks. Their activities must be within the "tolerance range" instead of fixed norms, which is a major problem with usual measurement. In other words, assessment must aim at (a) disability, (b) what behaviours are present that interface with individual functioning within the non-mature range, (c) what behaviours are present that represent the individuals effort to cope with the situation on an "instead" basis. The overall question of an adaptive behaviour approach is far reaching.

Behavioural assessment has been the most rapidly developing areas within the field of applied behaviour analysis, behaviour modification, and behaviour therapy. It is change oriented and has abandoned the standards of age norms for inter individual comparisons. In the total behavioural adjustment of an individual norm oriented assessment is of little value. It is rather necessary to follow the criterion referenced testing and observation index i.e., analysis of behaviour and condition that are relevant for an individual's environment. Three basic parametres are to be considered: onset time, frequency and duration. What is needed, therefore, are inter-observer and intra-observer agreement or "observer drit index".

Assessment in this area should reflect the basic objective i.e., learning deficit both qualitatively and quantitatively. This will enable for potentially beneficial placement of the disabled. Educational assessment should not only assess the child and the behaviour, and environmental contingencies which support the desired behaviour. There is a need for diagnostic psycho-educational report based on testing and observation appropriate for developmental intervention. Informal assessment should include teacher observation, teacher made tests, behaviour rating scales and checklists, precision teaching and formative assessment. Precision teaching not only charts current learning and growth but predicts future learning and growth. Teacher observation and assessment of classroom behaviour can be best accomplished it target behaviours are specific, observable and quantifiable. Child behaviour rating scales can come to help. Educational assessment must aim at educational intervention.

There is a felt need for assessment using both psychometric and behaviour observation-cum case study approach. The tests instead of being developed and/ or adapted at individual level may be undertaken by the respective National Institutes, IASE, CASE, CASP, etc. These tests should be disability or exceptionality specific with diagnostic purpose and be translated into regional and state level languages for ease and effective administration. Checklists of observation schedule and obtaining clinical data should also be developed both for assessing ability and achievement characteristics and levels. Cultural and sub-cultural experience are to find a place in developing tests and schedules with built in flexibility or alternatives to be appropriate enough for sampling behaviour in a pluralistic and multicultural society like ours. Norms are also to be developed for sub-cultural groups. Certification for test users should also be enforced and individual test developer must confirm to these norms or else such tests may be kept away from use with this population for any profitable purpose of identification, placement, and intervention (Panda, 1994).

Recent Developments and Research Focus

It is true that recent years have noticed a change from medical diagnosis. to multi-professional assessment, treatment to education, categorisation to individualised needs programme, Category specific needs (Evans and Verma, 1990; Pandey and Advani, 1995). Yet research in India has not made much headway in the field of special education. Perspectives for education of the disabled has been provided by Narsimhan and Mukherjee (1986), research (Panda, 1974) rehabilitation but most of what is. available in psycho educational research on disability are quite limited. A glance at the Indian Journal of Mental Retardation, Disability and Impairment, Journal of the Institute of Speech and Hearing would substantiate such observations although except for Disability and Impairment, the other two are virtually out of scene.

Quite a few significant studies have appeared under the guidance and involvement of individual researchers than of institutes, big and large. Noted amongst them are the contributions of Prof. A.K. Sen and Prof. (Mrs.) A. Sen at Delhi University with reference to mental retardation and specifically on learning and memory processes (Das, 1968; Goel and Sen, 1985), Psychosocial integration of the handicapped (Sen, A., 1983, 1988) and under the guidance of the present author (Prof. K.C. Panda) on response cost and positive reinforcement (Myreddi, 1995), peer modelling (Narayan, 1992), self injurious behaviour (Peshwaria, 1993), community attitudes (Panda, B., 1992), Integrated education of orthopaedially handicapped (Rath, 1993), Reading comprehension of the deaf (Sahoo, 1995), Personality structure of Blind (Khan, 1990), Isolation effect on learning (Panda, P. 1995), etc. are among the significant ones. NIMH has also researched into skill development in MR. Several research have also appeared o Blind, Blind Relief Association, National Association of the Blind, NIVH and individually (Pannikar, 1978; Panda and Panda, 1995).

The area of disability receiving much attention at the doctoral level research are mental retardation, visual impairment, gifted, hearing handicapped and learning disabled during the last decade but the number of researches are very few and quality wise are' only contributory to understanding the disabled.

Researches have concentrated more on, learning, memory, attention, personality, community attitudes, efficacy of systems but has hardly are oriented towards interventions but for rew which aimed skill development, development of learning package. National Institutes, NCERT, University Departments have not catered to significant research but contributed more to education and training of personnel for handling the disabled. Efficacy studies, have come up recently (Mani, 1993; Rath, 1993) but researches taken as a whole in the field of special education are in an embroyonic state.

There is no denying the fact that even till now the area of disability has remained as an area of welfare, rehabilitation and care than research, development and education. Both the directions are important and research can well integrate the two to the advantage of the disabled.

Future Prospects

This is a question which is difficult to answer but professionals irrespective of speciality in the field of disability must concentrate basically on issues and problems, which are relevant to educational and rehabilitation aspects by and large.

Areas of research would systematically include: assessment test/ checklist development in each area of disability; its regional translation and adaptation; standardisation of functional behaviour checklists even conditions of adaptation from western countries; measurement of change of progress in disabled children as a result of training, ecological intervention, parental involvement, and establishment of cultural norms for clinical as well as research use; prevalence of disability, its incidence in rural-urban set up, incidence rate, socio-demographic antecedents and consequences.

A major focus of our research endeavours must specify comparative studies on different therapeutic interventions and practices, sensory stimulations much early in the process of development and identify efficient procedures for developmental quotient and not merely IQ changes, competence, skills and social personal adjustment would be the primary focus leading to school readiness. Such research areas are painstaking and challenging but worth undertaking.

Special education in our country is an emerging field but there are many sound research generalisations elsewhere the field had an earlier origin. It is time for us to think and say on the basis of our own studies whether home based interventions are any way better than the institution based intervention, integrated system vs the special system, efficacy of community based rehabilitation and family studies. Public attitudes, acceptance and awareness are to be assessed and manipulated through various awareness programme since disability seen in home is sustained because of negative attitudes and stigma by the society.

How far rights of disabled are ensured or are they still discriminated against legal background? Disability occupation studies are essential for initiating training using a global socially desirable approach to draw attention or pay a lipservice to the vital areas.

Technology has come in a big way. How can it be used to the advantage of the disabled?-in terms of aids and appliances, classroom learning, teaching, self-learning, mastery learning, evaluation: diagnostic as well as normative, microprocessors and their use in case of teaching the disabled. Many such issues will appear. These are some directions only. While disability specific research is a matter of individual concern these are some of the area that come in any area of disability.

The Methodology

Behavioural scientists tend to be obsessed by their methods often at the expense of their results. It is not proper to enter into any philosophical debate on the process nor can any methodological formula for scientific research be formulated. The principal way of attending competence is to do it and develop insight. These methodological issues relate to designs in research, sampling frame and to size, qualitative vs quantitative research techniques. The field of special education is essential fraught with many such issues since researchers in special education have migrated from other disciplines with their well established rigid, hard core or soft-core training and temperament. The field of special education even without sacrificing research ethics, propriety and rigor can still follow a clinical model, a sample size of 1, a single subject research design using withdrawal or multiple base line data; across behaviours, across subjects, across situations, quasi-experimental design can take care of extreme groups in such research, as well as purposive sampling are acceptable practices inspite of procedural lapses and regression, when sample size is not large as it typical in the field of special education. What needed is that researchers in special education should take care of the methodological issues even when they use qualitative research techniques for fact finding, participant observation, interviewing, documentation and review. The fact should remain that it should maintain credibility, transferability, dependability, conformability, authenticity and fairness.

The Perspective

It is difficult at this stage to speculate and think of research on disability from a futuristic angle yet it is a part of programme building and research planning process. Research in future and particularly in 21st century will be more concerned with avoidance of discriminatory practices and maintenance of human rights so that disabled children have full participation in society. Hence, community research will get our priority besides legislative activism. But this is open direction, what is more crucial for this group is that disability is more often accompanied by mental problems. Hence, research in mental health, psychiatric social work, psychological interventions are and should be points of reference in planning research activities.

In the field of education, the year 2000 marked changes in educational index but what of disabled children? Can improved educational opportunities be extended to this group? Can inclusive education be benefiting the disabled or it is a medium of our self-preservation exercise and instinct. If not, research in the next decade should focus on the development of functional skill training, even using computer technology and computer aided instructions:

(a) Allow students to proceed at a more individual pace, thereby reducing stigmas.
(b) Enable developmentally disabled to work at home.
(c) Provide learning aids specifically designed for a group of disability.

In summary, research in the next decade and ahead should focus on:

(a) Identification of available services and resources.
(b) Development of learning potential assessment device test as basis of diagnosis.
(c) Epidemiological investigation of the disabled population.
(d) Research and advocacy of treatment approaches and techniques.
(e) Community integration with a comprehensive care system and a full operational prevention process.
(f) Identification of individually suitable teaching practices, peer tutoring and modelling, education and service delivery system.
(g) Family studies.

These are but a few reflections but there will be many more if really we are committed to the cause of helping disabled children in our society.

Highlights

Research in the field of exceptional children is taking off at a very slow and insignificant level in our country. Virtually it has low priority among professionals. The attempts to implant all Western ideas and principles will not pay divided unless indigenous techniques and procedures are developed through research and development of materials.

Research is in the areas of developing learning potential Assessment Device which is common to all areas of disability. Conceptually, it should focus on psycho-educational characteristics of the handicapped, efficacy of delivery system's community based programmes, curriculum modifications, developmental research on instructional system, management of educational environment, research in Piagetian Framework with the disabled, assessment techniques based on cultural specifics are in dire need in our country, with cooperative and partnership endeavour since the field of handicap is a complex area and therefore can rarely be handled at an individual level.

QUESTIONS

1. Which are the areas, where the research can be conducted ?
2. Which are the areas of concern for educational researches ?
3. What the conceptional issues ?

17

Programmes and Policies

Education and Training are the corner stones in the development of the potentialities of children, more so of children with special needs, or those categorised as exceptionals. Several policies and programmes have been undertaken in this field in our country. This chapter briefly describes these programmes.

- Recommendations of the Education Commission on the Handicapped.
- The National Policy for Children.
- Objectives of education for handicapped children in the International Year of Disabled Persons, 1981 with specific reference to India.
- Recommendations of the Working Group on Education of the Handicapped, 1981.
- Report of the Advisory Committee, 1981 on the Handicapped.
- National Policy on Education, 1986 on the Handicapped.
- Report of the Ramamurthy Committee, 1991.
- The Jannardan Reddy Committee Report 1992.
- Programme of Action, 1992.
- The Integrated Education Scheme 1992 for the Mildly Handicapped.
- Human Rights as per the United Nations' Standard Rules, 1994.

Indian Education Commission (1964-66)

The Education Commission was the first to suggest that the education of handicapped children has to be organised not merely on humanitarian- grounds, but also on grounds of utility. Proper education would enable handicapped children to overcome their disability, and make them useful citizens. It has to be remembered that the constitutional directives on compulsory education include handicapped children as well. Very little has been done in this field so far; and on account of several difficulties, any great improvement in the situation does not seem to be likely in the near future. All the same, it is important that a serious beginning is made. There is much in the field that can be learned from the educationally advanced countries which in recent years have developed new methods and techniques, based on advances in science and medicine.

It was further emphasized by the commission that the primary task of education for a handicapped child is to prepare him for adjustment to a socio-cultural environment designed to meet the needs of the normal. It is essential, therefore, that the education of handicapped children should be an inseparable part of the general educational system. The differences lie in the methods employed to teach the child and the means the child uses to acquire information. These differences in methodology do not influence the content or the goals of education. This form of education is, therefore, conveniently referred to as "Special Education". The Commission suggested educational facilities to be extended to four groups: the Blind, the Deaf, the Orthopaedically Handicapped, and the Mentally Retarded.

At the time, Education Commission (1964-66) made its recommendation, there were 115 schools for the Blind, 70 schools for the Deaf, 25 schools for the Orthopaedically Handicapped and 27 for the Mentally Retarded in the whole country. The Education Commission felt that the existing facilities were extremely inadequate. A carefully thought out plan for the development of educational services for the handicapped was therefore needed.

The Education Commission further felt that the progress in providing educational facilities to handicapped children will be limited by two main considerations: lack of teachers and of financial resources. A reasonable target will, therefore, be to provide by 1986, education for about 15 per cent of the blind, deaf and orthopaedically handicapped children and to about 5 per cent of the mentally retarded ones. This would mean the provision of educational facilities for about 10 per cent of the total number of handicapped children. As a part of the programme, it should be possible to have at least one good institution for the education of handicapped children in each district.

This goal was expected to be reached through the adoption of two programmes, the special and the integrated. In the special programme, the handicapped children are isolated from the normal ones and one placed in special institutions. In the other, handicapped children can be enrolled in regular school programmes. The second has several advantages of which two are important: reduction of costs, and promotion of mutual understanding between the handicapped and the non-handicapped children. There have also been disadvantages, for instance, many handicapped children find it psychologically disturbing to be placed in an ordinary school. An overall view of the problem show that experimentation with the integrated programmes is required and every attempt should be made to bring in as many children into integrated programmes as possible. With these salient suggestions the Commission left then implementation to planners of the country.

National Policy for Children

India is one of the few countries in the world with a comprehensive policy for children. The National Policy adopted in August 1974 is designed to provide guidelines to the Ministries of the Central Government, State Government and other agencies for an integrated approach to child development. The Ministry of Social Welfare coordinates action for the speedy implementation of measures contemplated in the National Policy for children. The measures are intended to cover all children belonging to the weaker sections of society and those who are handicapped. Then came the seminal International Year for Disabled Persons (IYDP) in 1981.

National Draft Plan

The General Assembly of the United Nations proclaimed 1981 as International Year for Disabled Persons in their Resolution No. 31/123 dated 16 December 1976. The United Nations, General Assembly set forth the following objectives:

— Helping disabled persons in their physical and psychological adjustments to society.
— Promoting all national and international efforts to provide disabled persons with proper assistance, training, care and guidance, to make available opportunities for suitable work and to ensure their full integration in society.
— Encouraging study and research projects designed to facilitate the practical participation of disabled persons in daily life, e.g. by improving their access to public buildings and transportation systems.
— Educating and informing the public about the rights of disabled persons to participate in and contribute to various aspects of economic, social and political life.
— Promoting effective measures for the prevention of disability and for the rehabilitation of disabled persons.

The theme of the year was "full participation with equality." In other words:

- integration should replace the present trends towards segregations;
- enrolment of handicapped children in ordinary schools should replace special residential schools;
- the development of sheltered workshops would remain a desirable programme;
- greater efforts would be made towards securing open employment for the handicapped.

India was one of the signatories to the resolution proclaiming IYDP, 1981. The Government of India endorsed the objectives set forth in the resolution of the General Assembly. Within the framework of the general objectives declared by the United Nations, the specific objectives to be achieved by India in the light of its present resources were the following:

— To evolve a National Policy on the handicapped, to include education, training, employment, measures to achieve full social integration, and protection and guarantees under the law.
— On the basis of this, to lay the foundation of a network of services for the handicapped that reaches the grassroot level,

so that a comprehensive rehabilitation service is eventually provided by preparing a prospective development plan for rehabilitation.

— To initiate in this chain a few practical programmes that would carry immediate and significant benefit to handicapped people themselves.

— To initiate concrete programmes aimed at bringing about the integration of handicapped people into the community and then utilisation in every way possible. Currently, there is a strong tendency to institutionalise handicapped people. This tends to inculcate among the handicapped a sense of dependence which prevents them from fully participating in community life even after they leave the protective walls of institutions. It also leads to maladjustment at work and in other social settings.

— To give a positive rural bias to services for the handicapped, since in India a great majority of handicapped persons live in rural communities. At present, practically all institutional programmes are located in urban areas. Most handicapped people from rural areas have to migrate to cities.

— To develop a strong national disability prevention programme. Currently, only a National Programme for the prevention of blindness is in operation. What is important is to develop and put into operation a comprehensive and pragmatic programme for the prevention of disabilities, where necessary, through legislative sanction so that wherever needed, social reforms could be brought to eliminate physical and mental disabilities.

— To prepare a base for research and development through the National Institutes, Institutes of Technology and other bodies so that in the years to come programmes for the rehabilitation of the handicapped should be responsive to change in the social or economic climate and to developments of techniques and technologies in various disciplines bearing on this field.

— To develop and initiate a planned network of information and publicity services for dissemination of information on new techniques, equipment programmes for the handicapped and for employers, teachers and social workers. The service should not only disseminate information but should also stimulate a greater awareness among opinion groups of the employment potential of the handicapped. Campaigns to eradicate social prejudice should form an integral part of the plan.

— To collect, with as wide a base as possible, all relevant data on the handicapped in the country.

In conformity with the National Plan of Action, State Governments have developed their own plan of action keeping in view the concepts and the priority areas as indicated in the plan of action. Special Education Cells have been set up in the states.

Working Group

Following the IYDP a working group was set up by the Govt. of India:

1. To suggest steps for
   - the adoption of proper legislative measures for the education and training of disabled.
   - publicity, and
   - action research.
2. To formulate the detailed action plan on "Education for the Disabled Child", including the Development of Skills in the context of observing 1981 as the International Year of the Disabled Persons, particularly with a view to enriching the existing services for the disabled; and
3. To give an idea of the financial requirements for implementing the various items of the Action Plan, keeping in view the feasibility of starting the programmes in IYDP, 1981.

The foremost task that emerged relates to the collection of reliable data on the basis of sample surveys in all the existing diversities of the country, according to social, economic, cultural and geographical factors.

The committee recommended that the following categories of handicapped children should be sovered:

1. The blind or the visually handicapped.
2. The deaf or the hearing handicapped.
3. The orthopaedically handicapped.
4. Educable and trainable mentally retarded children.
5. The cerebral palsied.

6. The neurologically handicapped, including the epileptic.
7. Children with speech and language disorders.
8. Children with speech and language disorders.
9. Children with minimal brain dysfunction including learning disabilities.

Experience indicated that quite a large number of multiple handicapped children need special services. Their problems are more complex.

What is of greatest importance is that a flexible and child-centred approach should be adopted. A child with a disability poses many complex infra-family, physical, social, economic and educational problems. To come to terms with such a staggering variety of problems no single approach is adequate. It is recommended, therefore, that for the pre-school handicapped children the following types of services may be organised:

1. Wide dissemination of information about the management and stimulation of various types of handicapped children at home may be undertaken through adequate literature in all Indian languages and publicity through all media of mass communication. In fact training of parents in the management and stimulation of disabled children may be a part of the functional literacy programmes being undertaken as part of various projects.
2. The publicity programme should be supported, by the worker at the district, block or village level, whose task should be to watch out for telltale signs of disability in children and to advise parents on the possibility of their children being at risk. This worker should undertake interpersonal discussion with the counselling of parents and other relatives or siblings.
3. Short courses for the training of parents, workshops and conferences for parents, and other forms of interaction between the parents and the professionals should be systematically organised with a view to enhancing the capability of parents to manage and enrich the pre-school education of disabled children at home.
4. Wherever possible, disabled children between three and six years of age may be integrated into ordinary nurseries or pre-

schools. To the extent possible, they should also be integrated into balwadis and other pre-school centres in rural areas.

5. Special pre-schools and balwadis may be set up for more severely handicapped children. These should be operated as day schools and maximum interaction between the disabled and normal children should be promoted.
6. For a small percentage of disabled children whose parents are totally unable to care for them, residential nursery schools should be set up, preferably one in each block, on to begin with, one in each district. Disabled children should be sent to residential nursery schools only as a last resort when they cannot benefit from other programmes.

For school age children the traditional approach has been to place handicapped children in special schools and especially in special residential schools. This has tended to isolate the disabled child. This trend is probably one of the most important factors contributing to the prevailing prejudice against disabled people. Moreover, our resources are limited and the cost of keeping disabled children in special residential schools is considerably greater than that in integrated settings and day schools. It is imperative, therefore, that a wide range of programmes should be taken up to suit the differing requirements of children with varying disabilities as well as in different social, cultural and economic circumstances.

The following types of programmes were recommended.

Integrated Programmes

a. Resource Teacher Programme
b. Itinerant Teacher Programme
c. The Special Class
d. Partial Integration

Special Schools

a. Day School
b. Special Residential Schools

While the placement of disabled children in integrated settings is expected to promote their social and psychological acceptance, it is often stressed that education of severely handicapped children needs certain supportive services like those of social workers, psychologists, physiotherapists, occupational therapists, speech therapists, and the like. It becomes the special responsibility of special schools, both day and residential to offer these supportive services in order to make the education of disabled children beneficial.

Further, special schools have often served as laboratories. They evolve special techniques which can later be applied even in integrated settings. Unfortunately, on account of the pressure of work in ordinary schools, it is by no means easy even for special teachers in integrated settings to devote time and energy to the development of new techniques and technologies.

The role of an innovative teacher in the education of disabled children can hardly be over-emphasised. A great deal of research is needed to arrive at the most effective techniques of imparting general education as well as vocational and professional skills to children with diverse disabilities. Some areas of specific research are listed below:

1. The chain of interpersonal interactions set off by the advent and management of a disabled child in the family.
2. Comparative study of academic and affective development of disabled children in various programmes.

The programme was proposed for a 20-year span.

Advisory Committee on Blind, Deaf, Orthopaedically Handicapped, and Mentally Retarded

The Ministry of Social Welfare and the Ministry of Education and Culture had appointed advisory committees to go into the details of the problems in these areas. These committees have met and discussed the following aspects in June and July, 1981.

a. Early detection, prevention, medical and physical rehabilitation.
b. Education and training of handicapped children and adults, including teacher training.
c. Employment.
d. General matters: role of voluntary organisations, creation of public awareness.

The salient recommendations with respect to training of teachers on education of the handicapped were:

a. Except for the severely orthopaedically handicapped and multiple handicapped children, no special education component is necessary. They should be integrated into regular schools. But for successful integration, teachers of regular schools should receive proper orientation. It was suggested that short term in-service teacher training programmes be conducted to meet this need.

b. In the area of education of the Blind, Deaf and Mentally Retarded, the prevailing conditions in rural areas were such that special schools were not available for hearing impaired children. Therefore, these children had to attend regular schools and teachers must be acquainted with the special needs and problems of these categories of handicapped.

c. The need for teacher training was highlighted by the inadequacies existing in the system. The dearth of teacher educators was stressed. The need for excellent models of teacher education and the need to strengthen the existing teacher training programmes were also recommended.

d. Appropriate curricula should be developed for use in special schools, special classes and remedial classes in rural and urban areas, by an agency such as NCERT and Regional College of Education.

e. There should be cooperation and coordination between all teacher training programmes in the country. It was suggested that the Ministry of Social Welfare and NCERT could undertake this.

National Policy on Education, 1986, 1992 (R)

The objective should be to integrate the physically and mentally handicapped with the general community as equal partners, to prepare them for normal growth and to enable them to face life with courage and confidence. The following measures were to be taken in this regard:

(i) Wherever it was feasible, the education of children with motor handicaps and other mild handicaps would be common with that of others.

(ii) Special schools with hostels would be provided, as far as possible at district headquarters, for the severely handicapped children.

(iii) Adequate arrangements would be made to give vocational training to the disabled.

(iv) Teacher's training programmes would be reoriented, in particular for teachers of primary classes, to deal with the special difficulties of handicapped children; and

(v) Voluntary effort for the education of the disabled would be encouraged in every possible manner.

Ramamurthy Committee, 1991

The Govt. of India set up the Ramamurthy Committee to comment upon NPE/POA stipulations. Some of the specific observations made on the handicapped as stated in the NPE 1986 were as follows.

NPE advocated the policy of integrating the physically and mentally handicapped with the general community as equal partners.

The POA mentioned the detailed measures to be taken, important amongst them being massive in-service training for teachers, orientation programmes for the administrators, development of supervisory expertise in the resource institutions like the SCERT and DIET, etc. It also called for provision of incentives like supply of aids, appliances, text books and free uniforms.

The reasons for the low coverage of handicapped children in education, are the following:

— Education of the handicapped is viewed as a social welfare activity.

— Child to child help leading to sensitization of the future generation, child to parent help for community sensitation and special and general pedagogy reinforcement were missed.

— Most of the special centres for the handicapped are located in metropolitan cities and urban centres. The non-government organisations barring a few exceptions have not significantly begun to operate at district or sub-district levels. Reportedly, 215 districts in the country do not have special schools for any disability though there are over 1000 documented special schools.

— The scheme of Integrated Education for Disabled Children which was conceptualised by the Department of Social Welfare in 1974 was implemented for several years in terms of running 'Mini Special Schools' within general schools. The reason was that there was no provision for sensitisation and involvement of all the teachers.

The NPE, so far as it relates to education of the handicapped, is inadequate in the following respects:

- It has not stressed the mobilisation of the total general education system for the education of the handicapped.
- Special schools have been treated in isolation from other educational institutions from the point of view of providing the educational supervisory infrastructure, leaving it to the Ministries of Welfare and HRD to co-operatively develop the same.

The merit of the POA is in its call for establishment of special schools at district and sub-district levels: curriculum development apart from provision of infrastructural facilities; and specific target setting for universal primary education of the handicapped. While special schools for the education of those with severe handicaps are rightly emphasised by the POA, they have not laid emphasis on multiple delivery of services in special schools. While single disability mode is required for research, development and rehabilitation work for delivery of educational services, multi-service mode in special schools should be given importance. This is particularly so because doctors, dispensaries, public health centres and development functionaries are multi-purpose in nature. The POA has not called for redefinition of the role of special schools.

The Department of Education has been implementing a scheme for the integrated education of the disabled under which 100% assistance is given to the States. The scheme is at present being implemented in nineteen States and Union Territories. The annual provision under the scheme is of the order of Rs. 2 crores and as of now 20,000 children are being covered. Assistance provided to the states under the scheme is expected to be utilised to provide for salaries and incentives for teachers, setting up of resource rooms, carrying out assessment of handicapped children, training of teachers, provision of instructional material, etc.

Having comprehensively taken into account the problems faced in providing education to the handicapped with reference to their special and diversified needs, and having studied the history of implementation of the educational programmes for the handicapped, the Committee gave the following recommendations:

(i) People should be made aware of the problems of the handicapped. The media should be effectively used for this purpose.

(ii) Every family with a handicapped child should be provided support through incentives, dialogue and periodic training and evaluation. Parents' groups and community education groups should be formed.

(iii) The educational system of the handicapped should be flexible. It should offer a range of education provisions-special schools for those who cannot be educated in general schools, special classes in general schools and integrated education for the disabled, vocational centres, etc.

(iv) Educational packages should be offered for hearing impaired children in a differentiated way-

- Purely oral oriented programmes for profoundly deaf children.
- Combined oral-manual programmes for profoundly deaf children for the education of whom pure oral programmes will not be adequate.
- Segregated programmes for those children for whom such programmes are essential.
- Integrated programmes for those whom this modality promises better emotive, cognitive, social and linguistic development.

(v) For making boys and girls of impaired hearing economically independent, vocational training has to be specially organised. Vocational training which is job-oriented and matched to the abilities and aptitudes of the hearing impaired, should be organised in a significantly diversified way.

(vi) Bharati Braille has been developed, at the National Institute for the Visually Handicapped (NIVH), Dehradun. This should be utilised maximally.

(vii) While work has been initiated for the development of Braille notations for mathematics and science, not much progress has been made.

(viii) For the moderately mentally retarded, special curricula should be developed and standardised not merely for the purpose of basic education in the three R's but also for training in self-care skills like motor integration, perceptual and motor skills, language, communication and conceptual skills.

(ix) Vocational schools for mentally retarded adults are not many. For their benefit jobs in sheltered workshops, farms and industries should be provided.

(x) In the pre-service teacher training programme, education of the handicapped, should be made part of the pedagogy and methodology.

(xi) A programme of sensitisation should be implemented for in-service teachers as well. This should include various components, namely, Non-formal Education, Vocationalisation of Education and Distance Education.

(xii) Teachers' training colleges should have special courses for teaching handicapped children; a special component on the education of the handicapped should be included in the B.Ed. courses as well.

(xiii) At least one resource faculty should be provided in each DIET to provide teacher training inputs in the context of education for the handicapped.

(xiv) The role of the special schools should be clearly redefined as spelt out below:

   (i) Early identification of children with handicaps and formulation of stimulation programmes for them.

   (ii) Education of the handicapped children who cannot be educated in general schools up to the point when they can be integrated-thus breaking the insulation between the general and special schools.

   (iii) Providing service as resource agencies for implementing the integrated education programmes in general schools.

   (iv) Bringing about mutual reinforcement of the pedagogies of special and general education.

(xv) A lot of development is taking place in the application of technology for the benefit of the handicapped. Several technological aids are already available, e.g., Brailleix produced in Germany which facilitates recording of whole encyclopaedia on cassettes, printing conversion devices like 'tactacon' which facilitates presentation of printed material in vibro-tactile form so as to enable blind persons to read, devices facilitating mobility of blind persons, etc. The technologies and techno-aids available for meeting the special needs of handicapped children should be reviewed, and measures for dissemination of information should be formulated.

(xvi) Sustained researches should be undertaken to determine the needs of the physically handicapped and produce technological aids capable of helping in overcoming handicaps.

These recommendations were very comprehensive to shape the programme planning effectively. Subsequently another Committee was set up by the government the Janardan Reddy Committee, which submitted its report in 1992.

The NPERC, 1992 felt that the NPE was inadequate in the following respects:

- NPE had not stressed the mobilisation of the total general education system for the education of the handicapped.
- Special schools had been treated in isolation from other educational institutions from the point of view of providing the educational supervisory infrastructure, leaving it to the Ministries of Welfare and HRD to co-operatively develop the same.

The NPERC made very useful recommendations relating to the modalities of implementing programmes for the education of the handicapped. Inter alia, it had advocated the use of media in creating awareness about the problems of the handicapped, providing support to every family with a handicapped child through incentives, dialogue and training and adopting a flexible approach to the education of the physically handicapped the NPERC examined at length the needs of different categories of the disabled such as the deaf, the blind and the mentally retarded, and made specific recommendations. The NPERC had also made important recommendations on the role of training, and of technological development in the education of the physically handicapped.

The Programme of Action which was formulated in 1992 by MHRD, Government of India took all these historical antecedents into account and focussed on an operational framework for implementing the plan of education of handicapped.

Programme of Action

The POA made a state of the art analysis of the situation. At the end of 1991-92 about 30,000 children with disability were availing special benefits under the scheme of Integrated Education for Disabled Children (IEDC). In addition, about 60,000 children with mild disabilities received resource support without special benefits. A large number of children with disability were also receiving education in special schools which numbered about 1035. The Project Integrated Education for Disabled (PIED) is being implemented, as a field demonstration, in one block each in ten States and Union Territories. In these blocks about 90 per cent of children with disability are receiving education in general schools. The cost per pupil in these blocks is now around Rs. 2000 but is likely to come down as the number of beneficiaries increases. General teachers feel confident and motivated as their status in the community has improved due to the services they provide. The innovative multi-category training of resource teachers has been found to be effective and has been institutionalised in the Regional Colleges and the training programmes organised by Non-governmental Organisations. Each DIET has been provided a resource centre for orienting elementary teachers and establishing field demonstrations in lab areas. Faculty from 102 DIETs have so far received induction training at the NCERT.

The Ministry of Welfare had taken steps to ensure supply of trained manpower to special schools and improve standards in these schools through the National Institute for the Handicapped and increased support to NGOs.

The Ministry of Labour manages 17 Vocational Rehabilitation Centres (VRCs) for the handicapped and helps in their placement. About 66,000 persons with disabilities had been rehabilitated under this scheme by September, 1991. Three per cent of seats for admission to ITIs and under the Apprenticeship Training Scheme are available for Handicapped persons. These seats are being fully utilised.

The evaluation of special schools and the scheme of IEDC has revealed some grey areas. The general education system has not yet been mobilised, to a noticeable extent, for education of the handicapped either at the Central or State Level. Inputs from different schemes like CBR, DRC, ECCE, non-formal education, adult education, vocational and technical education, etc. are not being brought together for the education of the physically handicapped. Some states are still reluctant to implement the Integrated Education for Disabled Children (IEDC) System, while some are implementing it rather indifferently. Few NGOs are active in rural areas. The standard of education in special schools needs improvement. Facilities for the education of children with multiple handicaps are yet to be developed. The early detection and intervention programmes so essential for education of these children have yet to be started. The goal of universalisation of elementary education for this disadvantaged group remains an unachievable dream unless concerted and urgent measures are taken.

For achieving equalisation of educational opportunities, children with disability should have access to quality education comparable to other children. However, considering the financial resources likely to be available the targets for education of disabled children should be as follows:

(i) Children who can be educated in general primary schools:
- (a) Universal enrolment by the end of ninth Five Year Plan.
- (b) Ensuring achievement of minimum level of learning through adjustment and adaptation of curriculum and teaching to special needs.

(ii) Children who require to be educated in special schools or special classes in general schools:
- (a) Universal enrolment by the end of the ninth Five Year Plan.
- (b) Ensuring achievement of level of learning commensurate with their potential.

(iii) Reduction of drop out rates to a level on par with other children:

(iv) Providing disabled children access to secondary and senior secondary schools with resource support and making special provision for vocational training of these children, particularly those with intellectual disabilities.

(v) Reorienting pre-service and in-service teacher education programmes including pre-school teachers training programmes to meet special needs.

(vi) Reorienting adult and non-formal education programmes to meet educational and vocational training needs of persons with disability.

The strategy of area-specific and population specific micro-planning for UEE is equally relevant for this disadvantaged group. Planning for UEE and adult literacy at all levels-centre, state, district, block and project-should provide for the educational needs of this category of children.

Education of children with disability will be a component in the training of educational planners and administrators as well as pre-service and in-service teachers. District Institutes of Education and Training (DIETS), Colleges of Teacher Education (CTEs) and the Institute of Advanced Study in Education (IASE) which have been provided with facilities for this component will have to pay particular attention to this aspect of teacher training. While drawing up schemes for strengthening SCERTs, cells for education of the handicapped may be considered as envisaged in IEDC.

The material supplied under Operation Blackboard will have to take into consideration special needs of these children. School buildings will have to take note of architectural adjustments needed to ensure access to children with disabilities, at the construction stage itself so as to avoid expenditure on modifications later on. Special schools need to be opened in the districts which have no special school facilities. The education of the handicapped should form an essential component in all externally assisted basic education projects being implemented or proposed to be implemented.

The following actions are needed for achieving the targets laid down:

(i) Adequate allocation or resources.

(ii) Provision for education of persons with disability should be made an integral component in externally assisted basic education projects.

(iii) Provision for education of the disabled should be made in the Centrally Sponsored Schemes of Operation Blackboard, Vocationalisation of Education and Non-formal Education.

(iv) There should be coordinated implementation of schemes like Community Based Rehabilitation, ECCE, VRCs and IEDC, so as to reduce cost and achieve higher coverage. This would require coordination among the Ministries/ Departments of Health, Welfare, Education, Women and Child Development and Labour.

(v) The NGOs have to be encouraged to implement IEDC, particularly in rural areas. The NGOs involved in other educational activities should be encouraged to work in this area also and should be assisted in developing their expertise.

The Ministry of Labour is providing vocational training for the handicapped through the Craftsman Training Scheme (CTS), the Apprenticeship Training Scheme and separate Vocational Rehabilitation Centres (VRCs). Three per cent of the seats for admission to ITIs under the Craftsman Training Scheme and Apprenticeship Training Scheme are reserved for candidates who are handicapped but have the aptitude and are otherwise fit to undergo the required training. The States/UTs have been advised from time to time to implement this reservation for the handicapped which will be continued during the eight-plan also. Seventeen VRCs will continue to provide training to a larger number of handicapped persons during the eight plan. The instructors in ITIs will receive orientation to meet special needs of handicapped persons. This components will be added in ITI instructor's training programme. Adjustment and adaptation of equipment to provide full access to disabled persons will be ensured.

Training of Teachers

All the DIETS established by the end of the eighth Plan have a resource room and trained faculty to teach the essential components of education of children with disability. They will also run orientation programmes for teachers, at least from lab areas and practising schools, to establish field demonstration of the IEDC programme. The SCERTs will support field demonstrations under the scheme of IEDC. Similar, actions is suggested for the 250 CTEs and 50 IASEs. The budget provision is available in the scheme itself. The pre-service training curriculum will induct essential components in these areas, wherever it has not been done so far.

All in-service teachers should receive awareness inputs on the education of children with disability in orientation programmes. In each area/ institution where IEDC is implemented all teachers should receive orientation as envisaged in the scheme of IEDC. The Heads of Institutions and educational administrators should also receive training.

Special Teachers

The NIHs and regional training centres have built up the capacity to train single disability special teachers for special schools. Besides meeting demands of the new special schools, the existing untrained teachers will be trained and backlog cleared by the end of the eighth Plan. Inservice training of special teachers will be planned in a way that each teacher receives a three-week course every four years.

Content and Process

Curriculum flexibility is of special significance for these children. Special needs of these children will be met, if child centred education is practised. The curriculum adjustment and adaptation of teaching methods and material will be worked out, field tried and provided to the users. The following actions will be taken:

(i) Guidelines for child centred education, including special needs in the classroom are being developed at the NCERT.

(ii) Guidelines for adjustment of curriculum and instructional material and methods for the visually and hearing handicapped at the primary level have been developed. These are available for use by teachers in IED/Special Schools.

(iii) The achievement of minimum levels of learning by children with mild disabilities should be ensured through resource support and alternative learning materials, wherever needed.

(iv) The Boards of Examination should make adjustments and adaptations in examinations for the handicapped children.

(v) Study of more than one language should not be compulsory for deaf children.

(vi) Teaching of Science and Mathematics is either not available to handicapped children or they opt for an easier substitute. Special efforts should be made by the NIHs and the NCERT to develop an action programme to improve access of disabled children to these important areas.

(vii) Child-to-child held in education of children with disabilities is an effective resource in view of large classes and multigrade teaching. NCERT should develop a package and make it available to teachers by end of 1993.

(viii) The special learning aids and equipment like braille books, braille kit, audio visual material will be developed and made available to schools by NIHs and NCERT.

Use of Mass Media

Radio and television are being used in a limited way both for advocacy as well as educational purposes. The CIETs, SIETs, NIHs and other organisations will develop a variety of programmes so that they can be regularly telecast/ broadcast. The MHRD will approach the Ministry of Information and Broadcasting for providing adequate time for this purpose.

Field publicity units should be utilised by states for advocacy programmes. Newspapers and magazines have started popular advocacy and educational writing in this area. The NCERT and the NIHs will develop packages and hand them over to journalists.

Monitoring and Evaluation

The availability of a reliable data base is essential for proper monitoring and evaluation of educational programmes for persons with disabilities. Towards this end the District Education Office, must with the help of other agencies, collect data about the number of disabled persons in the districts-disability wise, sex wise and age group wise, beneficiaries under IEDC, special schools, ITIs, VRCs, etc., number of special and resource teachers, their qualifications and pay scale, and budget utilisation. Similar information should also be included in the statistics collected by MHRD as also the Educational Surveys conducted by NCERT.

The MHRD and the Ministry of Welfare should make grants under IEDC and special schools contingent on the latter regularly giving the information. An inter-departmental Committee should be set up at the

State and Central levels for monitoring. In addition, regular visits by the officers of the MHRD, NCERT, Regional Colleges of Education and field offices, should lead to status reports.

Evaluation studies by external agencies, universities conducting courses on education, and rehabilitation of persons in specific geographical areas will be commissioned by MHRD and the Ministry of Welfare.

Integrated Education

The Government of India has given the education of disabled children special attention to achieve the goal of education for all. The objective is to integrate the handicapped with the general community at all levels as equal partners, to prepare them for normal growth and to enable them to face life with courage and confidence. This is operating through the centrally sponsored IEDC scheme. In addition, the disabled children who are placed in special schools should also be integrated in common schools once they acquire required communication and daily living skills. The Central Government assists the States/Union Territories in their implementation as per conditions laid down in the scheme. The scheme is implemented through the State Government/s UT Administrations/ Autonomous Organisations of stature having experience in the field of education and/or rehabilitation of the disabled. Because this scheme has to be implemented in schools, the Education Department is the implementing agency. The State Governments may take the assistance of voluntary organisations also for this purpose.

The scheme provides, educational facilities for children with disabilities who can be integrated in general schools. While rehabilitation assistance will be made available to all children with disabilities, student benefits will be extended on the recommendation by the Assessment Team. The scope of the scheme includes pre-school training for the disabled children and counselling for the parents. It would include, among other things, special training for hearing handicapped children, mobility and orientation training for the visually handicapped, daily living and communication skills training required by children with other disabilities, parental counselling and training in home management of these children. The education of the disabled children under this scheme will continue up to the senior secondary school level and include vocational courses equivalent to the senor secondary stage. A disabled child in receipt of any scholarship /assistance under some other scheme relating to disability from the State/Central Government will not be eligible for any of the benefits under this scheme unless he/she is willing to forego the other sources of assistance.

Implementing the Scheme

The implementing agency has set up an administrative cell under an officer not below the rank of Deputy Director to implement, monitor and evaluate the programme. These officials are chosen for their special qualifications in this field or if they are not so qualified, will be trained in a course conducted by the National Council of Educational Research and Training (NCERT). This cell will identify the areas and institutions for implementing the scheme.

It is preferable that in order to properly plan and supervise the implementation of the scheme a number of developmental blocks should be selected for its operation, rather than scattering the schools under this scheme all over the State. Within the area of the selected block all the desired inputs should be provided to the schools covered.

To identify disabled children in the blocks/ districts where the scheme is yet to be implemented, the first task should be to provide suitable orientation to all school teachers in the area for conducting a survey to identify disabled children in general schools. Teachers may be provided a small honorarium for conducting the survey. The IEDC cell should provide printed survey forms for identification of these children. Assistance up to Rs. 10,000 may be provided to the IEDC cell for this purpose. These efforts should be supplemented by publicity through the mass media.

The State-level cell will make arrangements for equipment, learning materials, staff, etc. in order to provide education to disabled children. The cell will also set up the machinery for assessment of a disabled children. Wherever a survey has been conducted by any other agency it should be utilised and augmented with the survey of disabilities not covered by the earlier survey. Monitoring and evaluation of the scheme at the State level will be carried out by the cell. The cell will ensure that the information regarding the scheme is widely known.

The Administrative Cell to be set up by the State Education Department will have a Deputy Director, a Coordinator (who will be a psychologist) a Special Educator, a Stenographer and a Lower Division Clerk.

The Assessment

The Coordinator of the programme will be responsible for arranging for the assessment of the children and monitoring their progress. A three-member assessment team, comprising a doctor, a psychologist and a special educator will be formed. The State/UT assessment team will function under the Administrative Cell. Specialists will be drawn upon in consultation with the State Health Department. Wherever district rehabilitation centres have been established, its resources for assessment may be used. The non-government organisations (NGOs) with infrastructural facilities may also be used for assessment purposes.

The average cost of an assessment should not exceed Rs. 150 per disabled child. It will be necessary to examine a large number of children to select those considered suitable for placement in an integrated programme.

The assessment report should be comprehensive enough for educational programming; a profile of what a particular child can or cannot do during testing situations should be adequately reported. The report should specifically indicate whether the child can be put directly into school or should receive preparation in special school/ special preparatory class in the Early Childhood Education Centre specially equipped for this purpose. Functional assessment can be carried out by the teacher if formal assessment is to take a long time so that the educational programme can be started for these children.

The Facilities

1. A disabled child may be given the following kinds of facilities. The facilities should, as far as possible, be given in kind. In case similar incentives are not being offered by the State Government/UT Administration under any other scheme, the following rates could be adopted.

a. Actual expenses on books and stationery up to Rs. 400 per annum.
b. Actual expenses on uniform up to Rs. 200 per annum.
c. Transport allowance up to Rs. 50 per month (if a disabled child admitted under the scheme resides in the school hostel within the school premises, no transportation charges would be admissible).
d. Reader allowance of Rs. 50 per month in case of blind children after class V.
e. Escort allowance for severally handicapped children with lower extremely disabilities at the rate of Rs. 75 per month.
f. Actual cost of equipment, subject to a maximum of Rs. 2000 per student for a period of five years.

2. In the case of severely orthopaedically handicapped children, it may be necessary to allow one attendant for 10 children in a school.
3. Disabled children residing in school hostels within the same institution where they are studying may also be paid boarding and lodging charges. Where there is no state, scheme of scholarships to hostel dwellers, the disabled children whose parental income does not exceed Rs. 5,000 per month may be paid actual boarding and lodging charges subject to a maximum of Rs. 200 per month. However disabled children should generally not be placed in hostels unless the required educational facilities are not available in nearby schools.
4. Severely orthopaedically handicapped children residing in school hostels may need the assistance of a helper or an ayah. A special pay of Rs. 50 per month is admissible to any employee of the hostel willing to extend such help to children in addition to his/her duties.

Special Teacher

Except for children with locomotor disabilities, special education teachers may be appointed in schools where the scheme is in operation to provide specific attention to the disabled children.

The teacher-pupil ratio for special education teachers envisaged under this scheme is 1:8. This ratio will be the same for normal classes as well as for preparatory pre-school classes. The same teacher will provide counselling to the parents. In accordance with this ratio the requisite number of special teachers may be appointed in schools (or for a cluster of schools) for children requiring special teacher support as per qualifications specified in the scheme.

The same scales of pay as available to the teachers of the corresponding category in that State/UT will be given to special teachers. Considering the special type of duties, these teachers will be given a special pay of Rs. 150 per month in urban areas and Rs. 200 per month in rural areas. The State Education Department may recruit such teachers for this purpose following the normal recruitment procedures.

Educational Measures

A resource room having all the essential equipment, learning aids and materials may be provided for a cluster of schools implementing the scheme of integrated education. The NCERT has prepared a handbook which also indicates the type of facilities which may be provided in the resource room. The average cost of such equipment is estimated at Rs. 30,000. The need for equipment would depend upon the disability types of the students enrolled in the associated schools. The resource room may be set up preferably in an existing room in the school. A new room may be built only where no accommodation is available to the satisfaction of the State Government. Grant shall be available for construction of a resource room in a school in such circumstances subject to a maximum of Rs. 50,000. NGOs/special schools wherever available should be used as resource centres for the IED programme in general schools.

Visually and hearing impaired children should be allowed to take only one language as already recommended. Provision for alternative modes of examination for blind and other children with physical disabilities coming in the way of writing should be considered and provided by the Boards of Examination.

Preparation of disabled children for education being essential, preference should be given to the blocks where the schemes of Integrated Child Development (ICD) and Early Childhood Centres of

Education (ECCE) exist while selecting blocks for implementation of the scheme. Support for services for disabled children will be available for instructional materials and training of teachers. Procedures of grant are governed as per scheme IEDC, 1992.

United Nations Standard Rules

The Rights of Disabled children have been greatly recognised and the UNO has stimulated several conditions on the Nation and State to plan for it. The following are the United Nations Standard Rules on the Equalisation of Opportunities for persons with disabilities duly adopted by the XI World Congress on Mental Retardation.

Equal Participation

1. States should take action to raise awareness in society about persons with disabilities; their rights, their needs their potential and their contribution.
2. States should ensure the provision of effective medical care to persons with disabilities.
3. States should ensure the provision of rehabilitation services to persons with disabilities in order for them to reach and substain their optimum level of independence and functioning.
4. States should ensure the development and supply of support services, including assistive devices for persons with disabilities, to assist them to increase their level of independence in their daily living and to exercise their rights.

Target Areas

5. States should recognize the overall importance of accessibility in the process of the equalization of opportunities in all spheres of society. For persons with disabilities of any kind states should (a) introduce programmes of action to make the physical environment accessible; and (b) undertake measures to provide access to information and communication.
6. States should recognize the principle of equal primary, secondary and tertiary educational opportunities for children, youth and adults with disabilities, in integrated settings. They

should ensure that the education of persons with disabilities is an integral part of the educational system.

7. States should recognize the principle that persons with disabilities must be empowered to exercise their human rights, particularly in the field of employment, in both rural and urban areas they must have equal opportunities for productive and gainful employment in the labour market.
8. States are responsible for the provision of social security and income maintenance for persons with disabilities.
9. States should promote the full participation of persons with disabilities in family life. They should promote their right to personal integrity and ensure that laws do not discriminate against persons with disabilities with respect to sexual relationships, marriage and parenthood.
10. States will ensure that persons with disabilities are integrated into and can participate in cultural activities on an equal basis.
11. States will take measures to ensure that persons with disabilities have equal opportunities for recreation and sports.
12. States will take measures for equal participation by persons with disabilities in the religious life of their communities.

Implementation Measures

13. States assume the ultimate responsibility for the collection and dissemination of information on the living conditions of persons with disabilities and promote comprehensive research on all aspects, including obstacles that affect the lives of persons with disabilities.
14. States will ensure that disability aspects are include in all relevant policy making and national planning.
15. States have a responsibility to create the legal bases for measures to achieve the objectives of full participation and equality for persons with disabilities.
16. States have the financial responsibility for national programmes and measures to create equal opportunities for persons with disabilities.

17. States are responsible for the establishment and strengthening of national coordinating committees, or similar bodies, to serve as a national focal point on disability matters.
18. States should recognize the right of the organizations of persons with disabilities to represent persons with disabilities at national, regional and local levels. States should also recognize the advisory role of organizations of person with disabilities in decision-making on disability matters.
19. States are responsible for ensuring the adequate training of personnel; at all levels, involved in the planning and provision of programmes and services concerning persons with disabilities.
20. States are responsible for the continuous monitoring and evaluation of the implementation of national programmes and services concerning the equalization of opportunities for persons with disabilities.
21. States, both industrialized and developing, have the responsibility to cooperate in and take measures for the improvement of the living conditions of persons with disabilities in developing countries.
22. States will participate actively in international cooperation concerning policies for the equalization of opportunities for persons with disabilities.

Development of special education perspectives have been well explained and described through the commissions, committees, programmes, policies of Government since Education Commission made is recommendation. The adoption of Integrated Education Schemes, and detailed programme of action have added seriousness of purpose to the education of disabled. Add to this is the role of United Nation's emphasis and declaration for the State to take up the responsibilities. The future only will show the progress.

Highlights

Interest in the education of the handicapped had a programatic development in our country. In 1964-66 the Education Commission made an analysis of the state of art in special education in the areas of Blind,

Deaf, Mentally Retarded and Orthopaedically Handicapped and observed inadequacy in the quantity and quality of institutions compared to magnitude of the problem. It was quite emphatic of the expansion of the movement which became consistent with National Policy on Children, 1974.

The IYDP, 1981 recommended education of the disabled, prevention, rehabilitation, and full participation with equality. India was one of the signatories which made series of attempts to evolve a National Policy on the Handicapped and a strong national disability prevention programme. Currently, prevention programme on Blindness is on its march. Specific planned network was established to provide education, legal protection, and employment.

The working groups, and various sub-committees set up by the Ministry of Welfare priortised the categories of disability to be taken care of. Initially, the Deaf, the Blind, the Orthopaedics and the Mentally Retarded were enrolled in different special schools. Long-term and Short-term teacher training courses were also conceptualised alongwith emphasis on awareness, generation and dissemination of information. Voluntary organisations also grew up in pace.

The National Policy on Education, 1986; 1992 (R) made recommendations on education of mild disabled children in regular schools, special residential schools in District HQs, vocational training, teacher training and initiating voluntary effort which were corroborated further by Ramamurthy and Janardan Reddy Committee Reports leading to a Programme of Action (POA) 1992. The POA made plans for implementation in the areas of: Integrated Education of the Disabled, support to families of disabled, development of educational packages, development of Braille, vocational schools, preservice teacher training programmes, inservice programme, early identification, use of technology in education of the handicapped, setting up VRCs, reorientation of the general education to take care of disability, Field Publicity Programmes, Convergence of ECCE, ICDS with PIED programmes etc. The PIED Scheme is a Centrally Sponsored Scheme.

The United Nations Standard Rules, 1994 operationalised and made mandatory recommendations to various States and Nations for protecting Rights of the Disabled in terms of equal participation in life, provision of equal educational opportunities for the disabled and responsibility of the State for complete care of disabled children and population. The National Disability Bill, 1996, in India is a step in this direction in our country.

QUESTIONS

1. What are the corner stones in the development of the potentialities of children ?
2. What are the two main considerations, limiting the progress in providing educational facilities to handicapped children ?
3. When was the National Policy on children adopted ?